enVision Mathematics
Common Core

Volume 1 Topics 1–6

Authors

Robert Q. Berry, III
Professor of Mathematics Education, Department of Curriculum, Instruction and Special Education, University of Virginia, Charlottesville, Virginia

Zachary Champagne
Assistant in Research Florida Center for Research in Science, Technology, Engineering, and Mathematics (FCR-STEM) Jacksonville, Florida

Eric Milou
Professor of Mathematics Rowan University, Glassboro, New Jersey

Jane F. Schielack
Professor Emerita Department of Mathematics Texas A&M University, College Station, Texas

Jonathan A. Wray
Mathematics Supervisor, Howard County Public Schools, Ellicott City, Maryland

Randall I. Charles
Professor Emeritus Department of Mathematics San Jose State University San Jose, California

Francis (Skip) Fennell
Professor Emeritus of Education and Graduate and Professional Studies, McDaniel College Westminster, Maryland

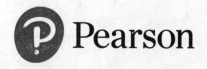
Pearson

Boston, Massachusetts   Chandler, Arizona
Glenview, Illinois   New York, New York

Pearson K12 Learning LLC. 221 River Street, Hoboken, NJ 07030

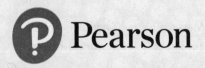

ISBN-13: 978-0-7685-7879-9
ISBN-10: 0-7685-7879-5

2 20

CONTENTS

TOPICS

DIGITAL RESOURCES

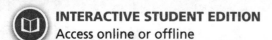 Go Online

INTERACTIVE STUDENT EDITION
Access online or offline

VISUAL LEARNING
Interact with visual learning animations

ACTIVITY
Use with *Solve & Discuss It, Explore It,*
and *Explain It* activities and Examples

VIDEOS
Watch clips to support *3-Act
Mathematical Modeling* Lessons
and *enVision® STEM Projects*

PRACTICE
Practice what you've learned and
get immediate feedback

TUTORIALS
Get help from *Virtual Nerd*
any time you need it

MATH TOOLS
Explore math with digital tools

GAMES
Play math games to help you learn

KEY CONCEPT
Review important lesson content

GLOSSARY
Read and listen to English and
Spanish definitions

ASSESSMENT
Show what you've learned

realize
Everything you need for
math anytime, anywhere.

TOPIC 1
Rational Number Operations

TOPIC 2 — Real Numbers

TOPIC 4

Analyze and Solve Percent Problems

TOPIC 5
Generate Equivalent Expressions

Solve Problems Using Equations and Inequalities

COMMON CORE STATE STANDARDS

GRADE 7

Standards for Mathematical Content

RATIOS AND PROPORTIONAL RELATIONSHIPS

7.RP.A Analyze proportional relationships and use them to solve real-world and mathematical problems.

1. Compute unit rates associated with ratios of fractions, including ratios of lengths, areas and other quantities measured in like or different units. *For example, if a person walks $\frac{1}{2}$ mile in each $\frac{1}{4}$ hour, compute the unit rate as the complex fraction $\frac{\frac{1}{2}}{\frac{1}{4}}$ miles per hour, equivalently 2 miles per hour.*

2. Recognize and represent proportional relationships between quantities.

   a. Decide whether two quantities are in a proportional relationship, e.g., by testing for equivalent ratios in a table or graphing on a coordinate plane and observing whether the graph is a straight line through the origin.

   b. Identify the constant of proportionality (unit rate) in tables, graphs, equations, diagrams, and verbal descriptions of proportional relationships.

   c. Represent proportional relationships by equations. *For example, if total cost t is proportional to the number n of items purchased at a constant price p, the relationship between the total cost and the number of items can be expressed as t = pn.*

   d. Explain what a point (x, y) on the graph of a proportional relationship means in terms of the situation, with special attention to the points (0, 0) and (1, r) where r is the unit rate.

3. Use proportional relationships to solve multistep ratio and percent problems. *Examples: simple interest, tax, markups and markdowns, gratuities and commissions, fees, percent increase and decrease, percent error.*

THE NUMBER SYSTEM

7.NS.A Apply and extend previous understandings of operations with fractions to add, subtract, multiply, and divide rational numbers.

1. Apply and extend previous understandings of addition and subtraction to add and subtract rational numbers; represent addition and subtraction on a horizontal or vertical number line diagram.

   a. Describe situations in which opposite quantities combine to make 0. *For example, a hydrogen atom has 0 charge because its two constituents are oppositely charged.*

   b. Understand $p + q$ as the number located a distance $|q|$ from p, in the positive or negative direction depending on whether q is positive or negative. Show that a number and its opposite have a sum of 0 (are additive inverses). Interpret sums of rational numbers by describing real-world contexts.

   c. Understand subtraction of rational numbers as adding the additive inverse, $p - q = p + (-q)$. Show that the distance between two rational numbers on the number line is the absolute value of their difference, and apply this principle in real-world contexts.

   d. Apply properties of operations as strategies to add and subtract rational numbers.

Standards for Mathematical Content

2. Apply and extend previous understandings of multiplication and division and of fractions to multiply and divide rational numbers.

   a. Understand that multiplication is extended from fractions to rational numbers by requiring that operations continue to satisfy the properties of operations, particularly the distributive property, leading to products such as $(-1)(-1) = 1$ and the rules for multiplying signed numbers. Interpret products of rational numbers by describing real-world contexts.

   b. Understand that integers can be divided, provided that the divisor is not zero, and every quotient of integers (with non-zero divisor) is a rational number. If p and q are integers, then $-\left(\frac{p}{q}\right) = \frac{(-p)}{q} = \frac{p}{(-q)}$. Interpret quotients of rational numbers by describing real-world contexts.

   c. Apply properties of operations as strategies to multiply and divide rational numbers.

   d. Convert a rational number to a decimal using long division; know that the decimal form of a rational number terminates in 0s or eventually repeats.

3. Solve real-world and mathematical problems involving the four operations with rational numbers.[1]

EXPRESSIONS AND EQUATIONS

7.EE.A Use properties of operations to generate equivalent expressions.

1. Apply properties of operations as strategies to add, subtract, factor, and expand linear expressions with rational coefficients.

2. Understand that rewriting an expression in different forms in a problem context can shed light on the problem and how the quantities in it are related. For example, $a + 0.05a = 1.05a$ means that "increase by 5%" is the same as "multiply by 1.05."

7.EE.B Solve real-life and mathematical problems using numerical and algebraic expressions and equations.

3. Solve multi-step real-life and mathematical problems posed with positive and negative rational numbers in any form (whole numbers, fractions, and decimals), using tools strategically. Apply properties of operations to calculate with numbers in any form; convert between forms as appropriate; and assess the reasonableness of answers using mental computation and estimation strategies. For example: If a woman making $25 an hour gets a 10% raise, she will make an additional $\frac{1}{10}$ of her salary an hour, or $2.50, for a new salary of $27.50. If you want to place a towel bar $9\frac{3}{4}$ inches long in the center of a door that is $27\frac{1}{2}$ inches wide, you will need to place the bar about 9 inches from each edge; this estimate can be used as a check on the exact computation.

4. Use variables to represent quantities in a real-world or mathematical problem, and construct simple equations and inequalities to solve problems by reasoning about the quantities.

   a. Solve word problems leading to equations of the form $px + q = r$ and $p(x + q) = r$, where p, q, and r are specific rational numbers. Solve equations of these forms fluently. Compare an algebraic solution to an arithmetic solution, identifying the sequence of the operations used in each approach. For example, the perimeter of a rectangle is 54 cm. Its length is 6 cm. What is its width?

   b. Solve word problems leading to inequalities of the form $px + q > r$ or $px + q < r$, where p, q, and r are specific rational numbers. Graph the solution set of the inequality and interpret it in the context of the problem. For example: As a salesperson, you are paid $50 per week plus $3 per sale. This week you want your pay to be at least $100. Write an inequality for the number of sales you need to make, and describe the solutions.

Standards for Mathematical Content

GEOMETRY

7.G.A **Draw, construct, and describe geometrical figures and describe the relationships between them.**

1. Solve problems involving scale drawings of geometric figures, including computing actual lengths and areas from a scale drawing and reproducing a scale drawing at a different scale.

2. Draw (freehand, with ruler and protractor, and with technology) geometric shapes with given conditions. Focus on constructing triangles from three measures of angles or sides, noticing when the conditions determine a unique triangle, more than one triangle, or no triangle.

3. Describe the two-dimensional figures that result from slicing three-dimensional figures, as in plane sections of right rectangular prisms and right rectangular pyramids.

7.G.B **Solve real-life and mathematical problems involving angle measure, area, surface area, and volume.**

4. Know the formulas for the area and circumference of a circle and use them to solve problems; give an informal derivation of the relationship between the circumference and area of a circle.

5. Use facts about supplementary, complementary, vertical, and adjacent angles in a multi-step problem to write and solve simple equations for an unknown angle in a figure.

6. Solve real-world and mathematical problems involving area, volume, and surface area of two- and three-dimensional objects composed of triangles, quadrilaterals, polygons, cubes, and right prisms.

STATISTICS AND PROBABILITY

7.SP.A **Use random sampling to draw inferences about a population.**

1. Understand that statistics can be used to gain information about a population by examining a sample of the population; generalizations about a population from a sample are valid only if the sample is representative of that population. Understand that random sampling tends to produce representative samples and support valid inferences.

2. Use data from a random sample to draw inferences about a population with an unknown characteristic of interest. Generate multiple samples (or simulated samples) of the same size to gauge the variation in estimates or predictions. *For example, estimate the mean word length in a book by randomly sampling words from the book; predict the winner of a school election based on randomly sampled survey data. Gauge how far off the estimate or prediction might be.*

7.SP.B **Draw informal comparative inferences about two populations.**

3. Informally assess the degree of visual overlap of two numerical data distributions with similar variabilities, measuring the difference between the centers by expressing it as a multiple of a measure of variability. *For example, the mean height of players on the basketball team is 10 cm greater than the mean height of players on the soccer team, about twice the variability (mean absolute deviation) on either team; on a dot plot, the separation between the two distributions of heights is noticeable.*

4. Use measures of center and measures of variability for numerical data from random samples to draw informal comparative inferences about two populations. *For example, decide whether the words in a chapter of a seventh-grade science book are generally longer than the words in a chapter of a fourth-grade science book.*

Standards for Mathematical Content

7.SP.C **Investigate chance processes and develop, use, and evaluate probability models.**

5. Understand that the probability of a chance event is a number between 0 and 1 that expresses the likelihood of the event occurring. Larger numbers indicate greater likelihood. A probability near 0 indicates an unlikely event, a probability around $\frac{1}{2}$ indicates an event that is neither unlikely nor likely, and a probability near 1 indicates a likely event.

6. Approximate the probability of a chance event by collecting data on the chance process that produces it and observing its long-run relative frequency, and predict the approximate relative frequency given the probability. *For example, when rolling a number cube 600 times, predict that a 3 or 6 would be rolled roughly 200 times, but probably not exactly 200 times.*

7. Develop a probability model and use it to find probabilities of events. Compare probabilities from a model to observed frequencies; if the agreement is not good, explain possible sources of the discrepancy.

   a. Develop a uniform probability model by assigning equal probability to all outcomes, and use the model to determine probabilities of events. *For example, if a student is selected at random from a class, find the probability that Jane will be selected and the probability that a girl will be selected.*

   b. Develop a probability model (which may not be uniform) by observing frequencies in data generated from a chance process. *For example, find the approximate probability that a spinning penny will land heads up or that a tossed paper cup will land open-end down. Do the outcomes for the spinning penny appear to be equally likely based on the observed frequencies?*

8. Find probabilities of compound events using organized lists, tables, tree diagrams, and simulation.

   a. Understand that, just as with simple events, the probability of a compound event is the fraction of outcomes in the sample space for which the compound event occurs.

   b. Represent sample spaces for compound events using methods such as organized lists, tables and tree diagrams. For an event described in everyday language (e.g., "rolling double sixes"), identify the outcomes in the sample space which compose the event.

   c. Design and use a simulation to generate frequencies for compound events. *For example, use random digits as a simulation tool to approximate the answer to the question: If 40% of donors have type A blood, what is the probability that it will take at least 4 donors to find one with type A blood?*

---

[1]Computations with rational numbers extend the rules for manipulating fractions to complex fractions.

COMMON CORE STATE STANDARDS

Standards for Mathematical Content

THE NUMBER SYSTEM

8.NS.A Know that there are numbers that are not rational, and approximate them by rational numbers.

1. Know that numbers that are not rational are called irrational. Understand informally that every number has a decimal expansion; for rational numbers show that the decimal expansion repeats eventually, and convert a decimal expansion which repeats eventually into a rational number.

2. Use rational approximations of irrational numbers to compare the size of irrational numbers, locate them approximately on a number line diagram, and estimate the value of expressions (e.g., π^2).

EXPRESSIONS & EQUATIONS

8.EE.A Work with radicals and integer exponents.

1. Know and apply the properties of integer exponents to generate equivalent numerical expressions.

2. Use square root and cube root symbols to represent solutions to equations of the form $x^2 = p$ and $x^3 = p$, where p is a positive rational number. Evaluate square roots of small perfect squares and cube roots of small perfect cubes. Know that $\sqrt{2}$ is irrational.

3. Use numbers expressed in the form of a single digit times an integer power of 10 to estimate very large or very small quantities, and to express how many times as much one is than the other.

4. Perform operations with numbers expressed in scientific notation, including problems where both decimal and scientific notation are used. Use scientific notation and choose units of appropriate size for measurements of very large or very small quantities (e.g., use millimeters per year for seafloor spreading). Interpret scientific notation that has been generated by technology.

Standards for Mathematical Content

8.EE.B Understand the connections between proportional relationships, lines, and linear equations.

5. Graph proportional relationships, interpreting the unit rate as the slope of the graph. Compare two different proportional relationships represented in different ways.

6. Use similar triangles to explain why the slope m is the same between any two distinct points on a non-vertical line in the coordinate plane; derive the equation $y = mx$ for a line through the origin and the equation $y = mx + b$ for a line intercepting the vertical axis at b.

8.EE.C Analyze and solve linear equations and pairs of simultaneous linear equations.

7. Solve linear equations in one variable.

   a. Give examples of linear equations in one variable with one solution, infinitely many solutions, or no solutions. Show which of these possibilities is the case by successively transforming the given equation into simpler forms, until an equivalent equation of the form $x = a$, $a = a$, or $a = b$ results (where a and b are different numbers).

   b. Solve linear equations with rational number coefficients, including equations whose solutions require expanding expressions using the distributive property and collecting like terms.

GEOMETRY

8.G.A Understand congruence and similarity using physical models, transparencies, or geometry software.

1. Verify experimentally the properties of rotations, reflections, and translations:

   a. Lines are taken to lines, and line segments to line segments of the same length.

   b. Angles are taken to angles of the same measure.

   c. Parallel lines are taken to parallel lines.

2. Understand that a two-dimensional figure is congruent to another if the second can be obtained from the first by a sequence of rotations, reflections, and translations; given two congruent figures, describe a sequence that exhibits the congruence between them.

3. Describe the effect of dilations, translations, rotations, and reflections on two-dimensional figures using coordinates.

4. Understand that a two-dimensional figure is similar to another if the second can be obtained from the first by a sequence of rotations, reflections, translations, and dilations; given two similar two-dimensional figures, describe a sequence that exhibits the similarity between them.

5. Use informal arguments to establish facts about the angle sum and exterior angle of triangles, about the angles created when parallel lines are cut by a transversal, and the angle-angle criterion for similarity of triangles.

Standards for Mathematical Content

8.G.B Understand and apply the Pythagorean Theorem.

6. Explain a proof of the Pythagorean Theorem and its converse.

7. Apply the Pythagorean Theorem to determine unknown side lengths in right triangles in real-world and mathematical problems in two and three dimensions.

8. Apply the Pythagorean Theorem to find the distance between two points in a coordinate system.

8.G.C Solve real-world and mathematical problems involving volume of cylinders, cones, and spheres.

9. Know the formulas for the volumes of cones, cylinders, and spheres and use them to solve real-world and mathematical problems.

Math Practices and Problem Solving Handbook

The **Math Practices and Problem Solving Handbook** is available online.

MP.1 Make sense of problems and persevere in solving them.

MP.2 Reason abstractly and quantitatively.

MP.3 Construct viable arguments and critique the reasoning of others.

MP.4 Model with mathematics.

MP.5 Use appropriate tools strategically.

MP.6 Attend to precision.

MP.7 Look for and make use of structure.

MP.8 Look for and express regularity in repeated reasoning.

Jordan helps his uncle set up for an event. Jordan's uncle drew a diagram to show Jordan how he wants the tables set up. Jordan needs to set up enough tables for 42 guests. How can Jordan figure out how many tables to set up?

Enough tables for 42 Guests

Can I see a pattern or structure in the problem or solution strategy?
I can see that each end table has 5 seats and each middle table has 4 seats. Each additional table increases the number of seats by 4.

How can I use the pattern or structure I see to help me solve the problem?
I can write an equation that includes a term for the two end tables and a term for the middle tables.

Do I notice any repeated calculations or steps? Each additional table adds 4 seats.

Are there general methods that I can use to solve the problem? I can multiply the number of middle tables by 4 and then add the seats on the two end tables.

Other questions to consider:
- Are there attributes in common that help me?
- Can I see the expression or equation as a single object? Or as a composition of several objects?

Other questions to consider:
- What can I generalize from one problem to another?
- Can I derive an equation from a series of data points?
- How reasonable are the results that I am getting?

Common Core State Standards
Standards for Mathematical Practice

MP.1 Make sense of problems and persevere in solving them.

Mathematically proficient students:
- can explain the meaning of a problem
- look for entry points to begin solving a problem
- analyze givens, constraints, relationships, and goals
- make conjectures about the solution
- plan a solution pathway
- think of similar problems, and try simpler forms of the problem
- evaluate their progress toward a solution and change pathways if necessary
- can explain similarities and differences between different representations
- check their solutions to problems.

MP.2 Reason abstractly and quantitatively.

Mathematically proficient students:
- make sense of quantities and their relationships in problem situations:
  - They *decontextualize*—create a coherent representation of a problem situation using numbers, variables, and symbols; and
  - They *contextualize* – attend to the meaning of numbers, variables, and symbols in the problem situation
- know and use different properties of operations to solve problems.

MP.3 Construct viable arguments and critique the reasoning of others.

Mathematically proficient students:
- use definitions and problem solutions when constructing arguments
- make conjectures about the solutions to problems
- build a logical progression of statements to support their conjectures and justify their conclusions
- analyze situations and recognize and use counterexamples
- reason inductively about data, making plausible arguments that take into account the context from which the data arose
- listen or read the arguments of others, and decide whether they make sense
- respond to the arguments of others
- compare the effectiveness of two plausible arguments
- distinguish correct logic or reasoning from flawed, and—if there is a flaw in an argument—explain what it is
- ask useful questions to clarify or improve arguments of others.

MP.4 › Model with mathematics.

Mathematically proficient students:
- can develop a representation—drawing, diagram, table, graph, expression, equation–to model a problem situation
- make assumptions and approximations to simplify a complicated situation
- identify important quantities in a practical situation and map their relationships using a range of tools
- analyze relationships mathematically to draw conclusions
- interpret mathematical results in the context of the situation and propose improvements to the model as needed.

MP.5 › Use appropriate tools strategically.

Mathematically proficient students:
- consider appropriate tools when solving a mathematical problem
- make sound decisions about when each of these tools might be helpful
- identify relevant mathematical resources, and use them to pose or solve problems
- use tools and technology to explore and deepen their understanding of concepts.

MP.6 › Attend to precision.

Mathematically proficient students:
- communicate precisely to others
- use clear definitions in discussions with others and in their own reasoning
- state the meaning of the symbols they use
- specify units of measure, and label axes to clarify their correspondence with quantities in a problem
- calculate accurately and efficiently
- express numerical answers with a degree of precision appropriate for the problem context.

MP.7 › Look for and make use of structure.

Mathematically proficient students:
- look closely at a problem situation to identify a pattern or structure
- can step back from a solution pathway and shift perspective
- can see complex representations, such as some algebraic expressions, as single objects or as being composed of several objects.

MP.8 › Look for and express regularity in repeated reasoning.

Mathematically proficient students:
- notice if calculations are repeated, and look both for general methods and for shortcuts
- maintain oversight of the process as they work to solve a problem, while also attending to the details
- continually evaluate the reasonableness of their intermediate results.

RATIONAL NUMBER OPERATIONS

? Topic Essential Question

How can the properties of operations be used to solve problems involving integers and rational numbers?

Topic Overview

Topic Vocabulary

- additive inverse
- complex fraction
- multiplicative inverse
- repeating decimal
- terminating decimal

Lesson Digital Resources

INTERACTIVE STUDENT EDITION
Access online or offline.

VISUAL LEARNING ANIMATION
Interact with visual learning animations.

ACTIVITY Use with *Solve & Discuss It, Explore It,* and *Explain It* activities, and to explore Examples.

VIDEOS Watch clips to support *3-Act Mathematical Modeling Lessons* and *STEM Projects*.

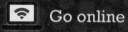 Go online

Win Some, Lose Some

Are you the kind of person who has a lot of knowledge about history, literature, or science? What about pop culture, music, sports, and current events? Some schools have an academic bowl team that competes in tournaments against other schools. The teams are made up of members with strengths in different subject areas.

In any quiz competition, it's important to understand the rules and scoring. Think about this during the 3-Act Mathematical Modeling lesson.

PRACTICE Practice what you've learned.

TUTORIALS Get help from *Virtual Nerd*, right when you need it.

MATH TOOLS Explore math with digital tools.

GAMES Play Math Games to help you learn.

KEY CONCEPT Review important lesson content.

GLOSSARY Read and listen to English/Spanish definitions.

ASSESSMENT Show what you've learned.

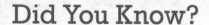 **enVision® STEM Project**

 VIDEO

Did You Know?

The **lowest recorded temperature in the world**, −136°F (−93.2°C), occurred in Antarctica.

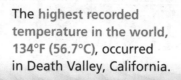

The **highest recorded temperature in the world**, 134°F (56.7°C), occurred in Death Valley, California.

The Celsius scale (°C) is commonly used for temperature measurement in most of the world.

Only a small number of nations, including the United States, regularly use the Fahrenheit scale (°F).

Windchill, based on the rate of heat loss from exposed skin, can make it feel colder outside than the actual air temperature indicates. Wind chills in some places of the world can dip into the −100°F range.

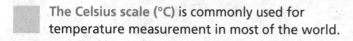

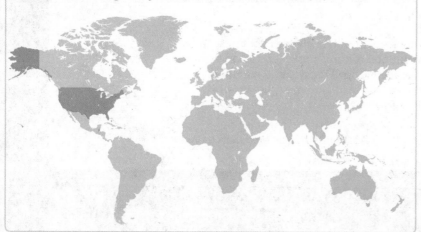

Your Task: How Cold is Too Cold?

There are many regions of the world with cold temperatures and extreme conditions. How do the inhabitants of these regions adapt and thrive? Do conditions exist that make regions too cold for human living? You and your classmates will explore and describe the habitability of regions with low temperatures.

Review What You Know!

Vocabulary

Choose the best term from the box. Write it on the blank.

absolute value
Associative Property
Commutative Property
Distributive Property
integers
rational number

1. The _____ explains why $a \times b = b \times a$ and $a + b = b + a$.

2. The _____ of -6 is 6, because it is 6 units from zero on the number line.

3. The number $\frac{5}{3}$ is a _____ because 5 and 3 are integers and $3 \neq 0$.

4. The set of _____ consists of the counting numbers, their opposites, and zero.

5. The sum of $(a + b) + c$ is equal to the sum of $a + (b + c)$ as explained

   by the _____ .

6. If you evaluate $n \times (y + z)$ by writing it as $(n \times y) + (n \times z)$, you have used

   the _____ .

Add and Subtract Fractions and Decimals

Add or subtract.

7. $2\frac{1}{3} + 6\frac{3}{5}$

8. $9\frac{1}{10} - 4\frac{3}{4}$

9. $19.86 + 7.091$

10. $57 - 10.62$

Multiply and Divide Fractions and Decimals

Multiply or divide.

11. 4.08×29.7

12. $15{,}183.3 \div 473$

13. $\frac{15}{16} \times 9\frac{1}{5}$

14. $4\frac{7}{9} \div 1\frac{7}{12}$

15. Byron has $1\frac{7}{10}$ kilograms of black pepper. He uses $\frac{7}{8}$ of the pepper and splits it between 7 pepper shakers. How much pepper will be in each shaker?

Ⓐ $\frac{119}{80}$ kg

Ⓒ 1.4125 kg

Ⓑ $\frac{1}{8}$ kg

Ⓓ $\frac{17}{80}$ kg

Language Development

Fill in the word map with new terms, definitions, and supporting examples or illustrations.

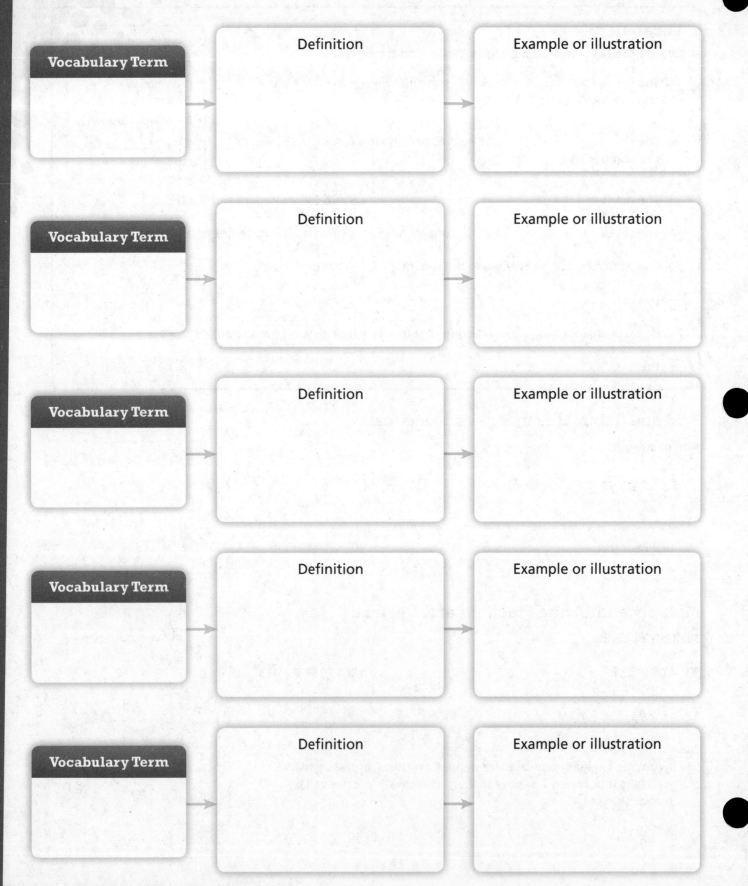

Vocabulary Term

Definition

Example or illustration

Vocabulary Term

Definition

Example or illustration

Vocabulary Term

Definition

Example or illustration

Vocabulary Term

Definition

Example or illustration

Vocabulary Term

Definition

Example or illustration

PROJECT
1A

What is something you can make?

PROJECT: DESIGN A HANDMADE ITEM TO SELL

PROJECT
1B

How old were you when petroglyphs were being painted?

PROJECT: MAKE A TIMELINE

PROJECT 1C

What makes an obstacle course fun?

PROJECT: BUILD A MODEL OF AN OBSTACLE COURSE

PROJECT 1D

What are your favorite ways to exercise?

PROJECT: FILM AN EXERCISE VIDEO

Solve & Discuss It!  ACTIVITY

When preparing for a rocket launch, the mission control center uses the phrase "T minus" before liftoff.

...T minus 3, T minus 2, T minus 1, ...

After the rocket has launched, "T plus" is used while the rocket is in flight.

...T plus 1, T plus 2, T plus 3, ...

When does the rocket launch?
What could "T" represent?

Reasoning What integers can you use to represent this situation?

I can...
relate integers, their opposites, and their absolute values.

© **Common Core Content Standards**
7.NS.A.1a

Mathematical Practices
MP.1, MP.2, MP.3, MP.4

Focus on math practices
Reasoning How are "T minus 4" and "T plus 4" related?

EXAMPLE 1 Combine Opposite Quantities to Make 0

Scan for Multimedia

Alexis was shopping on the ground floor of the mall when she realized she had left her phone in her car. She walks down 6 floors to her car in the underground parking garage.

How far will Alexis walk to get back to the ground floor? Use integers to explain.

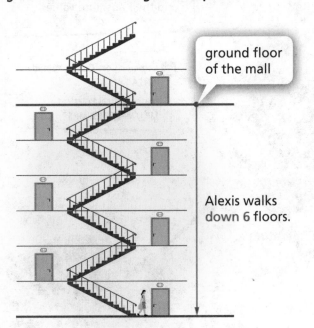

ground floor of the mall

Alexis walks down 6 floors.

Use integers on a number line to represent the situation.

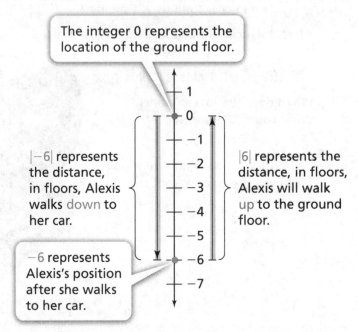

The integer 0 represents the location of the ground floor.

|−6| represents the distance, in floors, Alexis walks down to her car.

|6| represents the distance, in floors, Alexis will walk up to the ground floor.

−6 represents Alexis's position after she walks to her car.

$|-6| = |6| = 6$

−6 and 6 are opposites. Opposite quantities combine to make 0.

Alexis will walk the same distance, 6 floors, in the opposite direction to get back to the ground floor.

✓ Try It!

Xavier climbs 9 feet up into an apple tree. What integer represents the direction and how far he will climb to get back down to the ground? What does the integer 0 represent in this situation?

The integer ☐ represents Xavier's climb down.

The integer 0 represents ☐ .

Convince Me! How are the absolute values of opposite integers related?

EXAMPLE 2 ▸ **Combine Opposite Quantities**

Samuel has $20 in his savings account before he makes a deposit of $160. After 2 weeks, he withdraws $160. How did Samuel's savings account balance change?

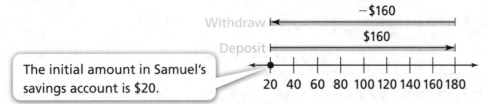

The initial amount in Samuel's savings account is $20.

The amounts deposited and withdrawn are opposite quantities and combine to make 0. Samuel's account balance did not change because the amounts deposited and withdrawn combine to make 0.

☑ **Try It!**

The temperature was 75°. At noon, the temperature increased 7°. By evening, the temperature decreased by 7°. How did the temperature change?

EXAMPLE 3 ▸ **Represent Change Using Integers**

One winter morning, the temperature was −2°C. By 11:00 A.M., the temperature had decreased by 3°. At 4:00 P.M., the temperature reached 0°C. What integer represents the temperature change from 11:00 A.M. to 4:00 P.M.?

Start at −2. The integer −3 represents the temperature decrease, so move 3 units left. The temperature has a change of −3.

Next, move 5 units right to show the temperature increase to 0°C. The temperature has a change of 5.

Increase of 5°

Decrease of 3°

At 11:00 A.M. the temperature was −5°C.

At 4:00 P.M. the temperature was 0°C.

The integer 5 represents the temperature change from 11:00 A.M. to 4:00 P.M.

☑ **Try It!**

Shaniqua has $45 in her wallet. She spends $4 on snacks and $8 on a movie ticket. What integer represents the change in the amount of money in Shaniqua's wallet? How much money does she have left?

An integer, *n*, and its opposite, −*n*, combine to make 0.

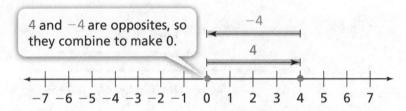

4 and −4 are opposites, so they combine to make 0.

Do You Understand?

1. **Essential Question** How are integers and their opposites related?

2. **Reasoning** In order for an atom to have a zero charge, every proton, which has a charge of +1, must be matched with an electron, which has a charge of −1. A helium atom has 2 protons and 2 electrons. Explain why a helium atom has a zero charge.

3. **Model with Math** Explain how to use a number line to show that opposite quantities combine to make 0.

Do You Know How?

4. Marcus dives from the surface of the ocean to a reef 18 meters below sea level. What integer represents Marcus's location relative to the surface? How far does Marcus have to go to return to the surface?

5. The temperature of the water in Emily's fish tank was 78°F on Sunday. The water temperature changed by −3° on Monday, and then by 3° on Tuesday. What integer represents the temperature change of the water from Sunday to Tuesday? What was the water temperature on Tuesday?

6. The scores of players on a golf team are shown in the table. The team's combined score was 0. What was Travis's score?

Golfer	Score
CELIA	−3
JANINE	3
SAMI	1
TED	4
TRAVIS	

Name: _____

Practice & Problem Solving

Scan for Multimedia

Leveled Practice In 7–9, write the integer that represents the situation.

7. Max spent $53 and now has no money left. He had $ [   ] before his purchase.

8. The temperature was 8°F. It dropped so that the temperature was 0°F.

   [   ] °F represents the change in temperature.

9. An airplane descended 4,000 feet before landing. The integer that represents how many feet the airplane was above the ground before

   its descent is [   ].

10. Carolyn says that point A and point B represent opposite integers.

    a. What is the opposite of the integer represented by point A? By point B?

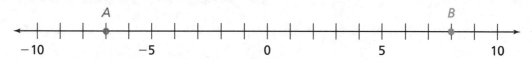

    b. **Construct Arguments** Do you agree with Carolyn? Explain.

11. A football team lost 9 yards during a play. The team had a combined gain or loss of 0 yards after the next play. What integer represents the yards gained or lost on the next play? Show this on the number line.

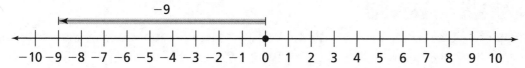

12. A roller coaster car goes above and below ground. Use the number line to show its changes in height. What is the height of the car at the end of the ride?

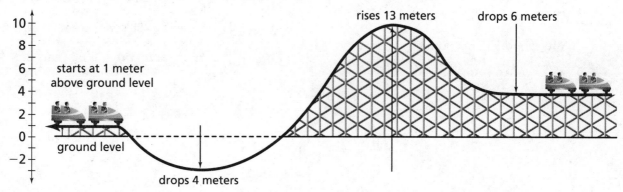

starts at 1 meter above ground level

ground level

rises 13 meters

drops 6 meters

drops 4 meters

13. Dimitri is buying a car. He chooses Option 1 to add a new sound system to his car. What integer represents the change from the base price of the car to its final price?

Used Car DEALER Price Sticker	20
	Base Price
Sale	–$700.00
Opt.1	+$1,400.00
Markdown	–$1,100.00
	?

14. Make Sense and Persevere What values do x and y have if $|x| = 16$, $|y| = 16$, and when x and y are combined they equal 0? Explain your reasoning.

15. Write a situation that can be represented by the opposite of –42.

16. Higher Order Thinking Three friends all live on the same street that runs west to east. Beth lives 5 blocks from Ann. Carl lives 2 blocks from Beth. If the street is represented by a number line and Ann's house is located at 0, what are the possible locations for Carl's house? Assume that each unit on the number line represents 1 block.

17. Which of these situations can be represented with an integer that when combined with –9 makes 0? Select all that apply.

☐ You walk down 9 flights of stairs.

☐ You climb up 9 flights of stairs.

☐ The temperature drops 9°F.

☐ You spend $9 on a book.

☐ You earn $9 from your job.

18. Which of these situations can be represented by the opposite of 80? Select all that apply.

☐ An airplane descends 80 m.

☐ An elevator ascends 80 m.

☐ The cost of a train ticket drops by $80.

☐ You remove 80 songs from an MP3 player.

☐ Suzy's grandmother is 80 years old.

Solve & Discuss It!  ACTIVITY

Calvin wants to customize his surfboard so that it is wider than the 82 model but narrower than the 92 model. What measurement could be the width of his surfboard? Explain.

I can...
recognize rational numbers and write them in decimal form.

 Common Core Content Standards
7.NS.A.2d

Mathematical Practices
MP.1, MP.2, MP.6, MP.7

Be Precise
Between which two numbers is the custom width located?

Model	82	92	102
	$22\frac{1}{2}$" wide	$23\frac{1}{4}$" wide	24" wide
	$3\frac{1}{4}$" thick	$3\frac{1}{2}$" thick	$3\frac{5}{8}$" thick

Focus on math practices

Use Structure Lindy's surfboard is $23\frac{1}{3}$ inches wide. Between which two surfboard models is her custom surfboard's width? How do you know?

? Essential Question How are rational numbers written as decimals?

EXAMPLE 1 **Write Rational Numbers in Decimal Form: Terminating Decimals**

Scan for Multimedia

Juanita is reporting on pitching statistics. Pedro's fastball statistic is $\frac{52}{80}$. How can Juanita write the fastball statistic in decimal form?

Make Sense and Persevere
How can you write a rational number as a decimal?

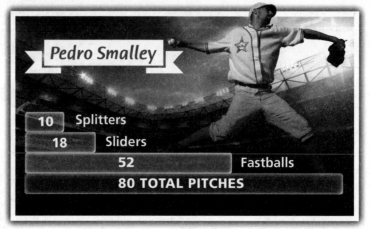

Pedro Smalley

10	Splitters
18	Sliders
52	Fastballs
80 TOTAL PITCHES

Make a bar diagram to show how the quantities are related.

52 Fastballs
80 TOTAL PITCHES

$\frac{52}{80}$

Divide the numerator by the denominator to convert the rational number $\frac{52}{80}$ to decimal form.

```
        0.65
   80)52.00
     −480
       400
      −400
         0
```

A **terminating decimal** is a decimal that ends in zero.

The remainder is 0, so the decimal form of $\frac{52}{80}$ is a terminating decimal.

Juanita can write $\frac{52}{80}$ as 0.65.

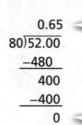 **Try It!**

In the next several games, the pitcher threw a total of 384 pitches and used a fastball 240 times. What decimal should Juanita use to update her report?

240 Fastballs
384 TOTAL PITCHES

Juanita should use the decimal ☐ to update her report.

Convince Me! How do you know that the answer is a terminating decimal?

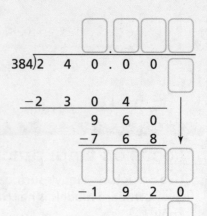

```
         .  ☐ ☐ ☐ ☐
              ☐
  384)2 4 0 . 0 0
    −2 3 0 4
         9 6 0
        −7 6 8
       ☐ ☐ ☐ ☐
        −1 9 2 0
              ☐
```

EXAMPLE 2 ▸ Write Rational Numbers in Decimal Form: Repeating Decimals

A class votes on whether to change their school mascot. How can you express the number of students in favor of a new mascot in decimal form?

In a class of **18** students, **5** voted to change their mascot.

Divide to write $\frac{5}{18}$ in decimal form.

$$
\begin{array}{r}
0.277 \\
18\overline{)5.000} \\
-36 \\
\hline
140 \\
-126 \\
\hline
140 \\
-126 \\
\hline
14
\end{array}
$$

A **repeating decimal** has a decimal expansion that repeats the same digit, or block of digits, without end.

The products and differences repeat. The remainder will never be 0.

The decimal form of $\frac{5}{18}$ is 0.277… or $0.2\overline{7}$.

The … means the decimal does not terminate.

A line over one or more digits indicates that those digits repeat.

✓ Try It!

What is the decimal form of $\frac{100}{3}$, $\frac{100}{5}$, and $\frac{100}{6}$? Determine whether each decimal repeats or terminates.

EXAMPLE 3 ▸ Recognize Rational Numbers in Decimal Form

Explain whether each of the following is a rational number.

a. −6.382

The decimal terminates, so this is a rational number.

b. 1.5399$\overline{81}$

The digits 8 and 1 repeat infinitely, so this is a rational number.

c. 0.43524982…

The decimal does not terminate and the digits do not repeat, so this is **NOT** a rational number.

✓ Try It!

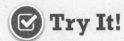

Is $-0.\overline{3}$ a rational number? Is 3.14144144414444… a rational number? Explain your reasoning.

To convert from the fraction form of a rational number to its decimal form, divide the numerator by the denominator. The decimal form of a rational number either terminates in 0s or eventually repeats.

Terminating Decimal	Repeating Decimal
$\dfrac{3}{4}$	$\dfrac{1}{6}$
$4\overline{)3.00}$ 0.75	$6\overline{)1.00}$ $0.1\overline{6}$

Do You Understand?

1. 🔑 **Essential Question** How are rational numbers written as decimals?

2. **Reasoning** How can you use division to find the decimal equivalent of a rational number?

3. **Be Precise** What is the difference between a terminating decimal and a repeating decimal?

Do You Know How?

4. What is the decimal equivalent of each rational number?

   a. $\dfrac{7}{20}$

   b. $-\dfrac{23}{20}$

   c. $\dfrac{1}{18}$

   d. $-\dfrac{60}{22}$

5. There are 5,280 feet in a mile. What part of a mile, in decimal form, will you drive until you reach the exit?

Name: _____

Practice & Problem Solving

Leveled Practice In 6–8, write the decimal equivalent for each rational number. Use a bar over any repeating digits.

6. $\frac{2}{3}$

7. $\frac{3}{11}$

8. $8\frac{4}{9}$

9. Is $1.02\overline{27}$ a rational number? Explain.

10. Which should Aaron use to convert a fraction to a decimal?

Ⓐ $\overline{\text{numerator})\text{denominator}}$

Ⓑ $\frac{\text{denominator}}{\text{numerator}} \cdot 100$

Ⓒ $\overline{\text{denominator})\text{numerator}}$

Ⓓ $\frac{\text{numerator}}{\text{denominator}} \cdot 100$

11. Is the fraction $\frac{1}{3}$ equivalent to a terminating decimal or a decimal that does not terminate?

12. Determine whether the given number belongs to each set.

	Whole Numbers	Integers	Rational Numbers
−34			

13. Ariel incorrectly says that $2\frac{5}{8}$ is the same as 2.58.

  a. Convert $2\frac{5}{8}$ to a decimal.

  b. What was Ariel's likely error?

14. Use Structure Consider the rational number $\frac{3}{11}$.

  a. What are the values of a and b in $a\overline{)b}$ when you use division to find the decimal form?

  b. What is the decimal form for $\frac{3}{11}$?

15. At a grocery store, Daniel wants to buy $3\frac{1}{5}$ lb of ham. What decimal should the digital scale show?

Write $3\frac{1}{5}$ as a fraction and then divide.

The scale should read [ ] lb.

16. Reasoning At a butcher shop, Hilda bought beef and pork. She left with $18\frac{8}{25}$ pounds of meat. Express the number of pounds of pork she bought using a decimal.

17. Be Precise Is 9.373 a repeating decimal? Is it rational? Explain your reasoning.

18. Reasoning Aiden has one box that is $3\frac{3}{11}$ feet tall and a second box that is 3.27 feet tall. If he stacks the boxes, about how tall will the stack be?

19. You are adding air to a tire. The air pressure in the tire should be $32\frac{27}{200}$ pounds per square inch. What decimal should you watch for on the digital pressure gauge?

20. Higher Order Thinking Dion has a pizza with a diameter of $10\frac{1}{3}$ in. Is the square box shown big enough to fit the pizza inside? Justify your answer.

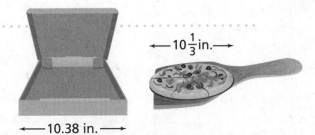

← $10\frac{1}{3}$ in. →

← 10.38 in. →

☑ Assessment Practice

21. Which of the following mixed numbers has the same decimal value as $110\frac{147}{168}$?

Ⓐ $110\frac{49}{56}$ Ⓑ $110\frac{170}{180}$ Ⓒ $110\frac{56}{72}$ Ⓓ $110\frac{247}{268}$

22. Select all the true statements about the negative fractions $-\frac{4}{5}$ and $-\frac{5}{6}$.

☐ $-\frac{4}{5}$ can be expressed as a repeating decimal.

☐ $-\frac{5}{6}$ can be expressed as a repeating decimal.

☐ Both fractions can be expressed as repeating decimals.

☐ The digit that repeats is 3.

☐ The digit that repeats is 8.

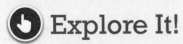

Explore It!

Rain increases the height of water in a kiddie pool, while evaporation decreases the height. The pool water level is currently 2 inches above the fill line.

 ACTIVITY

Go Online

I can...
add integers.

© **Common Core Content Standards**
7.NS.A.1b, 7.NS.A.1d

Mathematical Practices
MP.2, MP.3, MP.4, MP.5, MP.7

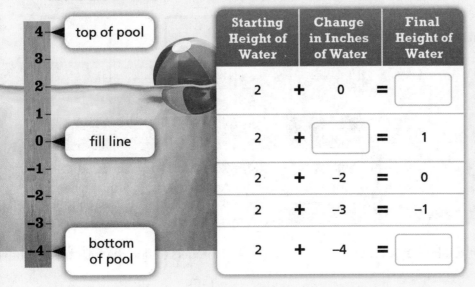

Starting Height of Water	Change in Inches of Water	Final Height of Water
2 +	0 =	
2 +	=	1
2 +	−2 =	0
2 +	−3 =	−1
2 +	−4 =	

A. Look for patterns in the equations in the table so you can fill in the missing numbers. Describe any relationships you notice.

B. Will the sum of 2 and (−6) be a positive or negative number? Explain.

Focus on math practices

Look for Relationships Suppose the water level of the pool started at 2 inches below the fill line. Make a table to show the starting height of the water, the change in inches, and the new final height of the water.

? **Essential Question** How do you use what you know about absolute value to add integers?

EXAMPLE 1 👁 Add Two Negative Integers

Scan for Multimedia

Nita wants to straighten a photo. She uses an app to adjust the tilt. What was the total tilt adjustment?

Reasoning Why is the total tilt adjustment negative?

Set at 0. | Adjust by −4 degrees. | Adjust by another −6 degrees.

Use a number line to represent the total tilt adjustment.

Then move 6 units left to show an adjustment of −6. The total adjustment was −10.

Start at 0. Move 4 units left to show an adjustment of −4.

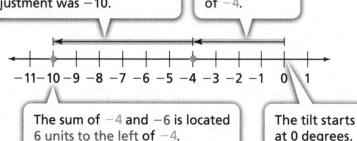

−11 −10 −9 −8 −7 −6 −5 −4 −3 −2 −1 0 1

The sum of −4 and −6 is located 6 units to the left of −4.

The tilt starts at 0 degrees.

Add integers to find the total tilt adjustment.

$-4 + (-6)$

Because you moved 4 units and then 6 units in the **same direction** on the number line, **add** the absolute values to find the amount of tilt.

$|-4| + |-6|$
$4 + 6 = 10$

10 represents the amount of tilt.

Because you moved to the **left** twice, the sum is negative.

$-4 + (-6) = -10$

Both adjustments are negative, so the tilt is negative.

The total tilt adjustment was −10.

✓ Try It!

Dana recorded a temperature drop of 2° and a second temperature drop of 3°. What is the total change in temperature?

[ ] + [ ] = [ ]

The sign of the sum is [   ]. The total change in temperature is [ ]°.

Convince Me! Would the sum of two positive integers be positive or negative? Explain.

EXAMPLE **2** Add Integers with Different Signs
  ACTIVITY ASSESS

Kara entered her chili recipe into the neighborhood cook-off. Nine judges rated each recipe with a thumbs up (+1) or thumbs down (−1). What was the final rating for Kara's recipe?

Reasoning There were more thumbs-down votes, so the final rating is negative.

Use a number line to represent Kara's final rating.

Start at 0. Move 5 units left for −5. Move 4 units right for 4. The final rating is −1.

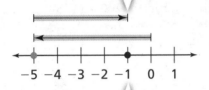

The sum of −5 and 4 is located 4 units to the right of −5.

Add integers to find Kara's final rating.

$-5 + 4$

Because you moved in **different directions** on the number line, **subtract** the absolute values.

$|-5| - |4|$

$5 - 4 = 1$

There is 1 more thumbs down vote than thumbs up.

Because you moved a **greater distance** to the left than to the right, the sum is negative.

$-5 + 4 = -1$

The sum is negative because $|-5|$ is greater than $|4|$.

The final rating for Kara's recipe was −1.

EXAMPLE **3** Identify Additive Inverses and Opposite Integers

Playing golf, Mike got a +2 on the first hole and −2 on the second hole. What is his combined score for the first two holes?

$2 + (-2)$

$|2| = 2$ and $|-2| = 2$

$2 - 2 = 0$

When the signs of the addends are different, subtract the absolute values.

So, $2 + (-2) = 0$.

Mike's combined score for the first two holes is 0.

Two numbers that have a sum of 0 are called **additive inverses**, or opposites.

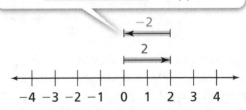

 Try It!

Find the sum for each expression.

a. $-66 + 42$
b. $-57 + 57$
c. $29 + (-28)$

When adding integers with the **same** sign, find the **sum** of the absolute values.

$(-36) + (-12)$

|−36| = 36 and |−12| = 12
36 + 12 = 48

So, $(-36) + (-12) = -48$ — Use the **same** sign as the addends.

When adding integers with **different** signs, find the **difference** of the absolute values.

$18 + (-14)$

|18| = 18 and |−14| = 14
18 − 14 = 4

So, $18 + (-14) = 4$ — Use the sign of the greater absolute value.

Do You Understand?

1. **Essential Question** How do you use what you know about absolute value to add integers?

2. **Reasoning** How can you tell the sign of the sum of a positive and negative integer without doing any calculations?

3. **Model with Math** How would you use a number line to determine the sum of two negative integers?

Do You Know How?

4. Sarah bought a bike that cost $260. She had a coupon that was worth $55 off the cost of any bike. Use the expression 260 + (−55) to find how much Sarah paid for her bike.

5. A shark is swimming 60 feet below the surface of the ocean. There is a fish that is 25 feet deeper in the water. Use the expression (−60) + (−25) to describe the fish's location relative to the surface of the ocean.

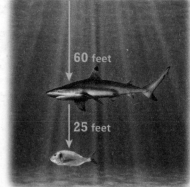

60 feet

25 feet

6. The high temperature one day was 30°F. Then the temperature dropped 23 degrees during the night. Does the expression 30 + (−23) represent the temperature at night? Explain.

Practice & Problem Solving

Leveled Practice For 7–9, use a number line to help find the sum.

7. 5 + (−3) is ☐ units from 5, in the ☐

direction.

Use the number line to find 5 + (−3).

8. −1 + (−3) is ☐ units from −1, in the ☐

direction.

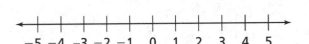

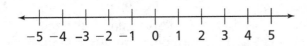

9. In City A, the temperature rises 9° from 8 A.M. to 9 A.M. Then the temperature drops 8° from 9 A.M. to 10 A.M. In City B, the temperature drops 5° from 8 A.M. to 9 A.M. Then the temperature drops 4° from 9 A.M. to 10 A.M.

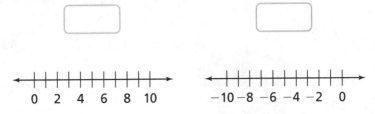

a. What expression represents the change in temperature for City A?

b. What integer represents the change in temperature for City A?

c. What expression represents the change in temperature for City B?

d. What integer represents the change in temperature for City B?

e. Which city has the greater change in temperature from 8 A.M. to 10 A.M.?

10. An airplane flying at an altitude of 30,000 feet flies up to avoid a storm. Immediately after passing the storm, the airplane returns to its original altitude.

a. What integer represents the airplane's change in altitude to avoid the storm?

b. What integer represents the airplane's change in altitude immediately after passing the storm?

c. Use Appropriate Tools Draw a number line to represent the airplane's change in altitude.

The airplane flies up to 38,000 feet to avoid a storm.

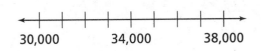

11. A deep-sea diver dives 81 feet from the surface. He then dives 14 more feet. The diver's depth can be represented by −81 + (−14). What is the diver's present location?

12. Rena's rowboat drifts 23 feet from shore, followed by 9 more feet. The rowboat's current position can be represented by −23 + (−9). What integer represents the rowboat's position?

13. **Critique Reasoning** A submarine traveling 200 meters below the surface of the ocean increases its depth by 45 meters. Adam says that the new location of the submarine is −155 meters. Describe an error Adam could have made that would result in the answer he gave.

14. Kim has $45 to spend for a day at the zoo. She pays $17 for admission, $8 for lunch, and $4 for a snack.

    a. **Model with Math** Use integers to write an addition expression that represents the amount of money Kim has left.

    b. Kim goes to the gift shop and finds a T-shirt she likes for $19. Does she have enough money to buy the T-shirt? Explain.

15. **Higher Order Thinking** Samantha has $300 for guitar lessons to learn her favorite song. Mrs. Jones charges $80 per lesson and requires three lessons to teach Samantha the song. Mr. Beliz charges $62 per lesson and will require four lessons to teach Samantha the song. Use integers to represent what each teacher charges. Which is the better deal for Samantha?

16. A fish swims at 10 ft below sea level, and then swims another 10 ft deeper to avoid a shark. Write an addition expression that represents this situation.

17. The temperature drops 10 degrees and then rises 10 degrees. Write an addition expression that represents this situation.

Solve & Discuss It!

A library database shows the total number of books checked out at any given time as a negative number. What are the possible numbers of books that were checked out and checked in on Monday? Explain.

MONDAY
Morning (–37)
Evening (–45)

Make Sense and Persevere How can you use the data to understand what happened during the day?

I can...
subtract integers.

Common Core Content Standards
7.NS.A.1c, 7.NS.A.1d

Mathematical Practices
MP.1, MP.2, MP.3, MP.4, MP.7

Focus on math practices

Reasoning Suppose the library database showed 0 for Monday evening. What do you know about the number of books checked out and checked in that day?

VISUAL LEARNING ASSESS

EXAMPLE 1 — Subtract Positive Integers

Scan for Multimedia

A football team gains 3 yards on first down. On second down, they lose 8 yards. What is the total change in yards after the first two downs?

Look for Relationships You can use what you know about adding integers to subtract integers.

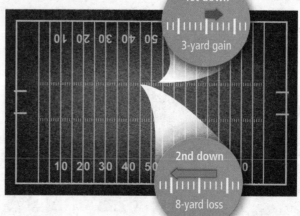

Use a number line to represent the team's total change in yards.

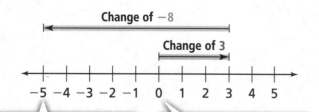

The team's final position represents a 5-yard loss.

0 represents the team's starting position.

Use a subtraction expression to represent the teams' change in yards.

$$3 - 8$$
$$= 3 + (-8)$$

Subtraction is the same as adding the opposite. To subtract 8, add its opposite, −8.

Now add.

$$|3| = 3 \text{ and } |-8| = 8$$
$$8 - 3 = 5$$
$$3 - 8 = -5$$

The total change in yards after the first two downs is represented by −5.

✓ Try It!

On the next play, the team gained 5 yards and then lost 6 yards. What is the total change in yards?

$$5 - \boxed{}$$
$$= 5 + \boxed{}$$
$$= \boxed{}$$

$\boxed{}$ -yard loss

$\boxed{}$ -yard gain

The total change in yards is $\boxed{}$, so they had a total loss of $\boxed{}$ yard.

Convince Me! Is the additive inverse of an integer always negative? Explain.

EXAMPLE **2** **Subtract Integers with Different Signs**

  ACTIVITY ASSESS

Ian's football team lost 2 yards on a running play. Then they received a 5-yard penalty. What is the team's total change in yards?

Write a subtraction expression to represent the change in yards.

$-2 - 5$

$= (-2) + (-5)$ ◁ Write an equivalent addition expression.

Add.

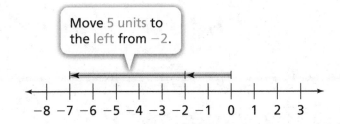

Move 5 units to the left from -2.

$|-2| = 2$ and $|-5| = 5$

$2 + 5 = 7$

$(-2) + (-5) = -7$

$-2 - 5 = -7$

The team's total change in yards is represented by -7, so they lost 7 yards.

EXAMPLE **3** **Subtract Negative Integers**

Find $-7 - (-8)$.

Write $-7 - (-8)$ as an equivalent addition expression. Then add.

$-7 + (8)$

$|-7| = 7$ and $|8| = 8$ ◁ The signs of the addends are different, so find the difference of the absolute values. The sum has the same sign as the greater absolute value.

$8 - 7 = 1$

$-7 + (8) = 1$

$-7 - (-8) = 1$

Subtracting -8 is the same as adding the opposite of -8, or $+8$.

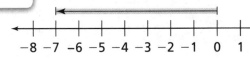

✓ Try It!

Subtract. Use a number line to help you find the answer.

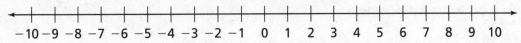

a. $-4 - 6$ **b.** $-6 - (-4)$ **c.** $4 - (-6)$

d. $6 - 4$ **e.** $4 - 6$ **f.** $-4 - (-6)$

When subtracting integers, such as $a - b$, you can use the additive inverse to write subtraction as an equivalent addition expression.

Subtracting b is the same as adding the opposite of b.

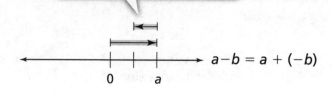

$$a - b = a + (-b)$$

Do You Understand?

1. **Essential Question** How is subtracting integers related to adding integers?

2. **Reasoning** Explain how to simplify the expression $-98 - 31$ using the additive inverse.

3. **Model with Math** How can you use a number line to represent the subtraction between two integers?

Do You Know How?

4. It was 12°C when Preston got home from school. The weather report shows a storm front moving in that will drop the temperature by 17°C. What is the expected temperature?

5. Complete the equation.

$$-67 - \boxed{} = 0$$

6. Find the difference.

   a. $41 - 275$

   b. $-15 - 47$

   c. $-72 - (-151)$

   d. $612 - (-144)$

Practice & Problem Solving

Scan for Multimedia

Leveled Practice In 7–8, fill in the boxes to solve.

7. What subtraction expression does the number line model show?

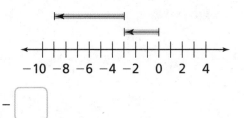

$$-10 \ -8 \ -6 \ -4 \ -2 \ \ 0 \ \ 2 \ \ 4$$

$\boxed{} - \boxed{}$

8. What is the value of the expression $-9 - (-5)$?

$$-9 - (-5)$$

$$= -9 \ \boxed{} \ 5$$

$$= \boxed{}$$

9. The temperature at the beginning of the day was 6°F. The temperature dropped 9°F by the end of the day. Use the number line to find the temperature at the end of the day.

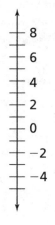

10. Murphy and Naryam do their math homework together. When they find $9 - (-8)$, they get different answers. Murphy claims the difference is 17. Naryam claims the difference is −1.

a. Who is correct?

b. What error likely led to the incorrect answer?

11. The news reports that today's high temperature is 16°F colder than yesterday's high temperature. Yesterday's high temperature was −2°F.

a. Write an expression to represent today's high temperature.

b. Reasoning Is today's high temperature positive or negative? Why?

12. Max sprints forward 10 feet and then stops and sprints back 15 feet. Use subtraction to explain where Max is relative to where he started.

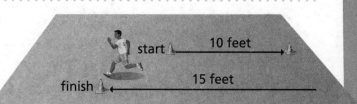

13. **Higher Order Thinking** Use the number line at the right.

a. What subtraction equation does the number line represent?

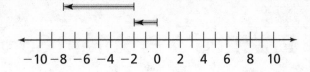

b. Use the number line to represent a different subtraction equation that has the same difference shown in the number line. Write the subtraction equation.

14. A crane lifts a pallet of concrete blocks 8 feet from the back of a truck. The truck drives away and the crane lowers the pallet 13 feet. What is the final position of the pallet relative to where it started in the back of the truck?

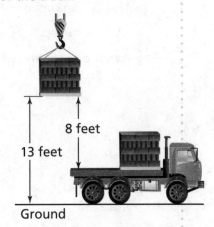

15. **Make Sense and Persevere** At its highest point, the elevation of a county is 5,762 feet above sea level. At its lowest point, the elevation of the county is 9 feet below sea level.

a. Write an expression using integers to represent the difference between the elevations.

b. Will the answer be written as a positive or negative integer?

c. What is the difference between the highest and lowest points of the county?

☑ Assessment Practice

16. Which number line model shows the subtraction 2 − 4?

Ⓐ
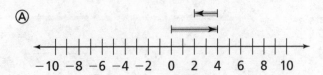

Ⓒ
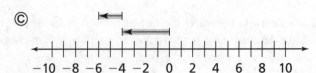

Ⓑ
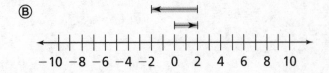

Ⓓ
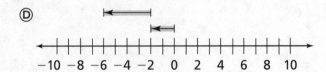

Solve & Discuss It!

ACTIVITY

Malik hikes Castle Trail from point A to point B. The elevation at point A is below sea level. What are possible beginning and ending elevations of Malik's hike?

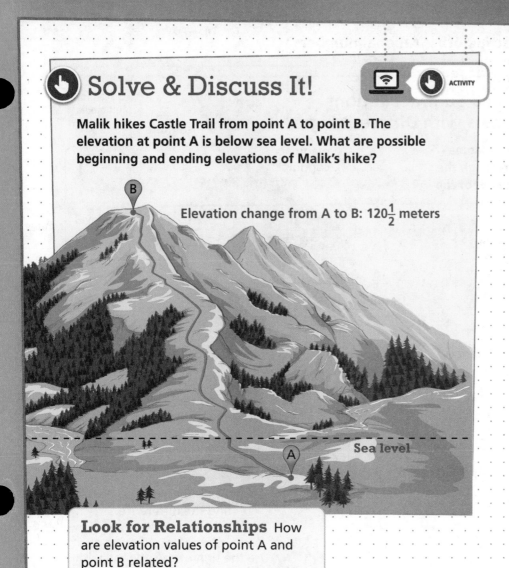

Elevation change from A to B: $120\frac{1}{2}$ meters

B

A

Sea level

I can...
add and subtract rational numbers.

© **Common Core Content Standards**
7.NS.A.1b, 7.NS.A.1c, 7.NS.A.1d

Mathematical Practices
MP.2, MP.3, MP.4, MP.7, MP.8

Look for Relationships How are elevation values of point A and point B related?

Focus on math practices

Reasoning What would be different about the hike from point B to point A?

EXAMPLE 1 · Add and Subtract Rational Numbers with Different Signs

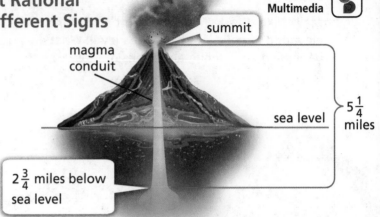

Lava flows from an active volcano's magma reservoir located below sea level through the magma conduit. How far is the summit of the volcano from sea level?

summit

magma conduit

sea level

$5\frac{1}{4}$ miles

$2\frac{3}{4}$ miles below sea level

> **Generalize** You can use the rules for adding integers to add all other rational numbers.

Use a number line to represent the distances.

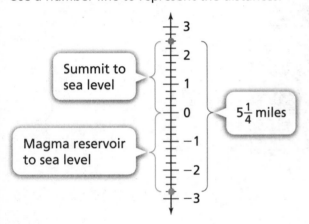

Summit to sea level

Magma reservoir to sea level

$5\frac{1}{4}$ miles

You can use the rules for adding integers to add any other rational numbers.

$\left(-2\frac{3}{4}\right) + 5\frac{1}{4}$ — Write an expression to represent the distance.

$\left|-2\frac{3}{4}\right| = 2\frac{3}{4}$ and $\left|5\frac{1}{4}\right| = 5\frac{1}{4}$

$5\frac{1}{4} - 2\frac{3}{4} = 2\frac{1}{2}$ — When the signs are different, find the difference.

$-2\frac{3}{4} + 5\frac{1}{4} = 2\frac{1}{2}$ — Use the sign of the addend with the greater absolute value.

The summit of the volcano is $2\frac{1}{2}$ miles above sea level.

☑ Try It!

A dolphin is at the surface of the water and then descends to a depth of $4\frac{1}{2}$ feet. Then the dolphin swims down another $2\frac{3}{4}$ feet. What is the location of the dolphin relative to the surface of the water?

$-4\frac{1}{2} - \boxed{}$

$-4\frac{1}{2} + \boxed{} = \boxed{}$

The location of the dolphin relative to the surface

of the water is $\boxed{}$ feet.

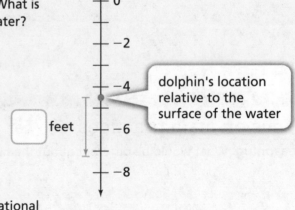

dolphin's location relative to the surface of the water

$\boxed{}$ feet

Convince Me! How are adding and subtracting two rational numbers with different signs related to adding and subtracting two integers with different signs?

EXAMPLE **2**

Use Properties of Operations to Add and Subtract

The force of gravity added to the force of thrust is the combined force at work on a model rocket. What is the combined force, in newtons, on the rocket?

$$-0.49 + 1\frac{1}{2}$$

> Use the Commutative Property and additive inverses as a strategy to add.

$$= 1\frac{1}{2} + (-0.49)$$

$$= 1\frac{1}{2} - 0.49$$

$$= 1.5 - 0.49$$

$$= 1.01$$

The combined force on the rocket is 1.01 newtons.

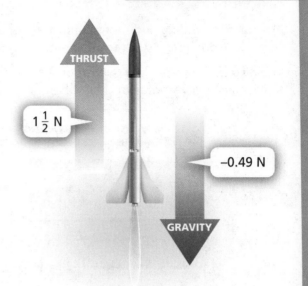

THRUST

$1\frac{1}{2}$ N

−0.49 N

GRAVITY

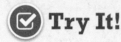 Try It!

Find the sum or difference of the rational numbers.

a. $-2.5 + \left(-5\frac{6}{10}\right)$ **b.** $-4.4 - \left(-1\frac{1}{2}\right)$ **c.** $-135.4 + 78\frac{1}{2}$

EXAMPLE **3**   **Find Distances on a Number Line**

Ruby looks over the edge of her boat and sees fish 0.4 meter below the surface of the water. If Ruby holds a 1-meter-long net at 0.5 meter above sea level, can she reach the fish? Explain.

ONE WAY

$$|0.5 - (-0.4)|$$

> To find the distance between any two points on a number line, find the absolute value of their difference.

$$= |0.5 + 0.4|$$

$$= |0.9|$$

$$= 0.9$$

ANOTHER WAY

$$|-0.4 - 0.5|$$

$$= |-0.4 + (-0.5)|$$

$$= |-0.9|$$

$$= 0.9$$

Yes. The fish are 0.9 meter below where Ruby holds the net, so Ruby can reach the fish with a 1-meter-long net.

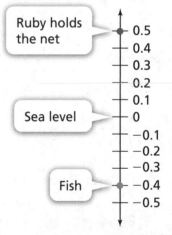

Ruby holds the net — 0.5
0.4
0.3
0.2
0.1
Sea level — 0
−0.1
−0.2
−0.3
Fish — −0.4
−0.5

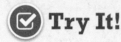 Try It!

Two divers are swimming at different depths below sea level. One diver is at −25.5 feet. The other diver is at −40.75 feet. How much farther below sea level is the diver who is farthest below sea level?

The rules for adding and subtracting all rational numbers are the same as those for adding and subtracting integers.

The distance between any two rational numbers p and q on a number line is the absolute value of their difference.

> The distance between p and q can be written as $|p - q|$ or $|q - p|$.

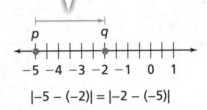

$$|-5 - (-2)| = |-2 - (-5)|$$

Do You Understand?

1. **? Essential Question** How are adding and subtracting integers related to adding and subtracting other rational numbers?

2. **Reasoning** When finding the distance between two rational numbers on a number line, does the order of the numbers you subtract matter? Explain.

3. **Critique Reasoning** Gwen says that the sum of $-1\frac{3}{4}$ and $2\frac{1}{2}$ is the same as the difference between $2\frac{1}{2}$ and $1\frac{3}{4}$. Is Gwen correct? Explain why or why not.

Do You Know How?

4. What is the distance between the top of the fishing pole and the fish?

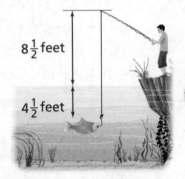

$8\frac{1}{2}$ feet

$4\frac{1}{2}$ feet

5. A shark began at 172.5 meters below sea level and then swam up 137.1 meters. Where is the shark's location now in relation to sea level?

6. Find the sum or difference.

   a. $-12\frac{1}{2} + 4\frac{1}{2}$

   b. $-0.35 - (-0.25)$

Practice & Problem Solving

Leveled Practice In 7–8, complete the expressions to find the sum or difference.

7. $3.2 - (-5.7)$

$= 3.2 + \boxed{}$

$= \boxed{}$

8. $\frac{12}{13} + \left(\frac{-1}{13}\right)$

$= \boxed{} - \boxed{}$

$= \boxed{}$

---

9. Reasoning When Tom simplified the expression $-2.6 + (-5.4)$, he got 2.8. What mistake did Tom likely make?

10. The temperature in a town is 36.6°F during the day and –12.6°F at night. What is the temperature change from day to night?

---

11. Simplify each expression.

a. $50\frac{1}{2} + (-12.3)$

b. $-50\frac{1}{2} + (-12.3)$

c. $-50\frac{1}{2} + 12.3$

---

12. At the beginning of the day, the stock market goes up $30\frac{1}{2}$ points. At the end of the day, the stock market goes down $120\frac{1}{4}$ points. What is the total change in the stock market from the beginning of the day to the end of the day?

13. A dolphin is swimming 18 feet below the surface of the ocean. There is a coast guard helicopter 75.5 feet above the surface of the water that is directly above the dolphin. What is the distance between the dolphin and the helicopter?

---

14. A bird flies from its nest to the bottom of the canyon. How far did the bird fly?

$528\frac{1}{5}$ feet —— nest

sea level

$-89\frac{3}{5}$ feet —— canyon floor

15. A scuba diving instructor takes a group of students to a depth of 54.96 feet. Then they ascend 22.38 feet to see some fish. Where are the fish in relation to the surface?

16. Model with Math Write an addition expression that is represented by the number line.

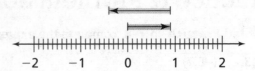

17. The roots of a plant reach down $3\frac{3}{4}$ inches below ground. How many inches is the plant above the ground?

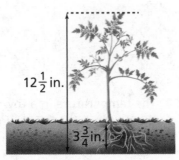

$12\frac{1}{2}$ in.

$3\frac{3}{4}$ in.

18. Higher Order Thinking

a. Simplify the expression $(-13.2) + 8.1$.

b. How are $(-13.2) + 8.1$ and $13.2 + (-8.1)$ related? Explain without computing.

c. Using a property of operations, what can you say about the sum of the two expressions?

![Assessment Practice]

19. The temperatures at sunrise and sunset are shown in the table.

PART A

Write an expression that represents the change in temperature for Day 1. Show how you can use properties of operations to find the value of the expression.

	Temperature at Sunrise (°F)	Temperature at Sunset (°F)
Day 1	−11.31	13.49
Day 2	−7.69	25.25

PART B

On which day did the temperature change more? Explain your reasoning.

20. Mischa dives from a platform that is 5 meters above water. Her dive takes her 2.1 meters below the surface of the water. Which expression could represent the distance, in meters, that Mischa dives? Select all that apply.

☐ $|5 - (-2.1)|$

☐ $|-(2.1) - (-5)|$

☐ $|2.1 - 5|$

☐ $|-(2.1) - 5|$

☐ $|5 + (-2.1)|$

1. **Vocabulary** How do you find the additive inverse of a number? Give an example of a number and its additive inverse. *Lesson 1-3*

2. A plastic toy submarine is held 15 centimeters below the water surface in a bath tub. The submarine is let go and rises 15 centimeters. What integer represents the toy submarine's position with respect to the surface of the water? *Lesson 1-1*

3. The temperature in the late afternoon was −7.5°C. It dropped 5 degrees by early evening and then dropped another 8.5 degrees by midnight. What was the temperature at midnight? *Lessons 1-3, 1-4, and 1-5*

4. The floor of an elevator in a building is 30 feet above ground level. It travels down to the lower level of the building, where the floor is 10 feet below ground level. What distance has the elevator's floor traveled? *Lessons 1-4 and 1-5*

5. Greg says that $3.\overline{3}$. is a rational number. Kari says $3.\overline{3}$ is not a terminating decimal. Who is correct and why? *Lesson 1-2*

6. Cece is hiking on a mountain and stops at $15\frac{5}{8}$ feet above sea level. The base of the mountain is 10.2 feet below sea level. What is the vertical distance between Cece and the base of the mountain? *Lesson 1-5*

Ⓐ 5.425 feet

Ⓑ 25.825 feet

Ⓒ $25\frac{3}{8}$ feet

Ⓓ $5\frac{1}{4}$ feet

How well did you do on the mid-topic checkpoint? Fill in the stars.

☆ ☆ ☆

MID-TOPIC PERFORMANCE TASK

An oceanographer, Dr. Price, is studying the types of sea life at various depths.

Location	Sea Life	Depth Relative to Sea Level (m)
A	Eels	−895.9
B	Eels	$-1{,}098\frac{3}{20}$
C	Shrimp	−2,784.75
D	Shrimp	$-3{,}259\frac{5}{8}$

PART A

Dr. Price uses a table to organize the types of sea life and the positions relative to sea level of each location.

Complete each sentence.

The difference between Location A and Location B is _____ meters.

The difference between Location B and Location C is _____ meters.

The difference between Location C and Location D is _____ meters.

PART B

After observing Location B, Dr. Price returns to Location A before descending to Location C. What is the total distance she travels?

PART C

Dr. Price descends to Location D to observe shrimp. She then ascends and stops to observe sea life that is halfway between Location B and Location C. What is the total distance between Location D and where Dr. Price stopped to observe?

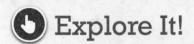

A popular beach erodes 4 inches per year on average.

Lesson 1-6
Multiply Integers

 Go Online

I can...
multiply integers.

© **Common Core Content Standards**
7.NS.A.2a, 7.NS.A.2c.

Mathematical Practices
MP.1, MP.2, MP.3, MP.4, MP.6,
MP.7, MP.8

A. How many years will it take for the coastline to erode one foot?

B. The number line below shows the expected change in the coastline as years pass. How could you use the number line to show the erosion after 10 years?

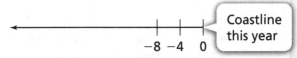

Coastline this year

−8 −4   0

Focus on math practices

Be Precise What expression could you use to represent the change in the coastline in 5 years?

VISUAL LEARNING ASSESS

EXAMPLE 1 Multiply a Negative Integer by a Positive Integer

Scan for Multimedia

While playing a board game, unlucky Lawrence had to move back 2 spaces for 4 turns in a row. What integer represents his change in position?

Model with Math What integer can you use to represent the number of spaces Lawrence had to move back each turn?

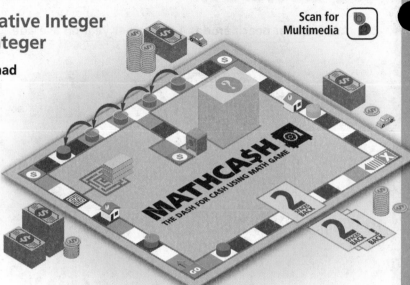

Use a number line to represent the change in position on the game board.

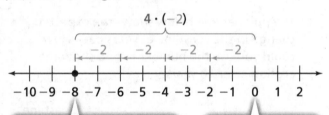

$$4 \cdot (-2)$$

−8 represents the change in position on the board.

0 represents the starting position.

The total change in position on the board is −8. Lawrence had to move back 8 spaces.

Use multiplication and properties of operations to show why $4 \cdot (-2) = -8$.

$$4 \cdot (-2 + 2) = 0$$

$$4 \cdot (-2) + 4 \cdot 2 = 0$$

Use additive inverses and the Zero Property of Multiplication to write a multiplication problem.

$$4 \cdot (-2) + 8 = 0$$

$$?\ + 8 = 0$$

You know that opposites add to 0, so $-8 + 8 = 0$.

So, $4 \cdot (-2) = -8$.

Generalize A rule for multiplication of integers is: positive • negative = negative.

✓ Try It!

A race car game takes 6 points from a player each time the player hits a cone. What integer represents the change in total points if the player hits 10 cones?

10 • [ ] = [ ]

The change in total points is [ ].

Convince Me! Could the product of a positive integer and a negative integer be positive? Explain.

EXAMPLE 2 Multiply a Positive Integer by a Negative Integer

What is the balloon's change in elevation in 3 minutes?

$-500 \cdot 3$

> Write an expression to represent the change in elevation.

$= 3 \cdot (-500)$

$= -1,500$

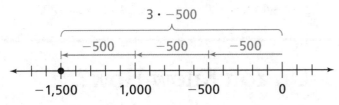

$3 \cdot -500$

The change in elevation for the balloon is $-1,500$ feet.

> **Generalize** A rule for multiplication of integers is: negative • positive = negative.

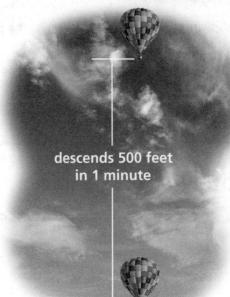

descends 500 feet in 1 minute

EXAMPLE 3 Multiply a Negative Integer by a Negative Integer

a. Use a number line to represent $-3 \cdot (-10)$.

$-(3 \cdot (-10))$ is the opposite of $3 \cdot (-10)$. So, $-3 \cdot (-10) = 30$.

$3 \cdot (-10) = -30$

> Opposites are the same distance from 0, but on opposite sides of 0.

b. Use multiplication and properties of operations to show why $-3 \cdot (-10) = 30$.

$-3 \cdot (-10 + 10) = 0$

> Use additive inverses and the Zero Property of Multiplication to write a multiplication problem.

$-3 \cdot (-10) + -3 \cdot 10 = 0$

$-3 \cdot (-10) + (-30) = 0$

$? \quad + (-30) = 0$

> You know that opposites add to 0, so $30 + (-30) = 0$.

So, $-3 \cdot (-10) = 30$.

> **Generalize** A rule for multiplication of integers is: negative • negative = positive.

 Try It!

Find each product.

a. $-7 \cdot (-2)$ **b.** $7 \cdot (-13)$ **c.** $-6 \cdot 8$ **d.** $(-1) \cdot (-1)$

When multiplying two integers, the sign of the product depends on the sign of the factors.

If the signs of the factors are the *same*, the product is positive.

$$7 \cdot 3 = 21 \qquad\qquad -7 \cdot (-3) = 21$$

If the signs of the factors are *different*, the product is negative.

$$-4 \cdot 5 = -20 \qquad\qquad 4 \cdot (-5) = -20$$

Do You Understand?

1. **? Essential Question** How do the signs of factors affect their product?

2. **Construct Arguments** What is the sign of the product if you multiplied three negative integers? Explain your answer.

3. **Reasoning** Explain why the product of two negative integers is not negative. Use $(-1)(-1)$ as an example.

4. **Use Structure** Is the product the same when multiplying $22 \times (-5)$ and multiplying $(-5) \times 22$? Explain.

Do You Know How?

5. Represent $2 \cdot (-3)$ on the number line.

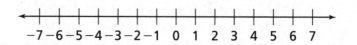

6. Which of these products is negative? Select all that apply.

☐ $-8 \cdot (-3)$

☐ $-2 \cdot 8$

☐ $0 \cdot (-2)$

☐ $15 \cdot (-5)$

☐ $-8 \cdot (-9)$

7. Find each product.

   a. $-9 \cdot (-4)$ **b.** $-7 \cdot 12$

   c. $8 \cdot (-8)$ **d.** $9 \cdot 15$

8. A game show contestant starts a game by answering two questions incorrectly. Each incorrect answer costs the contestant $600. Use a product of two integers to show the point total that would appear for the contestant.

Practice & Problem Solving

Scan for
Multimedia

In 9–14, multiply.

9. $(-6) \cdot (-2)$

10. $4 \cdot (-8)$

11. $7 \cdot (-5)$

12. $-5 \cdot 2$

13. $-1 \cdot (-24)$

14. $(5) \cdot (-9) \cdot (-2)$

15. A football team lost the same number of yards on each of 3 consecutive plays. What is the total change in yards from where the team started?

16. a. Find the product.

$-41 \cdot (-1)$

b. Construct Arguments Describe how you use the properties of multiplication to find the product.

17. Alex is working to simplify $5 \cdot (-8) \cdot 2$.

a. What is the product?

b. Suppose Alex found the opposite of the correct product. Describe an error he could have made that resulted in that product.

18. Which product is greater, $(-4) \cdot (-6)$ or $(-7) \cdot (-8)$? Explain.

19. Make Sense and Persevere While playing a board game, Cecilia had to move back 6 spaces 9 times. What integer represents Cecilia's movement on the board for those 9 turns?

20. Anya makes withdrawals from and deposits into her bank account.

   a. What integer represents the change in the amount in her account if Anya withdraws $12 once each day for four days?

   b. What integer represents the change in the amount in her account if Anya deposits $12 once each day for four days?

   c. Look for Relationships Explain the difference between the integer for the withdrawals and the integer for the deposits.

21. Higher Order Thinking A gold mine has two elevators, one for equipment and one for miners. One day, the equipment elevator begins to descend. After 28 seconds, the elevator for the miners begins to descend. What is the position of each elevator relative to the surface after another 14 seconds? At that time, how much deeper is the elevator for the miners?

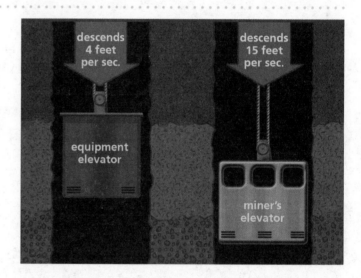

descends 4 feet per sec.

descends 15 feet per sec.

equipment elevator

miner's elevator

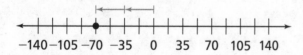
Assessment Practice

22. A number line is shown.

```
  |←——|←—|
——+++++++●++++++++++++++++++++——
-140 -105 -70 -35   0   35   70  105  140
```

Write a multiplication equation that is represented by the number line.

23. Which of these expressions have the same product as $(-6) \cdot 7$? Select all that apply.

☐ $(-3) \cdot 14$

☐ $16 \cdot (-3)$

☐ $-6 \cdot (-7)$

☐ $7 \cdot (-6)$

☐ $14 \cdot (-3)$

Solve & Discuss It!

ACTIVITY

Go Online

Stella is making the United States flag. She has blue fabric, red fabric, and white fabric. Choose a length for the flag. What length of blue fabric would Stella need to make this flag? Explain your thinking.

$\frac{2}{5}$ of the length of the flag

I can...
multiply rational numbers.

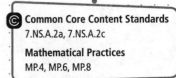

Common Core Content Standards
7.NS.A.2a, 7.NS.A.2c

Mathematical Practices
MP.4, MP.6, MP.8

Focus on math practices

Be Precise The blue region of the flag is $\frac{7}{13}$ the width and $\frac{2}{5}$ the length of the flag. What part of the total area is the blue region of the flag?

? Essential Question How is multiplying rational numbers like multiplying integers?

EXAMPLE 1  **Multiply a Negative Number by a Positive Rational Number**

Scan for Multimedia

Two hikers descend from the summit of a mountain. What is Petra's change in elevation?

Petra's change in elevation is 3.5 times as great as Ben's change in elevation.

−1.2 m change in elevation

Ben

Petra

Use a number line to represent Petra's change in elevation.

3.5 groups of −1.2

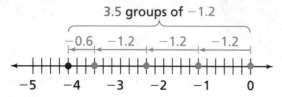

−0.6 −1.2 −1.2 −1.2

−5 −4 −3 −2 −1 0

Petra's change in elevation is −4.2 meters.

Use the rules for multiplying to find Petra's change in elevation.

3.5 • (−1.2)

Write an expression to represent the situation.

= −4.2

Petra's change in elevation is −4.2 meters.

Generalize The rules for multiplying integers apply to all rational numbers.

positive • negative = negative

✓ **Try It!**

Meghan's bank account is charged $9.95 per month for an online newspaper subscription. How could you represent the change in her account balance after three months of charges?

[ ] groups of [ ]

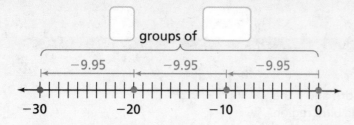

−9.95   −9.95   −9.95

−30   −20   −10   0

[ ] • −9.95 = [ ]

After three months, the change in her account balance is $ [ ].

Convince Me! Meghan's bank account is charged 3 times. Without calculating, how can you determine whether this is a negative or positive change to her account? Explain.

EXAMPLE **2** **Multiply a Positive Number by a Negative Rational Number**

Find the product of $-\frac{5}{6}$ and $\frac{2}{5}$.

$-\frac{5}{6} \cdot \frac{2}{5}$

$= \frac{-5 \cdot 2}{6 \cdot 5}$

$= \frac{-10}{30} = -\frac{1}{3}$ ◁ Multiply the numerators and the denominators and then simplify.

So, $-\frac{5}{6} \cdot \frac{2}{5} = -\frac{1}{3}$.

Plot the negative value and then find $\frac{2}{5}$ of that length.

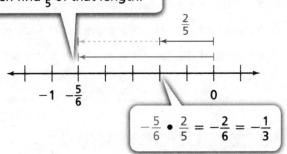

$-\frac{5}{6} \cdot \frac{2}{5} = -\frac{2}{6} = -\frac{1}{3}$

EXAMPLE **3** **Multiply a Negative Number by a Negative Rational Number**

Find the product of -0.3 and $-\frac{11}{30}$.

$-0.30 \cdot \left(-\frac{11}{30}\right)$

$= \frac{-3}{10} \cdot \left(-\frac{11}{30}\right)$ ◁ Convert one of the rational numbers so that they are both fractions or both decimals.

$= \frac{-3 \cdot (-11)}{10 \cdot 30}$

$= \frac{33}{300}$ or 0.11

Generalize The rules for multiplying integers apply to all rational numbers.

negative • negative = positive

So, $-0.3 \cdot \left(-\frac{11}{30}\right) = 0.11$ or $\frac{11}{100}$.

✓ **Try It!**

Find each product.

a. $-5.3 \cdot (-2.6)$

b. $-\frac{3}{5} \cdot 4\frac{1}{6}$

c. $0.2 \cdot (-1.78)$

d. $-2.5 \cdot \left(-\frac{7}{10}\right)$

The same rules for multiplying integers apply to multiplying all rational numbers.

When multiplying two rational numbers:

- If the signs of the factors are the *same*, the product is *positive*.
- If the signs of the factors are *different*, the product is *negative*.

Do You Understand?

1. 🔑 **Essential Question** How is multiplying rational numbers like multiplying integers?

2. How do you multiply a decimal greater than 0 and a fraction less than 0?

3. Model with Math How does this number line represent multiplication of a negative number by a positive number? Explain.

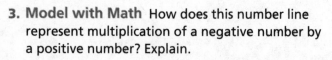

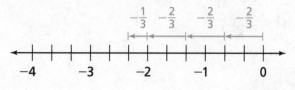

Do You Know How?

4. Use the number line to find the product

$$3 \cdot \left(-1\frac{1}{2}\right)$$

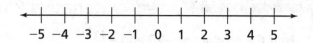

5. Which of these products is positive? Select all that apply.

- ☐ $-0.2 \cdot (12.5)$
- ☐ $-\frac{1}{12} \cdot \left(-6\frac{1}{2}\right)$
- ☐ $3.2 \cdot \left(-\frac{1}{900}\right)$
- ☐ $-3\frac{1}{2} \cdot 0$
- ☐ $-4.7 \cdot (-1)$

6. Find the product.

a. $-3.1 \cdot (-2.9)$

b. $1\frac{1}{2} \cdot \left(-\frac{5}{3}\right)$

c. $-3\frac{1}{2} \cdot 0.5$

d. $-\frac{4}{5} \cdot -\frac{1}{8}$

Name: _____

Practice & Problem Solving

In 7–14, multiply.

7. $(-2.655) \cdot (18.44)$

8. $-1\frac{5}{6} \cdot 6\frac{1}{2}$

9. $-2\frac{1}{2} \cdot \left(-1\frac{2}{3}\right)$

10. $-3\frac{7}{8} \cdot \left(-5\frac{3}{4}\right)$

11. $-7.5 \cdot -2\frac{3}{4}$

12. $-0.6 \cdot (-0.62)$

13. $-0.2 \cdot -\frac{5}{6}$

14. $-\frac{5}{6} \cdot \frac{1}{8}$

---

15. At the beginning of the season, Jamie pays full price for a ticket to see the Panthers, her favorite baseball team.

The Panthers currently have 33 wins and 31 losses.

a. Represent the total change in the cost of a ticket given their losses.

b. What is the cost of a ticket for the next game they play?

Ticket prices decrease $0.41 for every game the Panthers lose this season!

No: 01234567890
GAME ONE
VIP ZONE: C4 SEAT: 280
STANDARD Price **$49.64**
STADIUM
C1
Name
Sport
C1
VIP
Standard

16. The price per share of ENVX stock is dropping at a rate of $1.45 each hour.

   a. Write the rate as a negative number.

   b. What rational number represents the change in the price per share after 5 hours?

   c. What is the price per share after 5 hours?

17. Ming incorrectly says that this product is $\frac{4}{63}$.

$$-\left(-\frac{4}{9}\right) \cdot \left(-\frac{1}{7}\right)$$

   a. What is the correct product?

   b. What error could Ming have made?

18. Higher Order Thinking Place the products in order from least to greatest.

$$4\frac{4}{7} \cdot 4\frac{4}{7}$$

$$5\frac{6}{7} \cdot \left(-6\frac{6}{7}\right)$$

$$-5\frac{1}{8} \cdot \left(-2\frac{1}{4}\right)$$

Assessment Practice

19. Suppose there is a 1.3°F drop in temperature for every thousand feet that an airplane climbs into the sky. The temperature on the ground is −2.8°F.

PART A

Write a multiplication equation to represent the change in temperature after the plane ascends 10,000 feet.

PART B

What will the temperature be when the plane reaches an altitude of 10,000 feet?

  Ⓐ −15.8

  Ⓑ −10.2

  Ⓒ 10.2

  Ⓓ 15.8

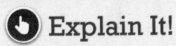

The shapes below are used to show the relationship between each of the four equations in the same fact family.

$8 \times 3 = 24$ ▨ × ● = ★

$3 \times 8 = 24$ ● × ▨ = ★

$24 \div 3 = 8$ ★ ÷ ● = ▨

$24 \div 8 = 3$ ★ ÷ ▨ = ●

I can...
divide integers.

Ⓒ **Common Core Content Standards**
7.NS.A.2b, 7.NS.A.2c

Mathematical Practices
MP.2, MP.4, MP.7, MP.8

A. Suppose the star represents −24. What values could the other shapes represent?

B. What do you know about the square and circle if the star represents a negative number?

C. What do you know about the star if the square and circle both represent a negative number?

Focus on math practices

Use Structure Suppose the square represents −8 and the circle represents 3. Use what you know about integer multiplication and the relationship between multiplication and division to write the complete fact family.

Essential Question How does dividing integers relate to multiplying integers?

 VISUAL LEARNING   ASSESS

EXAMPLE 1 ⊙ Divide Integers with Different Signs

Scan for Multimedia

A machine drill is used to access water under the ground. If the machine drills the same distance each day, what is the change in the location of the bottom of the hole each day?

DAY 1

DAY 2

DAY 3

DAY 4

water at 160 feet below ground level

Use a number line to represent the change each day.

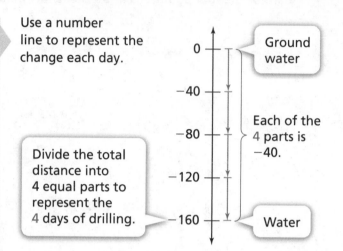

Ground water

Each of the 4 parts is −40.

Water

Divide the total distance into 4 equal parts to represent the 4 days of drilling.

The location of the bottom of the hole changed −40 feet, or 40 feet lower each day.

Use the inverse relationship between multiplication and division.

$-160 \div 4 = ?$

$4 \cdot ? = -160$

Write a related multiplication equation.

$4 \cdot (-40) = -160$

So, $-160 \div 4 = -40$.

When dividing integers with different signs, the quotient will be negative.

The location of the bottom of the hole changed by −40 feet, or decreased by 40 feet, each day.

☑ Try It!

Suppose the machine drilled the same distance into the ground for 3 days and reached water at 84 feet below ground level. What was the change in the location of the bottom of the hole each day?

Each day, the location of the bottom of the hole changed by [ ] feet, or decreased by [ ] feet.

Convince Me! Explain why the quotient of two integers with different signs is negative.

 [ ] ÷ 3 = ?

 3 · ? = [ ]

 3 · [ ] = −84

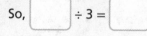 So, [ ] ÷ 3 = [ ].

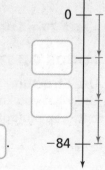

0

−84

EXAMPLE 2 Divide Integers with the Same Sign

Simplify $-27 \div (-3)$.

ONE WAY Use a related multiplication fact.

$-27 \div (-3) = ?$

$-3 \cdot ? = -27$ ◁ Write division as a product with a missing factor.

$-3 \cdot 9 = -27$

So, $-27 \div (-3) = 9$.

> When dividing integers with the **same** sign, the quotient will be **positive**.

ANOTHER WAY Write the division expression as a fraction and use properties of operations.

$\dfrac{-27}{-3}$

$= \dfrac{-1 \cdot 27}{-1 \cdot 3}$ ◁ Write negative numbers as a product, and then write as a product of fractions.

$= \dfrac{-1}{-1} \cdot \dfrac{27}{3}$

$= 1 \cdot 9$

$= 9$

So, $-27 \div (-3) = 9$.

Try It!

Simplify.

a. $-40 \div (-5)$ **b.** $40 \div (-5)$ **c.** $0 \div -40$

EXAMPLE 3 Write Equivalent Quotients of Integers

Are the following quotients equivalent? Justify your answer.

$-\left(\dfrac{18}{4}\right)$ $\dfrac{-18}{4}$ $\dfrac{18}{-4}$

$-\left(\dfrac{18}{4}\right) = -(18 \div 4)$ $\dfrac{-18}{4} = -18 \div 4$ $\dfrac{18}{-4} = 18 \div -4$

$\qquad\qquad = -(4.5)$ $= -4.5$ $= -4.5$

$\qquad\qquad = -4.5$

Yes, each expression is equivalent to -4.5.

> **Generalize** The value of $-\left(\dfrac{p}{q}\right)$ is equivalent to $\dfrac{-p}{q}$ and $\dfrac{p}{-q}$.

Try It!

Which of the following are equivalent to -5?

$\dfrac{55}{11}$ $-\left(\dfrac{55}{11}\right)$ $\dfrac{-55}{11}$ $\dfrac{-55}{-11}$ $\dfrac{55}{-11}$ $-\left(\dfrac{-55}{-11}\right)$

The rules for dividing integers are related to the rules for multiplying integers.

If the signs of the dividend and the divisor are the same, the quotient is positive.	If the signs of the dividend and the divisor are different, the quotient is negative.
$24 \div 4 = 6$ $-24 \div (-4) = 6$	$-15 \div 3 = -5$ $15 \div (-3) = -5$

Do You Understand?

1. **? Essential Question** How does dividing integers relate to multiplying integers?

2. **Reasoning** Why is the quotient of two negative integers positive?

3. Helen wrote the following facts to try to show that division by 0 results in 0. Explain her error.

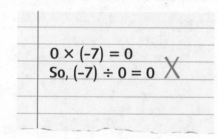

$0 \times (-7) = 0$
So, $(-7) \div 0 = 0$ ✗

Do You Know How?

4. Find each quotient.

    a. $-\dfrac{18}{3}$ b. $\dfrac{-5}{-1}$

    c. $\dfrac{24}{-6}$ d. $\dfrac{-10}{-1}$

    e. $\dfrac{-25}{5}$ f. $-\dfrac{8}{2}$

5. A scuba diver descends 63 feet in 18 seconds. What integer represents the change in the diver's position in feet per second?

6. Which of the following are equivalent to −7?

    ☐ $\dfrac{-49}{-7}$

    ☐ $\dfrac{0}{-7}$

    ☐ $\dfrac{49}{-7}$

    ☐ $\dfrac{-21}{3}$

    ☐ $\dfrac{21}{3}$

Practice & Problem Solving

Leveled Practice In 7–8, fill in the boxes to find each quotient.

7. $-16 \div 4 = ?$

$4 \cdot ? = \boxed{}$

$4 \cdot \boxed{} = \boxed{}$

So, $-16 \div 4 = \boxed{}$.

8. $-56 \div -7 = ?$

$\boxed{} \cdot ? = \boxed{}$

$\boxed{} \cdot \boxed{} = \boxed{}$

So, $-56 \div -7 = \boxed{}$.

9. Classify the quotient $-50 \div 5$ as positive, negative, zero, or undefined.

10. Is the expression $\frac{42}{-7}$ undefined? If not, find the quotient.

11. A company loses $780 as a result of a shipping delay. The 6 owners of the company must share the loss equally.

   a. Write an expression to show the change in profit for each owner.

   b. Evaluate the expression.

12. Which of the quotients are equivalent to 2.5? Select all that apply.

☐ $\frac{10}{-4}$

☐ $\frac{10}{4}$

☐ $\frac{-10}{-4}$

☐ $\frac{-5}{-2}$

☐ $\frac{-5}{2}$

☐ $\frac{5}{2}$

13. Use Structure The price of a stock steadily decreased by a total of $127 over 15 months. Which expression shows the change in the stock's value?

Ⓐ $\dfrac{-\$127}{-15 \text{ months}}$

Ⓒ $\dfrac{-\$127}{15 \text{ months}}$

Ⓑ $\dfrac{\$127}{15 \text{ months}}$

Ⓓ $\dfrac{\$15}{127 \text{ months}}$

14. Zak goes parachuting and descends at the rate shown. If he maintains a steady descent, what integer represents Zak's change in elevation in feet per second?

24 feet in 2 seconds

15. Model with Math Find each quotient and plot it on the number line. Which of the expressions are undefined?

$-8 \div 4 \qquad \dfrac{-21}{-7} \qquad -4 \div 0 \qquad -25 \div (-5) \qquad \dfrac{36}{-9} \qquad \dfrac{9}{0} \qquad 0 \div (-8)$

```
    ←——+——+——+——+——+——+——+——+——+——+——+——→
      -5  -4  -3  -2  -1   0   1   2   3   4   5
```

16. **Use Structure** The temperature in a town increased 16°F in 5 hours. The temperature decreased 31°F in the next 8 hours. Which of the expressions shows the rate of the total change in temperature?

   Ⓐ $\dfrac{-15°F}{13\ hours}$

   Ⓑ $\dfrac{47°F}{13\ hours}$

   Ⓒ $\dfrac{15°F}{10\ minutes}$

   Ⓓ $\dfrac{47°F}{-13\ hours}$

17. Camille takes a rock-climbing class. On her first outing, she rappels down the side of a boulder in three equal descents. What integer represents Camille's change in altitude in feet each time she descends?

Elevation 165 Feet

18. **Higher Order Thinking** If the fraction $\dfrac{396}{x-10}$ is equivalent to −22, find the value of x. Show your work.

✅ **Assessment Practice**

19. Which of the quotients is equivalent to $-\dfrac{5}{8}$? Select all that apply.

   ☐ $\dfrac{-5}{8}$

   ☐ $\dfrac{5}{8}$

   ☐ $\dfrac{5}{-8}$

   ☐ $-\left(\dfrac{5}{-8}\right)$

   ☐ $\dfrac{-5}{-8}$

20. Which of the following pairs of quotients are equivalent?

   Ⓐ $\dfrac{-4}{5}$ and $-\left(\dfrac{20}{25}\right)$

   Ⓑ $-\left(\dfrac{2}{-3}\right)$ and $\dfrac{-4}{6}$

   Ⓒ $\dfrac{-5}{7}$ and $\dfrac{35}{-40}$

   Ⓓ $\dfrac{1}{5}$ and $-\left(\dfrac{-2}{-10}\right)$

21. An elevator descends 36 feet in 3 seconds. What integer represents the elevator's change in elevation in feet per a second?

👆 Explore It!

ACTIVITY

The number line shows the movement of a glacier that retreats 8 meters every year.

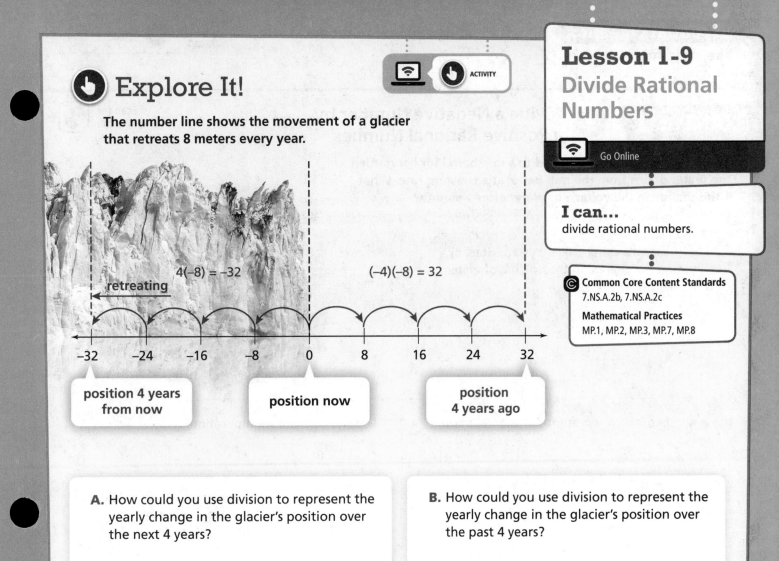

$4(-8) = -32$

retreating

$(-4)(-8) = 32$

−32   −24   −16   −8   0   8   16   24   32

position 4 years from now

position now

position 4 years ago

I can...
divide rational numbers.

© **Common Core Content Standards**
7.NS.A.2b, 7.NS.A.2c

Mathematical Practices
MP.1, MP.2, MP.3, MP.7, MP.8

A. How could you use division to represent the yearly change in the glacier's position over the next 4 years?

B. How could you use division to represent the yearly change in the glacier's position over the past 4 years?

C. Suppose the glacier retreated 8.25 meters every year. Draw a number line to represent this movement.

Focus on math practices

Reasoning If the number of meters the glacier retreats each year changes, does it affect the signs of each part of the division statement in Part A? Explain.

? **Essential Question** How is dividing rational numbers like dividing integers?

VISUAL LEARNING   ASSESS

EXAMPLE 1 👁 Divide a Negative Number by a Positive Rational Number

Scan for Multimedia

Yumiko has a drip hose attached to a rain barrel for her garden. The water drains from the rain barrel at a constant rate. What is the change in the volume of water after 1 minute?

Make Sense and Persevere Start by estimating the change in the volume of water after 1 minute.

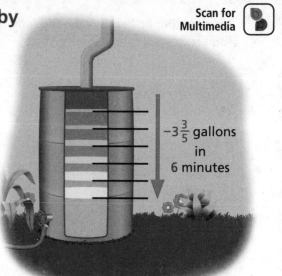

$-3\frac{3}{5}$ gallons in 6 minutes

Use a number line to represent the change in the volume.

Divide the given change in volume into 6 equal parts.

$-3\frac{3}{5} \div 6$

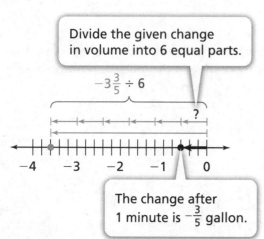

The change after 1 minute is $-\frac{3}{5}$ gallon.

Use the rules for multiplication.

$-3\frac{3}{5} \div 6$

$= -\frac{18}{5} \div \frac{6}{1}$

Two numbers whose product is 1 are **multiplicative inverses**, or reciprocals.

$= -\frac{18}{5} \cdot \frac{1}{6}$

$= -\frac{18}{30} = -\frac{3}{5}$

So, the change in the volume of water after 1 minute is $-\frac{3}{5}$ gallon.

Generalize You can extend what you know about multiplying rational numbers and dividing integers to division of rational numbers.

☑ **Try It!**

Suppose that the volume of water in the rain barrel decreased by $4\frac{5}{8}$ gallons in 4 minutes. What will be the change in the volume of water after 1 minute?

The rain barrel will lose ☐ gallons in 1 minute.

Convince Me! How are multiplicative inverses used in division with rational numbers?

$-\dfrac{\boxed{}}{8} \div \dfrac{4}{1}$

$= -\dfrac{\boxed{}}{8} \cdot \boxed{}$

$= -\dfrac{\boxed{}}{32}$, or $-1\dfrac{\boxed{}}{32}$

EXAMPLE 2 **Divide a Positive Number by a Negative Rational Number**

Simplify $\dfrac{3\frac{2}{3}}{-\frac{2}{3}}$.

> A **complex fraction** has a fraction in the numerator, the denominator, or both.

$3\frac{2}{3} \div \left(-\frac{2}{3}\right)$

$= \dfrac{11}{3} \div \left(-\dfrac{2}{3}\right)$

$= \dfrac{11}{3} \cdot \left(-\dfrac{3}{2}\right)$

> The multiplicative inverse of $-\frac{2}{3}$ is $-\frac{3}{2}$ because $-\frac{3}{2} \cdot -\frac{2}{3} = 1$.

$= \dfrac{11 \cdot (-3)}{3 \cdot 2}$

$= -\dfrac{33}{6} = -\dfrac{11}{2}$

$\qquad = -5\frac{1}{2}$

✅ Try It!

Find each quotient.

a. $\dfrac{1\frac{2}{5}}{-\frac{1}{5}}$

b. $-0.4 \div 0.25$

c. $\dfrac{7}{8} \div -\dfrac{3}{4}$

d. $0.7 \div -1\frac{1}{6}$

EXAMPLE 3  **Divide Rational Numbers with the Same Sign**

The location of a submarine changes by −0.06 kilometer each minute. How much time does it take to get to the sea bottom?

$-\dfrac{3}{4} \div (-0.06)$ ·········· Divide the location of the sea bottom by the change in the location of the submarine.

$= -0.75 \div (-0.06)$

$= 12.5$

> The rules for dividing integers apply to all rational numbers.
> negative ÷ negative = positive

$-\dfrac{3}{4}$ km

It takes 12.5 minutes to reach the sea bottom.

✅ Try It!

Find each quotient.

a. $-1\frac{1}{3} \div (-1.6)$

b. $\dfrac{-\frac{2}{3}}{-\frac{1}{4}}$

c. $-\dfrac{9}{10} \div \left(-\dfrac{3}{10}\right)$

d. $-0.5 \div \left(-\dfrac{3}{13}\right)$

The same rules for dividing integers apply to dividing rational numbers. When dividing two rational numbers:

- If the signs of the dividend and divisor are the same, the quotient is positive.

- If the signs of the dividend and divisor are different, the quotient is negative.

Do You Understand?

1. **? Essential Question** How is dividing rational numbers like dividing integers?

2. **Use Structure** How do you know the sign of the quotient $-\frac{4}{5} \div \frac{1}{6}$?

3. **Reasoning** When -4 is divided by a rational number between 0 and 1, where would the quotient be located on the number line? Why?

Do You Know How?

4. Find each quotient.

   a. $-\frac{7}{12} \div \frac{1}{7}$

   b. $-0.05 \div \left(-\frac{5}{8}\right)$

   c. $6\frac{1}{4} \div \left(-\frac{5}{16}\right)$

   d. $-1 \div \left(-\frac{10}{13}\right)$

5. Simplify the complex fraction.

   a. $\dfrac{-\frac{2}{7}}{1\frac{1}{3}}$

   b. $\dfrac{-\frac{3}{5}}{2\frac{1}{4}}$

   c. $\dfrac{-\frac{9}{10}}{1\frac{3}{5}}$

Practice & Problem Solving

Leveled Practice In 6–7, fill in the boxes to find the quotient.

6. Find the quotient $\frac{5}{7} \div \left(-\frac{11}{5}\right)$.

$$\frac{5}{7} \div \left(-\frac{11}{5}\right) = \frac{5}{7} \cdot \boxed{}$$

$$= -\frac{\boxed{}}{\boxed{}}$$

7. Simplify the complex fraction $\dfrac{-\frac{4}{5}}{\frac{3}{10}}$.

Rewrite the complex fraction: $\boxed{} \div \boxed{}$

Write the division as multiplication: $\boxed{} \cdot \boxed{}$

The product is $\boxed{}$.

8. Which multiplication expression is equivalent to the division expression $-\frac{7}{17} \div \frac{13}{34}$?

Ⓐ $-\frac{17}{7} \times \frac{13}{34}$

Ⓒ $-\frac{17}{7} \times \frac{34}{13}$

Ⓑ $-\frac{7}{17} \times \frac{13}{34}$

Ⓓ $-\frac{7}{17} \times \frac{34}{13}$

9. Derek says that the quotient $-\frac{2}{7} \div \left(-\frac{2}{21}\right)$ is $-\frac{1}{3}$.

a. What is the correct quotient?

b. What mistake did Derek likely make?

10. The water level of a lake fell by $1\frac{1}{2}$ inches during a $1\frac{2}{3}$-week-long dry spell. Simplify the complex fraction below to find the average rate at which the water level changed every week.

$$\dfrac{-1\frac{1}{2}}{1\frac{2}{3}} \text{ inches/week}$$

Water level dropped $1\frac{1}{2}$ inches

11. Complete the table. Simplify expressions.

	Dividend	Divisor	Quotient
a.	$-\frac{3}{4}$	$\frac{2}{5}$	
b.	-0.75	0.4	
c.	$\frac{3}{4}$	$-\frac{2}{5}$	

12. a. Find the reciprocal of $-1\frac{1}{17}$.

b. Find the reciprocal of $-\frac{17}{18}$.

c. Reasoning Explain why the answer for part a is the multiplicative inverse of the answer for part b.

13. Use numbers $-\frac{7}{13}$, $1\frac{6}{7}$, $-1\frac{6}{7}$, $\frac{7}{13}$

   a. Which is the reciprocal of $1\frac{6}{7}$?

   b. Which is the reciprocal of $\frac{7}{13}$?

   c. Reasoning What do you notice about the reciprocals of $1\frac{6}{7}$ and $\frac{7}{13}$?

14. A water tank in Stewart's home had a small, steady leak.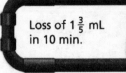

 Loss of $1\frac{3}{5}$ mL in 10 min.

   a. Use a complex fraction to represent the change in the volume of water in 1 minute.

   $\dfrac{\boxed{}\text{ milliliters}}{10 \text{ minutes}}$

   b. Simplify the complex fraction to find the change in the volume of water in the tank in 1 minute.

15. Find the quotient. Express your answer as a simplified fraction.

$$\frac{3}{10} \div 3.8$$

16. Higher Order Thinking Between 10 P.M. and 7:45 A.M., the water level in a swimming pool decreased by $\frac{13}{16}$ inch.

Assuming that the water level decreased at a constant rate, how much did it drop each hour?

The water level decreased by $\boxed{}$ inch each hour.

17. Critique Reasoning Kayla wants to find $2\frac{2}{3} \div \left(-1\frac{3}{7}\right)$. She first rewrites the division as $\left(2\frac{2}{3}\right)\left(-1\frac{7}{3}\right)$. What is wrong with Kayla's reasoning?

✓ Assessment Practice

18. Which is an equivalent multiplication expression for $\dfrac{-\frac{3}{8}}{\left(-\frac{7}{54}\right)}$?

   Ⓐ $-\frac{3}{8} \cdot \left(\frac{7}{54}\right)$

   Ⓒ $-\frac{3}{8} \cdot \left(\frac{54}{7}\right)$

   Ⓑ $-\frac{3}{8} \cdot \left(-\frac{54}{7}\right)$

   Ⓓ $-\frac{8}{3} \cdot \left(-\frac{7}{54}\right)$

19. Which is NOT a step you perform to divide $-2\frac{1}{8} \div 6\frac{4}{5}$. Select all that apply.

   ☐ Rewrite the mixed numbers as fractions.

   ☐ Divide 8 by 4.

   ☐ Multiply by the multiplicative inverse of $\frac{34}{5}$.

   ☐ Multiply by the multiplicative inverse of $\frac{17}{8}$.

   ☐ Multiply 8 and 34.

Lesson 1-10
Solve Problems
with Rational
Numbers

 Go Online

I can...
solve problems with rational
numbers.

© **Common Core Content Standards**
7.NS.A.3, 7.EE.B.3

Mathematical Practices
MP.1, MP.2, MP.3, MP.4, MP.8

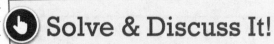 Solve & Discuss It!   ACTIVITY

Stefan estimates the income and expenses for renting
a phone accessory store in the mall. He enters the
amounts in the table below. Should Stefan
rent a phone accessory store? Explain.

Estimated Income and Expenses

Type	Amount	Frequency
Sales	$950	Each week
Services	$2,875	Each month
Rent	−$4,500	Each month
Travel	−$7.50	Each day
Merchandise	−$1,650	Each month

Focus on math practices

Reasoning How can you assess the reasonableness of
your solution using mental math or estimation strategies?

Essential Question How do you decide which rational number operations to use to solve problems?

VISUAL LEARNING   ASSESS

EXAMPLE 1 ⊙ **Decide Which Operations to Use to Solve Problems**

Scan for Multimedia

Water drains steadily out of a lock to lower a boat from one level to another. What is the boat's change in position each minute?

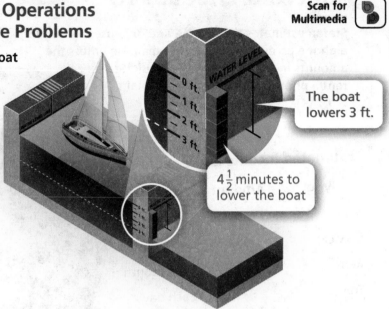

The boat lowers 3 ft.

$4\frac{1}{2}$ minutes to lower the boat

Reasoning Which operation can you use to find the boat's change in position in 1 minute?

STEP 1 Use a bar diagram to represent the time it takes the boat to lower 3 feet in the lock.

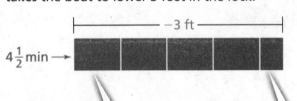

Each whole box represents the boat's change in position in 1 minute.

This $\frac{1}{2}$ box represents the boat's change in position in $\frac{1}{2}$ minute.

STEP 2 Decide which operation to use to find the boat's change in position in 1 minute.

$\frac{-3}{4\frac{1}{2}}$

Divide to find the boat's change in position in 1 minute.

$= -3 \div \frac{9}{2}$

$= -3 \cdot \frac{2}{9}$

$= -\frac{6}{9} = -\frac{2}{3}$

So, the boat's change in position each minute is $-\frac{2}{3}$ feet. The boat lowers $\frac{2}{3}$ feet each minute.

✓ **Try It!**

A weather balloon ascended from an elevation of 18 feet below sea level to an elevation of $19\frac{1}{2}$ feet above sea level. What distance did the weather balloon rise?

The distance between two points is the absolute value of their [_____].

So, $|-18 \bigcirc 19\frac{1}{2}| =$ [_____].

The weather balloon rose a distance of [____] feet.

Convince Me! How can you decide which operation to use to solve a problem?

EXAMPLE 2

 Use Properties of Operations with Rational Numbers

Kevin played a trivia game. Each correct answer is worth $2\frac{1}{4}$ points, and each incorrect answer is worth $-\frac{1}{2}$ point. What was Kevin's score?

Use Structure How are the two methods of solving the problem alike? How are they different?

ONE WAY

$(15)2\frac{1}{4} + (15)\left(-\frac{1}{2}\right)$

$= \frac{9}{4}(15) + \left(-\frac{1}{2}\right)(15)$ ⟵ Multiply first. Then add.

$= \frac{135}{4} + \left(-\frac{15}{2}\right)$

$= \frac{135}{4} + \left(-\frac{30}{4}\right)$

$= \frac{105}{4} = 26\frac{1}{4}$

Kevin's score was $26\frac{1}{4}$ points.

ANOTHER WAY

$(15)2\frac{1}{4} + (15)\left(-\frac{1}{2}\right)$

$= 15\left[2\frac{1}{4} + \left(-\frac{1}{2}\right)\right]$

$= 15\left(1\frac{3}{4}\right)$

$= 15\left(\frac{7}{4}\right)$

$= \frac{105}{4} = 26\frac{1}{4}$

Since Kevin had the same number of correct and incorrect answers, use the Distributive Property.

Kevin's score was $26\frac{1}{4}$ points.

 Try It!

Rashida had 18 correct answers and 12 incorrect answers. What was Rashida's score?

EXAMPLE 3

 Solve Multi-Step Problems with Rational Numbers

The temperature at 4:00 P.M. was 2.5°F. It dropped 0.75°F each hour for the next 4 hours. What was the temperature at 8:00 P.M.?

STEP 1 Multiply to find the total change in temperature.

$-0.75 \times 4 = -3$

The total change in temperature was −3 degrees.

STEP 2 Add the total change in temperature to the initial temperature.

$2.5 + (-3) = -0.5$

The temperature at 8:00 P.M. was −0.5°F.

Reasoning Use multiplication if a value is given per hour and you need to find the value after several hours.

 Try It!

The temperature at 10:00 A.M. was −3°F and increased 2.25°F each hour for the next 5 hours. What was the temperature at 3:00 P.M.?

You can solve a problem with rational numbers by making sense of the problem and deciding which operations to use.

Do You Understand?

1. **? Essential Question** How do you decide which rational number operations to use to solve problems?

2. **Reasoning** A truck's position relative to a car's position is −60 feet. The car and the truck move in the same direction, but the car moves 5 feet per second faster for 8 seconds. What operations could be used to find the truck's relative position after 8 seconds? Explain.

3. **Construct Arguments** Emilio used addition of two rational numbers to solve a problem. Jim used subtraction to solve the same problem. Is it possible that they both solved the problem correctly? Use a specific example to explain.

Do You Know How?

4. Kara had a savings account balance of $153 on Monday. On Tuesday, she had six withdrawals of $15.72 and a deposit of $235.15. What was her account balance after these transactions?

5. A scuba diver is swimming at the depth shown, and then swims 0.5 foot toward the surface every 3 seconds. What is the location of the scuba diver, relative to the surface, after 15 seconds?

−46 feet

6. The temperature of a cup of coffee changed by −54°F over $22\frac{1}{2}$ minutes. What was the change in temperature each minute?

Practice & Problem Solving

7. Suppose there is a 1.1°F drop in temperature for every thousand feet that an airplane climbs into the sky. If the temperature on the ground is 59.7°F, what will be the temperature at an altitude of 11,000 ft?

Altitude: 11,000 ft

59.7°F at ground level

8. A farmer sells an average of $15\frac{3}{5}$ bushels of corn each day. What integer represents the change in bushels of corn in his inventory after 6 days?

9. A certain plant grows $1\frac{1}{6}$ inches every week. How long will it take the plant to grow $6\frac{1}{6}$ inches?

10. An object is traveling at a steady speed of $8\frac{2}{3}$ miles per hour. How long will it take the object to travel $5\frac{1}{5}$ miles?

11. Brianna works as a customer service representative. She knows that the amount of her yearly bonus is $155, but $2.50 is taken away for each customer complaint about her during the year. What is her bonus if there are 12 complaints about her in the year?

12. Make Sense and Persevere There are ten birdbaths in a park. On the first day of spring, the birdbaths are filled. Several weeks later, the overall change in the water level is found. The results are shown in the table. What is the range of the data?

Changes in Water Level (inches)									
2.4	1.4	−2.3	2.9	2.3	−1.2	−1.4	−1.8	2.5	0.9

13. Model with Math Marcelo played a carnival game at the Interstate Fair 6 times. He spent 3 tokens to play each game, and he won 7 tokens each game. Write two different expressions that can be used to find the total profit in tokens that Marcelo made.

14. The temperature of a pot of water is shown. The temperature of the water changed −2.5°F per minute.

180.3 °F

a. What was the temperature after 20 minutes?

b. Make Sense and Persevere How many minutes did it take to cool to 100.3°F?

15. Higher Order Thinking The table shows the relationship between a hedgehog's change in weight and the number of days of hibernation.

a. What number represents the change in weight for each day of hibernation?

b. What number represents the change in weight in ounces for the hedgehog in 115 days of hibernation?

Weight Loss of Hedgehog

Days of Hibernation	Change in Weight (oz)
8	−0.24
28	−0.84
75	−2.25
93	−2.79

✓ Assessment Practice

16. A basketball team played six games. In those games, the team won by 7 points, lost by 20, won by 8, won by 11, lost by 3, and won by 9. Which was the mean amount by which the team won or lost over the six games?

Ⓐ −3 points

Ⓑ 2 points

Ⓒ 3 points

Ⓓ 6 points

17. In digging a hole, the construction crew records the location of the bottom of the hole relative to ground level. After 3 hours the hole is 8.25 feet deep.

PART A

What number represents the change in location in feet after 1 hour?

PART B

If the crew were to continue digging at the same rate, what number would they record for the location in feet after 8 hours?

3-ACT MATH ▷ ▷ ▷

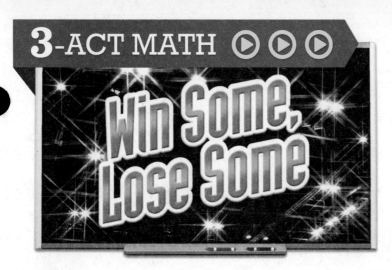

Win Some, Lose Some

3-Act Mathematical Modeling:
Win Some, Lose Some

📶 Go Online

© **Common Core Content Standards**
7.NS.A.1

Mathematical Practices
MP.4, MP.1, MP.2, MP.3, MP.5, MP.7, MP.8

ACT 1

1. After watching the video, what is the first question that comes to mind?

2. Write the Main Question you will answer.

3. Make a prediction to answer this Main Question.

The person who will win is [   ].

4. Construct Arguments Explain how you arrived at your prediction.

5. What information in this situation would be helpful to know? How would you use that information?

6. **Use Appropriate Tools** What tools can you use to solve the problem? Explain how you would use them strategically.

7. **Model with Math** Represent the situation using mathematics. Use your representation to answer the Main Question.

8. What is your answer to the Main Question? Does it differ from your prediction? Explain.

9. Write the answer you saw in the video.

10. Reasoning Does your answer match the answer in the video? If not, what are some reasons that would explain the difference?

11. Make Sense and Persevere Would you change your model now that you know the answer? Explain.

Reflect

12. **Model with Math** Explain how you used a mathematical model to represent the situation. How did the model help you answer the Main Question?

13. **Reasoning** How is each person's starting score related to their final score?

14. **Construct Arguments** If there were one final round where each contestant chooses how much to wager, how much should each person wager? Explain your reasoning.

$100	$200	$300	$400
$500	$100	$400	$300
$400	$500	$200	$500
	$300		$100

? Topic Essential Question

How can the properties of operations be used to solve problems involving integers and rational numbers?

Vocabulary Review

Complete each definition and then provide an example of each vocabulary word.

Vocabulary   additive inverses   complex fraction   terminating decimal   repeating decimal

Definition	Example
1. A _____ is a fraction $\frac{a}{b}$ where a and/or b are fractions and b is not equal to 0.	
2. A decimal that ends is a(n) _____.	
3. Two numbers that have a sum of 0 are _____.	

Use Vocabulary in Writing

Explain how you could determine whether $\frac{\frac{21}{3}}{\frac{120}{12}}$ and $\frac{7}{9}$ have the same decimal equivalent. Use vocabulary words in your explanation.

Concepts and Skills Review

Quick Review

Integers are the counting numbers, their opposites, and 0. Opposite integers are the same distance from 0 in opposite directions. Opposite quantities combine to make 0.

Example

A climber descends 3 miles into a canyon. What integer represents the descent of her climb? How far does she have to climb to return to her starting point?

The descent of her climb is represented by −3. She has to climb 3 miles to return to her starting point.

Practice

1. On a cold winter morning, the temperature was −4°F. By noon, the temperature increased 4°. What was the temperature at noon?

2. Audrey deposits $27 in her account. Then she makes two withdrawals, one for $15 and one for $12. What is the total change to the balance of Audrey's account? Explain.

Quick Review

All rational numbers have an equivalent decimal form. The decimal equivalent will be either a terminating decimal or a repeating decimal. A terminating decimal ends in repeating zeros. A repeating decimal has a never-ending pattern of the same digits.

Example

Write the decimal equivalents for $\frac{5}{8}$ and $\frac{8}{11}$. Are the decimals terminating or repeating?

The decimal equivalent for $\frac{5}{8}$ = 0.625, which is a terminating decimal.

The decimal equivalent for $\frac{8}{11}$ = 0.7272... = $0.\overline{72}$, which is a repeating decimal.

Practice

1. Which fractions have a decimal equivalent that is a repeating decimal? Select all that apply.

   ☐ $\frac{13}{65}$ ☐ $\frac{141}{47}$

   ☐ $\frac{11}{12}$ ☐ $\frac{19}{3}$

2. Greg bought $19\frac{11}{16}$ gallons of gas. What decimal should the meter on the gas pump read?

3. What is the decimal equivalent of each rational number?

   a. $\frac{9}{11}$ b. $\frac{4}{5}$

   c. $-\frac{17}{5}$ d. $\frac{5}{9}$

LESSON 1-3 Add Integers

Quick Review

To add integers with the same sign, add the absolute value of each integer. The sign of the sum will be the same as the sign of the addends. To add integers with different signs, find the difference of the absolute value of each integer. The sign of the sum will be the same as the sign of the greater addend.

Example

Find the sum of (−28) + (−19).

$|-28| + |-19| = 28 + 19 = 47$

The sum of $(-28) + (-19) = -47$.

Find the sum of (−28) + 19.

$|-28| - |19| = 28 - 19 = 9$

The sum of $(-28) + 19 = -9$, because $|-28| > |19|$.

Practice

1. Jonah's cell phone came with 64 GB of memory. He has used 15 GB. He then uses 5 MB of memory to record photos and videos from a trip. Use the addition expression $64 + (-15) + (-5)$ to find how much memory is left on his phone.

2. Stella walks down a flight of stairs to the basement. Then she walks back up the stairs and up another flight of stairs to the second floor of her house. Each flight of stairs represents a change of 12 feet in height. How far is Stella above the ground?

3. Find the sum.
   a. $64 + (-15)$ b. $-121 + (-34)$
   c. $-86 + 92$ d. $109 + (-162)$

LESSON 1-4 Subtract Integers

Quick Review

To subtract integers, use the additive inverse to write an equivalent addition expression. Then follow the rules for addition. When the signs are the same, find the sum of the absolute values. When the signs are different, find the difference. Use the sign of the number with the greater absolute value.

Example

Find −7 − (8).

$-7 + (-8) = -15$

The signs are the same, so the sum has the same sign as the addends.

Find −7 − (−8).

$-7 + 8 = 1$

The signs are different, so the sign of the difference is the same sign as the integer (8) with the greater absolute value, which is positive.

Practice

1. The temperature is 1°F at dusk. It is 8 degrees colder at dawn. What is the temperature at dawn?

2. Kyle and Nadim are on the same space on a board game they are playing. Kyle moves back 2 spaces in one turn and moves back 3 more spaces in his second turn. Nadim has remained in the same place. What integer represents Kyle's location relative to Nadim's location on the game board?

3. Find the difference.
   a. $82 - (-14)$ b. $-18 - (-55)$
   c. $-17 - 44$ d. $70 - (-101)$

Quick Review

Positive and negative rational numbers and decimals can be added and subtracted following the same rules as adding and subtracting integers.

Example

Find $-5\frac{1}{2} - 1.75$.

Convert 1.75 to an equivalent fraction, $1\frac{3}{4}$.

$$-5\frac{1}{2} - 1\frac{3}{4}$$

$$= -5\frac{2}{4} + (-1\frac{3}{4})$$

$$= -6\frac{5}{4}$$

$$= -7\frac{1}{4}$$

Practice

1. Doug digs a hole that is 1.7 feet below ground level. He plants a bush that is $3\frac{2}{10}$ feet tall from the bottom of the root to the top branch. How much of the bush is above the ground?

2. Penelope has a birdhouse that is $4\frac{9}{10}$ feet above the roof of her garage. She has a second birdhouse that is 5.36 feet below the roof of her garage. What is the distance between the birdhouses?

3. Find the sum or difference.

  a. $-2.63 + 3\frac{1}{4}$ **b.** $-4\frac{1}{2} - (-1.07)$

  c. $0.74 + \left(-\frac{3}{5}\right)$ **d.** $-\frac{1}{8} - 0.356$

Quick Review

Multiply integers the same way you multiply whole numbers. If the signs of the factors are the same, the product is positive. If the signs of the factors are different, the product is negative.

Example

$-9 \cdot -8 = 72$

$-9 \cdot 8 = -72$

Practice

1. Marisa buys 4 books at $13 per book. What integer represents the total change in the amount of money Marisa has?

2. Which expressions have a product of -18? Select all that apply.

  ☐ $-2 \cdot -9$ ☐ $-6 \cdot 3$

  ☐ $-3 \cdot 6$ ☐ $-9 \cdot 2$

3. Find the product.

  a. $-7 \cdot -14$ **b.** $-15 \cdot 12$

  c. $9 \cdot -20$ **d.** $-11 \cdot -16$

Quick Review

The same rules for multiplying integers apply to multiplying rational numbers. If the signs of the factors are the same, the product will be positive. If the signs of the factors are different, the product will be negative.

Example

$-9.6 \cdot 1.8 = -17.28$

$-9.6 \cdot -1.8 = 17.28$

Practice

1. Jason spends $2.35 to buy lunch at school. If he buys a lunch on 9 days, what number represents the total change in the amount of money Jason has?

Multiply.

2. $-2\frac{2}{3} \cdot -4\frac{3}{7}$

3. $-3\frac{4}{9} \cdot 5\frac{2}{5}$

4. $6\frac{2}{3} \cdot -4\frac{1}{5}$

Quick Review

Divide integers the same way you divide whole numbers. The quotient is positive if the signs of the dividend and divisor are the same. The quotient is negative if the signs of the dividend and divisor are different.

Example

$-39 \div 3 = -13$

$-39 \div -3 = 13$

Practice

1. Which expressions have a quotient of −4? Select all that apply.

☐ $\frac{-24}{6}$ ☐ $-36 \div -9$

☐ $-72 \div 18$ ☐ $\frac{84}{-21}$

2. Whitney rolls a ball down a ramp that is 18 feet long. If the ball rolls down 2 feet each second, what integer represents the amount of time, in seconds, the ball takes to reach the end of the ramp?

3. Find the quotient.

a. $\frac{81}{-9}$ b. $-123 \div -4$

c. $-\frac{94}{4}$ d. $65 \div (-5)$

Quick Review

The same rules for dividing integers apply to dividing all rational numbers. The quotient is positive when the numbers being divided have the same signs. The quotient is negative when the numbers being divided have different signs. **Complex fractions** have a fraction in the numerator, the denominator, or both. To divide by a fraction, rewrite as multiplication by its **multiplicative inverse, or reciprocal.**

Example

Simplify $\dfrac{-\frac{3}{4}}{\frac{15}{24}}$.

$$-\frac{3}{4} \div \frac{15}{24} = -\frac{3}{4} \cdot \frac{24}{15} = -\frac{72}{60} = -\frac{6}{5} = -1\frac{1}{5}$$

Practice

Find the quotient.

1. $\dfrac{8}{9} \div -1\dfrac{4}{15}$

2. $-3.6 \div 2\dfrac{1}{7}$

3. A boat drops an anchor 17.5 feet to the bottom of a lake. If the anchor falls at a rate of 0.07 feet each second, how long will it take the anchor to reach the bottom of the lake?

Quick Review

You can use rational numbers to solve problems in the same way that you use whole numbers. Be sure to make sense of the problem you are solving to help you choose the correct operations and determine which values will be positive and which will be negative.

Example

During a 15-day dry spell, the water level in a lake changed by $-2\frac{3}{8}$ inches. What rational number represents the average change in the water level per day?

$$-2\frac{3}{8} \div 15$$

$$= -\frac{19}{8} \cdot \frac{1}{15}$$

$$= -\frac{19}{120} \text{ inch}$$

Practice

1. In 5 rounds of a game, Jill scored −3, 8, 9 −7, and 13. What integer represents her average score for the 5 rounds?

2. Peter signed up for a program that costs $10.50 per month to stream movies to his computer. He decided to cancel his service after $\frac{5}{6}$ month. He only has to pay for the amount of time he used the service. What number represents the total change in the amount of money Peter has after paying for the service?

3. Maggie spent $4.05 on cheese and fruit at the farmer's market. She bought $\frac{1}{8}$ pound of apples, $\frac{1}{4}$ pound of pears, and 1.25 pounds of bananas. If fruit cost $0.80 per pound, how much did Maggie spend on cheese?

Crisscrossed

Find each sum, difference, product, or quotient. Write your answers in the cross-number puzzle below. Each digit and negative sign in your answers goes in its own box.

I can...
add, subtract, multiply, and divide integers. © 7.NS.A.1, 7.NS.A.2

Across

2. 248 + (−1,027)
5. 818 − (−1,021)
6. −516 + 774
8. 242 + (−656)
9. 2,087 + (−1,359)
10. 631 − 897
11. −342 + 199
12. −49 • −27
13. −321 − 987
14. 2,988 ÷ −3
15. 2,580 ÷ 6
16. 4,592 ÷ −82
17. 48 • −27
18. −24 • 83
21. −118 + 1,201
22. −45 • −59

Down

1. 246 + 173
2. 22 • −22
3. 726 − (−219)
4. 501 − 699
7. −10,740 ÷ 15
8. 6,327 ÷ −9
10. 144 • −16
11. 15 • −67
12. 7,164 ÷ 4
13. −33 • 63
14. −2,695 ÷ 55
17. −1,032 − (−285)
18. 512 − 720
19. −729 + 951
20. −17 • −25

TOPIC 2 · REAL NUMBERS

? Topic Essential Question

What are real numbers? How are real numbers used to solve problems?

Topic Overview

2-1 Rational Numbers as Decimals

2-2 Understand Irrational Numbers

2-3 Compare and Order Real Numbers

2-4 Evaluate Square Roots and Cube Roots

2-5 Solve Equations Using Square Roots and Cube Roots

2-6 Use Properties of Integer Exponents

2-7 More Properties of Integer Exponents

2-8 Use Powers of 10 to Estimate Quantities

2-9 Understand Scientific Notation

3-Act Mathematical Modeling: Hard-Working Organs

2-10 Operations with Numbers in Scientific Notation

Topic Vocabulary

- cube root
- irrational number
- Negative Exponent Property
- perfect cube
- perfect square
- Power of Powers Property
- Power of Products Property
- Product of Powers Property
- Quotient of Powers Property
- scientific notation
- square root
- Zero Exponent Property

Lesson Digital Resources

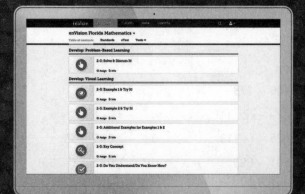

INTERACTIVE STUDENT EDITION
Access online or offline.

INTERACTIVE ANIMATION
Interact with visual learning animations.

ACTIVITY Use with *Solve & Discuss It*, *Explore It*, and *Explain It* activities, and to explore Examples.

VIDEOS Watch clips to support *3-Act Mathematical Modeling Lessons* and *STEM Projects*.

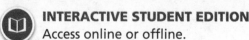

Go online

Hard-Working Organs

▶ Hard-Working Organs

Did you know you have seven pulse points on your body? If you took your pulse recently, you probably used the one in your neck or the one in your wrist. Try to take your resting pulse right now.

Monitoring your pulse while you exercise helps you make sure you are getting the most out of your workout. Your heart rate varies greatly between resting, sleeping, and working out. Think about this during the 3-Act Mathematical Modeling lesson.

PRACTICE Practice what you've learned.

TUTORIALS Get help from *Virtual Nerd*, right when you need it.

MATH TOOLS Explore math with digital tools.

GAMES Play Math Games to help you learn.

KEY CONCEPT Review important lesson content.

GLOSSARY Read and listen to English/Spanish definitions.

ASSESSMENT Show what you've learned.

ënVision® STEM Project

 VIDEO

Did You Know?

Natural resources are materials that occur in nature, such as water, fossil fuels, wood, and minerals. Natural resources not only meet basic human needs, but also support industry and economy.

Minerals are used in the manufacturing of all types of common objects, including cell phones, computers, light bulbs, and medicines.

Water, oil, and forests are some of the natural resources that are in danger of someday being depleted.

Each person in the United States needs over 48,000 pounds of minerals each year.

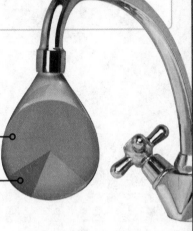

70% of available fresh water is used in agriculture...

...and 10% for human consumption.

About 18 million acres of forest are lost to deforestation each year.

Solar power, wind power and other renewable energy sources are helping to lessen the dependency on oil and fossil fuels.

Fossil fuels are expected to supply almost 80% of world energy use through 2040.

Your Task: Going, Going, Gone? ▶

Natural resource depletion is an important issue facing the world. Suppose a natural resource is being depleted at the rate of 1.333% per year. If there were 300 million tons of this resource in 2005, and there are no new discoveries, how much will be left in the year 2045? You and your classmates will explore the depletion of this resource over time.

Review What You Know!

Vocabulary

Choose the best term from the box. Write it on the blank.

fraction
integer
repeating decimal
terminating decimal

1. A(n) _____ is a decimal that ends in repeating zeros.

2. A(n) _____ is a decimal in which a digit or digits repeat endlessly.

3. A(n) _____ is either a counting number, the opposite of a counting number, or zero.

4. A(n) _____ is a number that can be used to describe a part of a whole, a part of a set, a location on a number line, or a division of whole numbers.

Terminating and Repeating Decimals

Determine whether each decimal is terminating or repeating.

5. 5.692

6. −0.222222…

7. 7.0001

8. $7.2\overline{8}$

9. $1.\overline{178}$

10. −4.03479

Multiplying Integers

Find each product.

11. $2 \cdot 2$

12. $-5 \cdot (-5)$

13. $7 \cdot 7$

14. $-6 \cdot (-6) \cdot (-6)$

15. $10 \cdot 10 \cdot 10$

16. $-9 \cdot (-9) \cdot (-9)$

Simplifying Expressions

Simplify each expression.

17. $(4 \cdot 10) + (5 \cdot 100)$

18. $(2 \cdot 100) + (7 \cdot 10)$

19. $(6 \cdot 100) - (1 \cdot 10)$

20. $(9 \cdot 1{,}000) + (4 \cdot 10)$

21. $(3 \cdot 1{,}000) - (2 \cdot 100)$

22. $(2 \cdot 10) + (7 \cdot 100)$

Language Development

Fill in the word map with new terms, definitions, and supporting examples or illustrations.

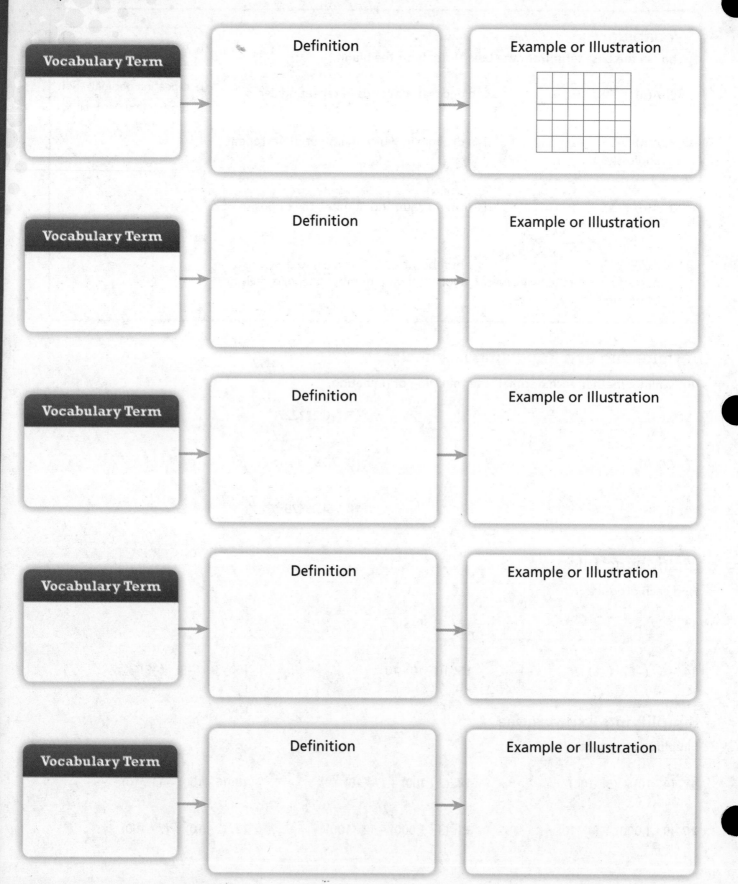

Vocabulary Term	Definition	Example or Illustration

PROJECT 2A

Who is your favorite poet, and why?

PROJECT: WRITE A POEM

PROJECT 2B

If you moved to a tiny house, what would you bring with you?

PROJECT: DESIGN A TINY HOUSE

PROJECT 2C

If you could travel anywhere in space, where would you go?

PROJECT: PLAN A TOUR OF THE MILKY WAY

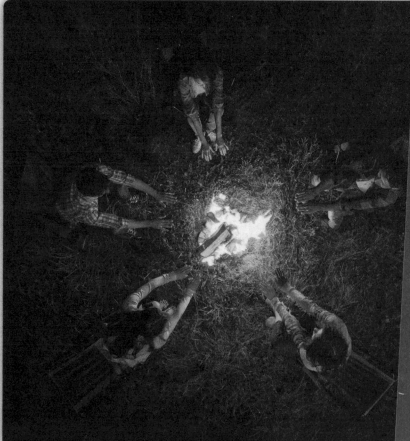

PROJECT 2D

Why do you think people tell stories around a campfire?

PROJECT: TELL A FOLK STORY

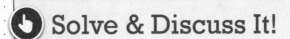

Solve & Discuss It!  ACTIVITY

Jaylon has a wrench labeled 0.1875 inch and bolts labeled in fractions of an inch. Which size bolt will fit best with the wrench? Explain.

$\frac{3}{8}$ in. $\frac{1}{8}$ in. $\frac{3}{16}$ in. $\frac{1}{4}$ in.

Reasoning How can you write these numbers in the same form?

I can...
write repeating decimals as fractions.

© **Common Core Content Standards**
8.NS.A.1

Mathematical Practices
MP.2, MP.6, MP.7

Focus on math practices

Reasoning Why is it useful to write a rational number as a fraction or as a decimal?

 VISUAL LEARNING   ASSESS

EXAMPLE 1 **Write Repeating Decimals as Fractions**

Scan for Multimedia

The Sluggers baseball team ended the season with the highest win percentage in their division. What is the Slugger's winning percentage written as a fraction?

Statistics are often rounded. Here, the decimal 0.555... or $0.\overline{5}$ is rounded to the thousandths place.

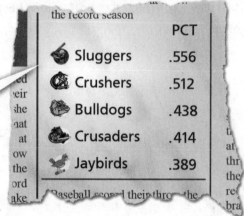

	the record season	PCT
	Sluggers	.556
	Crushers	.512
	Bulldogs	.438
	Crusaders	.414
	Jaybirds	.389

Baseball scored their through the

Locate 0.555... on a number line.

The decimal number 0.555... is between 0.5 and 0.6; so it is between $\frac{1}{2}$, or $\frac{5}{10}$, and $\frac{6}{10}$.

0.5 0.6

```
◄──┼──┼──┼──┼──┼──┼──┼──┼──┼──┼──►
   0                             1
```

$\frac{5}{10} = \frac{1}{2}$ $\frac{6}{10}$

Reasoning How do you know that the repeating decimal 0.555... can be written as a fraction?

Write the repeating decimal as a fraction.

Assign a variable to represent the repeating decimal.

Let $x = 0.\overline{5}$.

$10 \cdot x = 10 \cdot 0.\overline{5}$

Because $0.\overline{5}$ has 1 repeating digit, multiply each side of the equation by 10^1, or 10.

$10x = 5.\overline{5}$

$10x - x = 5.\overline{5} - 0.\overline{5}$

$9x = 5$

Subtract $0.\overline{5}$ from each side of the equation, then solve for x. Because $x = 0.\overline{5}$, you can subtract x from one side and $0.\overline{5}$ from the other side.

$\frac{9x}{9} = \frac{5}{9}$

$x = \frac{5}{9}$

The Sluggers won $\frac{5}{9}$ of their games.

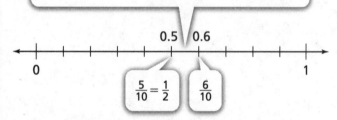 **Try It!**

In another baseball division, one team had a winning percentage of 0.444.... What fraction of their games did this team win?

The team won ☐ of their games.

Convince Me! How do you know what power of ten to multiply by in the second step at the right?

Let $x = 0.\overline{4}$.

☐ $\cdot x =$ ☐ $\cdot 0.\overline{4}$

☐ $x =$ ☐

☐ $- x =$ ☐ $- 0.\overline{4}$

☐ $x =$ ☐

$x =$ ☐

ACTIVITY ASSESS

Sabine entered a division expression into her calculator. The quotient is shown on the calculator screen. What expression could Sabine have entered?

0.266666666667

Let $x = 0.2\overline{6}$.

$10x = 2.\overline{6}$

> Multiply by 10^1, or 10, because the decimal has 1 repeating digit.

$10x - x = 2.\overline{6} - 0.2\overline{6}$

> Subtract $0.2\overline{6}$ from each side of the equation, and then solve for x. Because $x = 0.2\overline{6}$, you can subtract x from one side and $0.2\overline{6}$ from the other side.

$9x = 2.4$

$\dfrac{9x}{9} = \dfrac{2.4}{9}$

$x = \dfrac{24}{90}$

> Write an equivalent fraction so that the numerator and denominator are integers.

Sabine could have entered $24 \div 90$, or an equivalent expression such as $8 \div 30$.

 Try It!

Write the repeating decimal 0.63333… as a fraction.

EXAMPLE 3 **Write Decimals with Multiple Repeating Digits as Fractions**

Write $2.\overline{09}$ as a mixed number.

Let $x = 2.\overline{09}$.

$100 \cdot x = 100 \cdot 2.\overline{09}$

> The repeating decimal has 2 repeating digits, so multiply each side of the equation by 10^2, or 100.

$100x - x = 209.\overline{09} - 2.\overline{09}$

$99x = 207$

$x = \dfrac{207}{99}$ or $2\dfrac{1}{11}$

> Subtract x from one side of the equation and its equivalent $2.\overline{09}$ from the other side of the equation.

> **Use Structure** How do you know that subtracting x from one side of the equation and subtracting $2.\overline{09}$ from the other side results in an equivalent equation?

 **Try It!**

Write the repeating decimal 4.1363636… as a fraction.

 KEY CONCEPT

Because repeating decimals are rational numbers, you can write them in fraction form.

STEP 1 Assign a variable to represent the repeating decimal.

STEP 2 Write an equation: *variable = decimal*.

STEP 3 Multiply each side of the equation by 10^d, where d is the number of repeating digits in the repeating decimal.

STEP 4 Subtract equivalent expressions of the variable and the repeating decimal from each side of the equation.

STEP 5 Solve for the variable. Write an equivalent fraction so that the numerator and denominator are integers, if necessary.

Do You Understand?

1. **Essential Question** How can you write repeating decimals as fractions?

2. **Use Structure** Why do you multiply by a power of 10 when writing a repeating decimal as a rational number?

3. **Be Precise** How do you decide by which power of 10 to multiply an equation when writing a decimal with repeating digits as a fraction?

Do You Know How?

4. A survey reported that $63.\overline{63}\%$ of moviegoers prefer action films. This percent represents a repeating decimal. Write it as a fraction.

5. A student estimates the weight of astronauts on the Moon by multiplying their weight by the decimal 0.16666.... What fraction can be used for the same estimation?

6. Write 2.3181818… as a mixed number.

Practice & Problem Solving

Leveled Practice In **7** and **8**, write the decimal as a fraction or mixed number.

7. Write the number 0.21212121... as a fraction.

Let $x = $ [   ].

$100x = $ [   ]

$100x - x = $ [   ] − [   ]

$99x = $ [   ]

$x = $ [   ]

So 0.2121... is equal to [   ].

8. Write 3.7 as a mixed number.

Let $x = $ [   ].

$10x = $ [   ]

$9x = $ [   ]

$x = $ [   ]

So 3.$\overline{7}$ is equal to [   ].

9. Write the number shown on the scale as a fraction.

10. Tomas asked 15 students whether summer break should be longer. He used his calculator to divide the number of students who said yes by the total number of students. His calculator showed the result as 0.9333....

a. Write this number as a fraction.

b. How many students said that summer break should be longer?

11. Write 0.$\overline{87}$ as a fraction.

12. Write 0.$\overline{8}$ as a fraction.

13. Write $1.\overline{48}$ as a mixed number.

14. Write $0.\overline{6}$ as a fraction.

15. A manufacturer determines that the cost of making a computer component is $2.161616. Write the cost as a fraction and as a mixed number.

$2.161616

16. Reasoning When writing a repeating decimal as a fraction, does the number of repeating digits you use matter? Explain.

17. Higher Order Thinking When writing a repeating decimal as a fraction, why does the fraction always have only 9s or 9s and 0s as digits in the denominator?

✅ Assessment Practice

18. Which decimal is equivalent to $\frac{188}{11}$?

Ⓐ $17.\overline{09}$

Ⓑ $17.0\overline{09}$

Ⓒ $17.\overline{1709}$

Ⓓ $17.\overline{17090}$

19. Choose the repeating decimal that is equal to the fraction on the left.

	$0.\overline{17}$	$0.\overline{351}$	$0.1\overline{7}$	$0.3\overline{51}$	$0.35\overline{1}$
$\frac{58}{165}$	☐	☐	☐	☐	☐
$\frac{79}{225}$	☐	☐	☐	☐	☐
$\frac{13}{37}$	☐	☐	☐	☐	☐
$\frac{8}{45}$	☐	☐	☐	☐	☐
$\frac{17}{99}$	☐	☐	☐	☐	☐

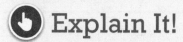 **Explain It!**

ACTIVITY

Sofia wrote a decimal as a fraction. Her classmate Nora says that her method and answer are not correct. Sofia disagrees and says that this is the method she learned.

$$0.12112111211112.... =$$
$$x = 0.\overline{12}$$
$$100 \cdot x = 100 \cdot 0.\overline{12}$$
$$100x = 12.\overline{12}$$
$$99x = 12$$
$$x = \frac{12}{99}$$

I can...
identify a number that is irrational.

 Common Core Content Standards
8.NS.A.1

Mathematical Practices
MP.1, MP.2, MP.3, MP.7, MP.8

A. Construct Arguments Is Nora or Sofia correct? Explain your reasoning.

B. Use Structure What is another nonterminating decimal number that can not be written as a fraction.

Focus on math practices

Construct Arguments Is 0.12112111211112… a rational number? Explain.

95

? Essential Question How is an irrational number different from a rational number?

  VISUAL LEARNING ASSESS

EXAMPLE 1 **Identify Irrational Numbers**

Scan for Multimedia

The Venn diagram shows the relationships among rational numbers.

How would you classify the number 0.24758326... ?

Reasoning How can you use the definition of each number set to classify numbers?

Rational Numbers: $-\frac{4}{5}$, 0.75, 31.8

Integers: -5, $-\frac{16}{4}$, $-1,000$

Whole Numbers: 0

Natural Numbers: 19, $\sqrt{4}$

0.24758326...

The decimal expansion does not terminate or repeat, so it cannot be written as a ratio of two integers.

The number 0.24758326... is not a rational number.

Numbers that are not rational are called *irrational*. An **irrational number** is a number that cannot be written in the form $\frac{a}{b}$, where a and b are integers and $b \neq 0$.

Rational Numbers: $-\frac{4}{5}$, 0.75, 31.8

Integers: -5, $-\frac{16}{4}$, $-1,000$

Whole Numbers: 0

Natural Numbers: 19, $\sqrt{4}$

Irrational Numbers: $\sqrt{2}$, 1.121121112..., π, $-\sqrt{3}$

The number 0.24758326... is irrational because the decimal expansion is nonrepeating and nonterminating.

☑ Try It!

Classify each number as rational or irrational.

π 3.565565556...

0.04053661... -17

$0.\overline{76}$ 3.275

Rational	Irrational

Convince Me! **Construct Arguments** Jen classifies the number 4.567 as irrational because it does not repeat. Is Jen correct? Explain.

EXAMPLE 2 — Identify Square Roots as Irrational Numbers

Classify $\sqrt{3}$.

$\sqrt{3}$ means "the nonnegative square root of 3."

The **square root** of a number is a number that when multiplied by itself equals the original number. The radical symbol $\sqrt{}$ is used to denote the nonnegative square root.

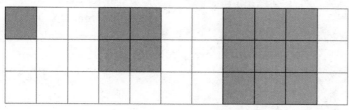

$1 \cdot 1 = 1$	$2 \cdot 2 = 4$	$3 \cdot 3 = 9$
$\sqrt{1} = 1$	$\sqrt{4} = 2$	$\sqrt{9} = 3$

The number 3 is not a perfect square, so $\sqrt{3}$ cannot be written as an integer. So, $\sqrt{3}$ is irrational.

> A **perfect square** is a number that is the square of an integer. The first three integer perfect squares are 1, 4, and 9.

> **Generalize** For any whole number b that is not a perfect square, $\sqrt{b}$ is irrational.

EXAMPLE 3 — Classify Numbers as Rational or Irrational

Classify each number as rational or irrational. Explain how you classified each number.

$$-81,572 \qquad \sqrt{11} \qquad 5.636336333\ldots \qquad \sqrt{16}$$

> $-81,572$ is an integer and can be written as the fraction $\frac{-81,572}{1}$, so it is rational.

Rational	Irrational
$-81,572$	$\sqrt{11}$
$\sqrt{16}$	$5.636336333\ldots$

> 11 is not a perfect square, so $\sqrt{11}$ is irrational.

> The number 16 is a perfect square, so $\sqrt{16} = 4$ is rational.

> This decimal expansion does not repeat or terminate, so it is irrational.

 Try It!

Classify each number as rational or irrational and explain.

$$\frac{2}{3} \qquad \sqrt{25} \qquad -0.7\overline{5} \qquad \sqrt{2} \qquad 7,548,123$$

Numbers that are not rational are called **irrational numbers**.

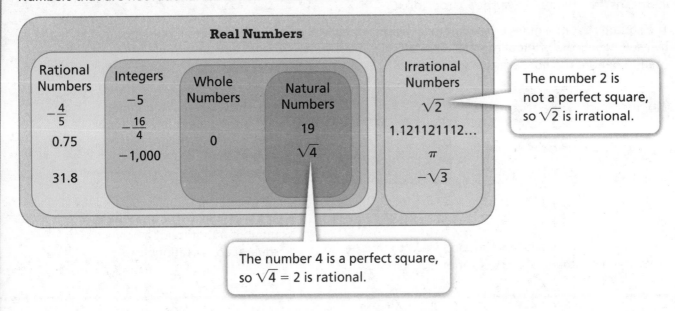

Do You Understand?

1. **? Essential Question** How is an irrational number different from a rational number?

2. **Reasoning** How can you tell whether a square root of a whole number is rational or irrational?

3. **Construct Arguments** Could a number ever be both rational and irrational? Explain.

Do You Know How?

4. Is the number 65.4349224... rational or irrational? Explain.

5. Is the number $\sqrt{2,500}$ rational or irrational? Explain.

6. Classify each number as rational or irrational.

   $4.2\overline{7}$ 0.375 $0.232342345...$ $\sqrt{62}$ $\dfrac{13}{1}$

Rational	Irrational

Practice & Problem Solving

Scan for
Multimedia

7. Is 5.787787778... a rational or irrational number? Explain.

8. Is $\sqrt{42}$ rational or irrational? Explain.

9. A teacher places seven cards, lettered A–G, on a table. Which cards show irrational numbers?

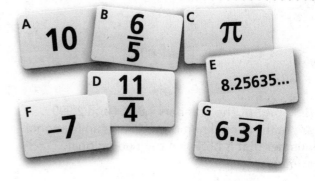

10. Circle the irrational number in the list below.

$7.\overline{27}$ $\frac{5}{9}$ $\sqrt{15}$ $\sqrt{196}$

11. Lisa writes the following list of numbers.

5.737737773..., 26, $\sqrt{45}$, $-\frac{3}{2}$, 0, 9

a. Which numbers are rational?

b. Which numbers are irrational?

12. Construct Arguments Deena says that 9.565565556... is a rational number because it has a repeating pattern. Do you agree? Explain.

13. Is $\sqrt{1,815}$ rational? Explain.

14. Is the decimal form of $\frac{13}{3}$ a rational number? Explain.

15. Write the side length of the square rug as a square root. Is the side length a rational or irrational number? Explain.

Area = 100 ft^2

16. Reasoning The numbers 2.888... and 2.999... are both rational numbers. What is an irrational number that is between the two rational numbers?

17. Higher Order Thinking You are given the expressions $\sqrt{76 + n}$ and $\sqrt{2n + 26}$. What is the smallest value of n that will make each number rational?

Assessment Practice

18. Which numbers are rational?

   I.   1.1111111...

   II. 1.567

   III. 1.101101110...

   Ⓐ II and III

   Ⓑ III only

   Ⓒ II only

   Ⓓ I and II

   Ⓔ I only

   Ⓕ None of the above

19. Determine whether the following numbers are rational or irrational.

	Rational	Irrational
$\frac{8}{5}$	☐	☐
π	☐	☐
0	☐	☐
$\sqrt{1}$	☐	☐
4.46466...	☐	☐
-6	☐	☐
$\sqrt{2}$	☐	☐

Solve & Discuss It!  ACTIVITY

Courtney and Malik are buying a rug to fit in a 50-square-foot space. Which rug should they purchase? Explain.

$99 Rug Sale!

7 ft x 7 ft   8 ft diameter   6 ft x 8½ ft

Rug Emporium has your floors covered.

Focus on math practices

Make Sense and Persevere How did you decide which rug Courtney and Malik should purchase?

? **Essential Question** How can you compare and order rational and irrational numbers?

 VISUAL LEARNING   ASSESS

EXAMPLE 1 **Approximate an Irrational Number**

Scan for Multimedia

Darcy wants to add the ribbon shown along the diagonal of the rectangular flag she is designing. Does Darcy have enough ribbon? Explain.

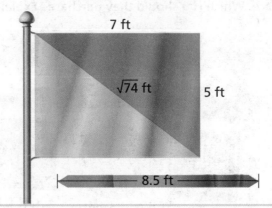

7 ft

$\sqrt{74}$ ft   5 ft

8.5 ft

Approximate $\sqrt{74}$ using perfect squares.

Because 74 lies between the two consecutive perfect squares 64 and 81, $\sqrt{74}$ is located between $\sqrt{64}$ and $\sqrt{81}$.

> Because 74 is closer to 81 than 64, $\sqrt{74}$ is closer to $\sqrt{81}$, or 9.

$\sqrt{64}$ $\sqrt{74}$ $\sqrt{81}$

8   9

Find a better approximation by squaring decimals between 8 and 9. Then compare.

> **Reasoning** Which decimals can you use to find a better approximation?

$8.5 \times 8.5 = 72.25$ This approximation is too low.

$8.6 \times 8.6 = 73.96$ This is a good approximation.

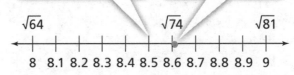

$\sqrt{64}$ $\sqrt{74}$ $\sqrt{81}$

8 8.1 8.2 8.3 8.4 8.5 8.6 8.7 8.8 8.9 9

The length of the diagonal, $\sqrt{74}$, is about 8.6 feet. Darcy does not have enough ribbon.

 **Try It!**

Between which two whole numbers is $\sqrt{12}$?

$\boxed{}$ < 12 < $\boxed{}$

$\boxed{}$ < $\sqrt{12}$ < $\boxed{}$

$\boxed{}$ < $\sqrt{12}$ < $\boxed{}$

Convince Me! Which of the two numbers is a better estimate for $\sqrt{12}$? Explain.

EXAMPLE **2** Compare Irrational Numbers

  ACTIVITY ASSESS

Compare $\sqrt{32}$ and 5.51326... . Plot each number at its approximate location on a number line.

STEP 1 Approximate $\sqrt{32}$ by using perfect squares.

$$25 < 32 < 36$$
$$\sqrt{25} < \sqrt{32} < \sqrt{36}$$
$$5 < \sqrt{32} < 6$$

> **Look for Relationships**
> To compare irrational numbers and locate them on a number line, you can use their rational approximations.

Then find a better approximation by using decimals.

$$5.5 \times 5.5 = 30.25 \qquad 5.6 \times 5.6 = 31.36 \qquad 5.7 \times 5.7 = 32.49$$
$$5.6 < \sqrt{32} < 5.7$$

STEP 2 Approximate 5.51326... as a rational number by rounding to the nearest tenth.

$$5.51326... \approx 5.5$$

STEP 3 Plot each approximation on a number line to compare.

So, $5.51326... < \sqrt{32}$.

EXAMPLE **3** Compare and Order Rational and Irrational Numbers

Compare and order the numbers below.

$$\pi^2, 9\frac{1}{2}, 9.8, 9.\overline{5}, \sqrt{94}$$

STEP 1 Use rational approximation to estimate the values of irrational numbers.

$$\pi^2 \approx 3.14 \times 3.14 \approx 9.8596$$
$$9\frac{1}{2} = 9.5$$
$$9.8$$
$$9.\overline{5} = 9.5555...$$
$$\sqrt{94} \approx 9.7$$

STEP 2 Plot each approximation on a number line.

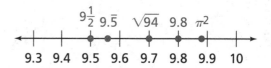

So, $9\frac{1}{2} < 9.\overline{5} < \sqrt{94} < 9.8 < \pi^2$.

☑ **Try It!**

Compare and order the following numbers:

$$\sqrt{11}, 2\frac{1}{4}, -2.5, 3.\overline{6}, -3.97621 ...$$

To compare rational and irrational numbers, you must first find rational approximations of the irrational numbers. You can approximate irrational numbers using perfect squares or by rounding.

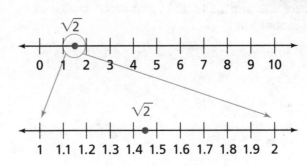

Do You Understand?

1. **Essential Question** How can you compare and order rational and irrational numbers?

2. **Reasoning** The "leech" is a technical term for the slanted edge of a sail. Is the length of the leech shown closer to 5 meters or 6 meters? Explain.

3. **Construct Arguments** Which is a better approximation of $\sqrt{20}$, 4.5 or 4.47? Explain.

Do You Know How?

4. Approximate $\sqrt{39}$ to the nearest whole number.

5. Approximate $\sqrt{18}$ to the nearest tenth and plot the number on a number line.

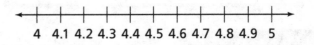

6. Compare 5.7145… and $\sqrt{29}$. Show your work.

7. Compare and order the following numbers:

    $5.2,\ -5.\overline{6},\ 3\frac{9}{10},\ \sqrt{21}$

Practice & Problem Solving

8. Leveled Practice Find the rational approximation of $\sqrt{15}$.

a. Approximate using perfect squares.

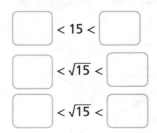

$\boxed{} < 15 < \boxed{}$

$\boxed{} < \sqrt{15} < \boxed{}$

$\boxed{} < \sqrt{15} < \boxed{}$

b. Locate and plot $\sqrt{15}$ on a number line.

Find a better approximation using decimals.

$3.8 \times 3.8 = \boxed{}$

$3.9 \times 3.9 = \boxed{}$

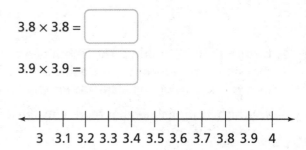

9. Compare $-1.96312\ldots$ and $-\sqrt{5}$. Show your work.

10. Does $\frac{1}{6}$, -3, $\sqrt{7}$, $-\frac{6}{5}$, or 4.5 come first when the numbers are listed from least to greatest? Explain.

11. A museum director wants to hang the painting on a wall. To the nearest foot, how tall does the wall need to be?

$\sqrt{90}$ ft

12. Dina has several small clay pots. She wants to display them in order of height, from shortest to tallest. What will be the order of the pots?

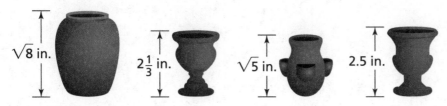

$\sqrt{8}$ in. $2\frac{1}{3}$ in. $\sqrt{5}$ in. 2.5 in.

13. Rosie is comparing $\sqrt{7}$ and 3.44444... . She says that $\sqrt{7} > 3.44444...$ because $\sqrt{7} = 3.5$.

   a. What is the correct comparison?

   b. **Critique Reasoning** What mistake did Rosie likely make?

14. **Model with Math** Approximate $-\sqrt{23}$ to the nearest tenth. Draw the point on the number line.

15. **Higher Order Thinking** The length of a rectangle is twice the width. The area of the rectangle is 90 square units. Note that you can divide the rectangle into two squares.

   Area = 90 square units

   a. Which irrational number represents the length of each side of the squares?

   b. Estimate the length and width of the rectangle.

☑ Assessment Practice

16. Which list shows the numbers in order from least to greatest?

   Ⓐ $-4, -\frac{9}{4}, \frac{1}{2}, 3.7, \sqrt{5}$

   Ⓑ $-4, -\frac{9}{4}, \frac{1}{2}, \sqrt{5}, 3.7$

   Ⓒ $-\frac{9}{4}, \frac{1}{2}, 3.7, \sqrt{5}, -4$

   Ⓓ $-\frac{9}{4}, -4, \frac{1}{2}, 3.7, \sqrt{5}$

17. The area of a square poster is 31 square inches. Find the length of one side of the poster. Explain.

   PART A

   To the nearest whole inch

   PART B

   To the nearest tenth of an inch

Solve & Discuss It!

ACTIVITY

Matt and his dad are building a tree house. They buy enough flooring material to cover an area of 36 square feet. What are all possible dimensions of the floor?

Look for Relationships
Can different floor dimensions result in the same area?

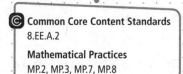

I can...
find square roots and cube roots of rational numbers.

© **Common Core Content Standards**
8.EE.A.2

Mathematical Practices
MP.2, MP.3, MP.7, MP.8

Focus on math practices

Reasoning Why is there only one set of dimensions for a square floor when there are more sets for a rectangular floor? Are all the dimensions reasonable? Explain.

? Essential Question > How do you evaluate cube roots and square roots?

  VISUAL LEARNING · ASSESS

EXAMPLE 1 **Evaluate Cube Roots to Solve Problems**

Scan for Multimedia

Leah is building a bird house for purple martins, birds that prefer cube-shaped birdhouses. What are the dimensions of each square piece of wood Leah needs to build the 216 cubic-inch birdhouse?

Reasoning What do you know about the length, width, and height of the birdhouse?

Draw and label a cube to represent the birdhouse.

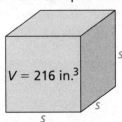

$V = 216$ in.^{3}

$216 = s \cdot s \cdot s$

$216 = s^3$

A number that is a cube of an integer is a **perfect cube**.

The number 216 is also a perfect cube.

To find the value of s, find the cube root of 216. The **cube root** of a number is a number whose cube is equal to that number.

The symbol $\sqrt[3]{}$ means the cube root of a number.

$$\sqrt[3]{216} = \sqrt[3]{6 \cdot 6 \cdot 6}$$
$$= \sqrt[3]{6^3}$$
$$= 6$$

Taking the cube root and cubing a number are inverse operations.

The dimensions of each square piece of wood are 6 inches by 6 inches.

☑ **Try It!**

A cube-shaped art sculpture has a volume of 64 cubic feet. What is the length of each edge of the cube?

The length of each edge is ☐ feet.

$\sqrt[3]{64} = \sqrt[3]{\boxed{} \cdot \boxed{} \cdot \boxed{}}$

$\sqrt[3]{64} = \sqrt[3]{\boxed{}^3}$

$\sqrt[3]{64} = \boxed{}$

Convince Me! How can you find the cube root of 64?

EXAMPLE 2 ▶ Evaluate Perfect Squares and Perfect Cubes

Evaluate.

A. $\sqrt[3]{64}$

$\sqrt[3]{64} = \sqrt[3]{4 \cdot 4 \cdot 4}$

$= \sqrt[3]{4^3}$

$= 4$

B. $\sqrt{100}$

$\sqrt{100} = \sqrt{10 \cdot 10}$

$= \sqrt{10^2}$

$= 10$

C. $\sqrt{49}$

$\sqrt{49} = \sqrt{27 \cdot 7}$

$= \sqrt{7^2}$

$= 7$

D. $\sqrt[3]{8}$

$\sqrt[3]{8} = \sqrt[3]{2 \cdot 2 \cdot 2}$

$= \sqrt[3]{2^3}$

$= 2$

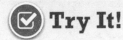 **Try It!**

Evaluate.

a. $\sqrt[3]{27}$
b. $\sqrt{25}$
c. $\sqrt{81}$
d. $\sqrt[3]{1}$

EXAMPLE 3 ▶ Evaluate Square Roots to Solve Problems

Sean cuts one sheet of colorful poster paper to cover the bulletin board exactly. What are the dimensions of the poster paper?

Find the square root of the area to find the side lengths of the bulletin board.

$\sqrt{144} = \sqrt{12 \cdot 12}$

$= \sqrt{12^2}$

$= 12$

Each side of the bulletin board measures 12 inches. Sean will need to cut a 12-inch by 12-inch sheet of poster paper.

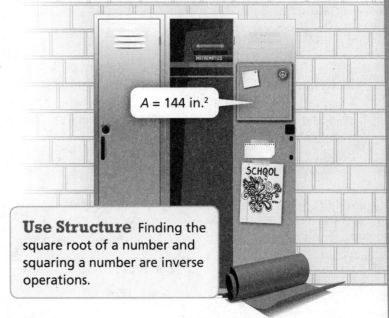

$A = 144$ in.^{2}

Use Structure Finding the square root of a number and squaring a number are inverse operations.

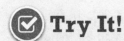 **Try It!**

Emily wants to buy a tablecloth to cover a square card table. She knows the tabletop has an area of 9 square feet. What are the minimum dimensions of the tablecloth Emily needs?

Emily should buy a tablecloth that measures at least

[ ] feet by [ ] feet.

$\sqrt{9} = \sqrt{\boxed{} \cdot \boxed{}}$

$= \sqrt{\boxed{}^2}$

$= \boxed{}$

The cube root of a number is a number whose cube is equal to that number.

$$\sqrt[3]{125} = \sqrt[3]{5 \cdot 5 \cdot 5}$$
$$= \sqrt[3]{5^3}$$
$$= 5$$

Cubing a number and taking the cube root of the number are inverse operations.

The square root of a number is a number whose square is equal to that number.

$$\sqrt{4} = \sqrt{2 \cdot 2}$$
$$= \sqrt{2^2}$$
$$= 2$$

Squaring a number and taking the square root of the number are inverse operations.

Do You Understand?

1. **? Essential Question** How do you evaluate cube roots and square roots?

2. **Generalize** A certain number is both a perfect square and a perfect cube. Will its square root and its cube root always be different numbers? Explain.

3. **Critique Reasoning** A cube-shaped box has a volume of 27 cubic inches. Bethany says each side of the cube measures 9 inches because $9 \times 3 = 27$. Is Bethany correct? Explain your reasoning.

Do You Know How?

4. A cube has a volume of 8 cubic inches. What is the length of each edge of the cube?

5. Below is a model of the infield of a baseball stadium. How long is each side of the infield?

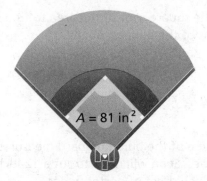

$A = 81 \text{ in.}^2$

6. Julio cubes a number and then takes the cube root of the result. He ends up with 20. What number did Julio start with?

Practice & Problem Solving

Leveled Practice In **7** and **8**, evaluate the cube root or square root.

7. Relate the volume of the cube to the length of each edge.

$V = 8 \text{ cm}^3$

Edge length   Edge length   Edge length

☐ cm × ☐ cm × ☐ cm

$\sqrt[3]{8} =$ ☐

8. Relate the area of the square to the length of each side.

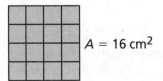

$A = 16 \text{ cm}^2$

Side length   Side length

☐ cm × ☐ cm

$\sqrt{16} =$ ☐

9. Would you classify the number 169 as a perfect square, a perfect cube, both, or neither? Explain.

10. The volume of a cube is 512 cubic inches. What is the length of each side of the cube?

11. A square technology chip has an area of 25 square centimeters. How long is each side of the chip?

12. Would you classify the number 200 as a perfect square, a perfect cube, both, or neither? Explain.

13. A company is making building blocks. What is the length of each side of the block?

$V = 1 \text{ ft}^3$

14. Mrs. Drew wants to build a square sandbox with an area of 121 square feet. What is the total length of wood Mrs. Drew needs to make the sides of the sandbox?

15. Construct Arguments Diego says that if you cube the number 4 and then take the cube root of the result, you end up with 8. Is Diego correct? Explain.

16. Higher Order Thinking Talia is packing a moving box. She has a square-framed poster with an area of 9 square feet. The cube-shaped box has a volume of 30 cubic feet. Will the poster lie flat in the box? Explain.

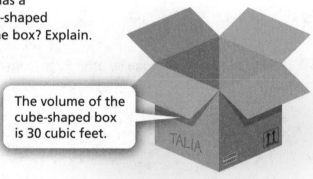

The volume of the cube-shaped box is 30 cubic feet.

✓ Assessment Practice

17. Which expression has the greatest value?

Ⓐ $\sqrt{49} \cdot 2$

Ⓑ $\sqrt{49} - \sqrt{16}$

Ⓒ $\sqrt{25} + \sqrt{16}$

Ⓓ $\sqrt{25} \cdot 3$

18. A toy has various shaped objects that a child can push through matching holes. The area of the square hole is 8 square centimeters. The volume of a cube-shaped block is 64 cubic centimeters.

PART A

Which edge length can you find? Explain.

PART B

Will the block fit in the square hole? Explain.

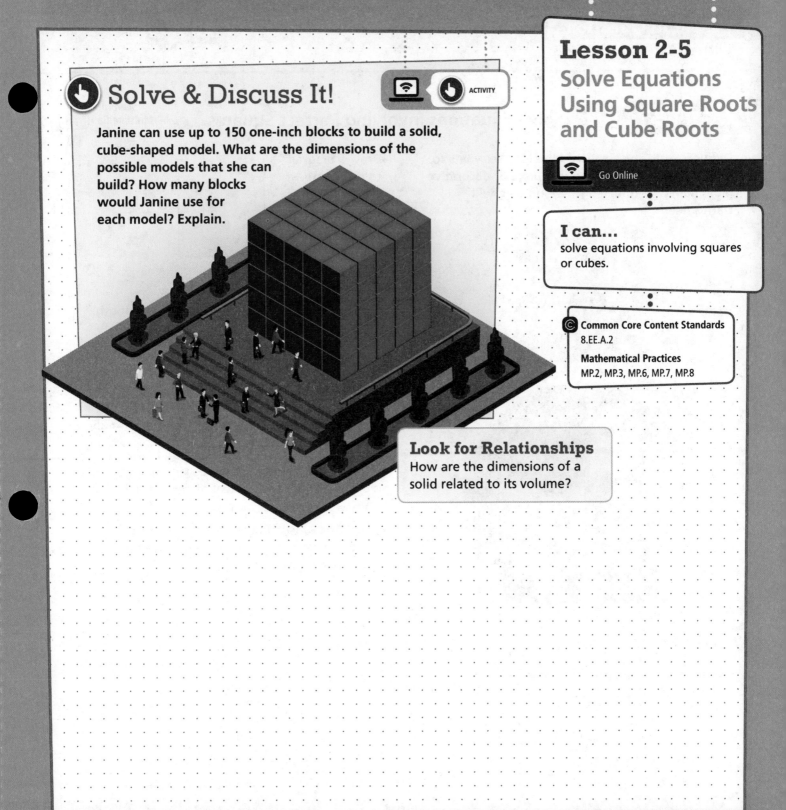

Solve & Discuss It! 🖐

ACTIVITY

Janine can use up to 150 one-inch blocks to build a solid, cube-shaped model. What are the dimensions of the possible models that she can build? How many blocks would Janine use for each model? Explain.

Look for Relationships
How are the dimensions of a solid related to its volume?

I can...
solve equations involving squares or cubes.

© **Common Core Content Standards**
8.EE.A.2

Mathematical Practices
MP.2, MP.3, MP.6, MP.7, MP.8

Focus on math practices

Reasoning Janine wants to build a model using $\frac{1}{2}$-inch cubes. How many $\frac{1}{2}$-inch cubes would she use to build a solid, cube-shaped model with side lengths of 4 inches? Show your work.

? Essential Question How can you solve equations with squares and cubes?

VISUAL LEARNING   ASSESS

EXAMPLE 1 **Solve Equations Involving Perfect Squares**

Scan for Multimedia

Darius is restoring a square tabletop. He wants to finish the outside edges with a piece of decorative molding. What total length of molding will Darius need?

A = 25 ft²

Draw a diagram to represent the tabletop.

s

$A = 25 \text{ ft}^2$ s

Use the formula $A = s^2$ to find each side length. To solve, take the square root of both sides of the equation.

$$A = s^2$$
$$25 = s^2$$
$$\sqrt{25} = \sqrt{s^2}$$
$$\pm 5 = s$$

Because $5^2 = 5 \times 5 = 25$ and $(-5)^2 = -5 \times -5 = 25$, $s = 5$ and $s = -5$, or $s = \pm 5$.

Since length is positive, each side length of the tabletop is 5 feet. Darius needs 20 feet of decorative molding.

Generalize In general, an equation of the form $x^2 = p$, where p is a positive rational number, has two solutions, $x = \pm\sqrt{p}$.

☑ **Try It!**

What is the side length, s, of the square below?

$A = 100 \text{ m}^2$

$$A = s^2$$
$$\boxed{} = s^2$$
$$\boxed{} = \sqrt{s^2}$$
$$\pm \boxed{} = s$$

Each side of the square measures meters.

Convince Me! Why are there two possible solutions to the equation $s^2 = 100$? Explain why only one of the solutions is valid in this situation.

EXAMPLE 2 Solve Equations Involving Perfect Cubes

Kyle has a large, cube-shaped terrarium for his iguana. He wants to cover the opening with a square screen. What are the dimensions, s, for the screen?

$V = s^3$

$343 = s^3$

$\sqrt[3]{343} = \sqrt[3]{s^3}$

$7 = s$

> The value of s is not $\pm \sqrt[3]{343}$ because $(-7)^3 = -7 \times -7 \times -7 = -343$.

$V = 343 \text{ ft}^3$

Each edge of the terrarium is 7 feet, so the dimensions of the screen are 7 feet by 7 feet.

 Try It!

Solve $x^3 = 64$.

EXAMPLE 3 Solve Equations Involving Imperfect Squares and Cubes

Solve for x.

A. $x^2 = 50$

$\sqrt{x^2} = \sqrt{50}$

$x = \pm\sqrt{50}$

> Because 50 is not a perfect square, write the solution using the square root symbol.

There are two possible solutions, $x = +\sqrt{50}$ and $x = -\sqrt{50}$.

B. $x^3 = 37$

$\sqrt[3]{x^3} = \sqrt[3]{37}$

$x = \sqrt[3]{37}$

> $x = \sqrt[3]{37}$ is an exact solution of the equation.

There is one possible solution, $x = \sqrt[3]{37}$.

 **Try It!**

a. Solve $a^3 = 11$.

b. Solve $c^2 = 27$.

You can use square roots to solve equations involving squares.

$$x^2 = a$$
$$\sqrt{x^2} = \sqrt{a}$$
$$x = +\sqrt{a}, -\sqrt{a}$$

You can use cube roots to solve equations involving cubes.

$$x^3 = b$$
$$\sqrt[3]{x^3} = \sqrt[3]{b}$$
$$x = \sqrt[3]{b}$$

Do You Understand?

1. **? Essential Question** How can you solve equations with squares and cubes?

2. **Be Precise** Suri solved the equation $x^2 = 49$ and found that $x = 7$. What error did Suri make?

3. **Construct Arguments** There is an error in the work shown below. Explain the error and provide a correct solution.

$$x^3 = 125$$
$$\sqrt[3]{x^3} = \sqrt[3]{125}$$
$$x = 5 \text{ and } x = -5$$

4. Why are the solutions to $x^2 = 17$ irrational?

Do You Know How?

5. If a cube has a volume of 27 cubic centimeters, what is the length of each edge? Use the volume formula, $V = s^3$, and show your work.

6. Darius is building a square launch pad for a rocket project. If the area of the launch pad is 121 square centimeters, what is its side length? Use the area formula, $A = s^2$, and show your work.

$A = 121 \text{ cm}^2$

7. Solve the equation $x^3 = -215$.

Practice & Problem Solving

Leveled Practice In **8** and **9**, solve.

8. $z^2 = 1$

$$\sqrt{\boxed{}} = \sqrt{\boxed{}}$$

$$z = \pm\boxed{}$$

The solutions are $\boxed{}$ and $\boxed{}$.

9. $a^3 = 216$

$$\sqrt[3]{\boxed{}} = \sqrt[3]{\boxed{}}$$

$$a = \boxed{}$$

---

10. Solve $v^2 = 47$.

11. The area of a square photo is 9 square inches. How long is each side of the photo?

---

12. Solve the equation $y^2 = 81$.

13. Solve the equation $w^3 = 1,000$.

---

14. The area of a square garden is shown. How long is each side of the garden?

$A = 121 \text{ ft}^2$

s

15. Solve $b^2 = 77$.

---

16. Find the value of c in the equation $c^3 = 1,728$.

17. Solve the equation $v^3 = 12$.

18. Higher Order Thinking Explain why

$$\sqrt[3]{-\frac{8}{27}} \text{ is } -\frac{2}{3}$$

19. Critique Reasoning Manolo says that the solution of the equation $g^2 = 36$ is $g = 6$ because $6 \times 6 = 36$. Is Manolo's reasoning complete? Explain.

20. Evaluate $\sqrt[3]{-512}$.

   a. Write your answer as an integer.

   b. Explain how you can check that your result is correct.

21. Yael has a square-shaped garage with 228 square feet of floor space. She plans to build an addition that will increase the floor space by 50%. What will be the length, to the nearest tenth, of one side of the new garage?

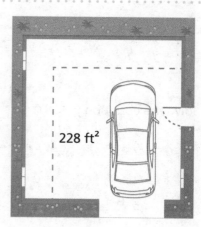

228 ft²

☑ Assessment Practice

22. The Traverses are adding a new room to their house. The room will be a cube with a volume of 6,859 cubic feet. They are going to put in hardwood floors, which costs $10 per square foot. How much will the hardwood floors cost?

23. While packing for their cross-country move, the Chen family uses a crate that has the shape of a cube.

PART A

If the crate has the volume $V = 64$ cubic feet, what is the length of one edge?

PART B

The Chens want to pack a large, framed painting. If the framed painting has the shape of a square with an area of 12 square feet, will the painting fit flat against a side of the crate? Explain.

1. **Vocabulary** How can you show that a number is a rational number? *Lesson 2-2*

2. Which shows $0.2\overline{3}$ as a fraction? *Lesson 2-1*

   Ⓐ $\frac{2}{33}$

   Ⓑ $\frac{7}{33}$

   Ⓒ $\frac{23}{99}$

   Ⓓ $\frac{7}{30}$

3. Approximate $\sqrt{8}$ to the nearest hundredth. Show your work. *Lesson 2-3*

4. Solve the equation $m^2 = 14$. *Lesson 2-5*

5. A fish tank is in the shape of a cube. Its volume is 125 ft³. What is the area of one face of the tank? *Lessons 2-4 and 2-5*

6. Write $1.\overline{12}$ as a mixed number. Show your work. *Lesson 2-1*

How well did you do on the mid-topic checkpoint? Fill in the stars.

MID-TOPIC PERFORMANCE TASK

Six members of the math club are forming two teams for a contest. The teams will be determined by having each student draw a number from a box.

Student	Number Drawn
Lydia	$\sqrt{38}$
Marcy	$6.3\overline{4}$
Caleb	$\sqrt{36}$
Ryan	6.343443444...
Anya	$6.\overline{34}$
Chan	$\sqrt{34}$

PART A

The table shows the results of the draw. The students who drew rational numbers will form the team called the Tigers. The students who drew irrational numbers will form the team called the Lions.

List the members of each team.

PART B

The student on each team who drew the greatest number will be the captain of that team. Who will be the captain of the Tigers? Show your work.

PART C

Who will be the captain of the Lions? Show your work.

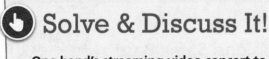 Solve & Discuss It!

One band's streaming video concert to benefit a global charity costs $1.00 to view.

The first day, the concert got 2,187 views. The second day, it got about three times as many views. On the third day, it got 3 times as many views as on the second day. If the trend continues, how much money will the band raise on Day 7?

I can...
use the properties of exponents to write equivalent expressions.

© **Common Core Content Standards**
8.EE.A.1

Mathematical Practices
MP.3, MP.4, MP.7

Focus on math practices

Use Structure Use prime factorization to write an expression equivalent to the amount of money raised by the band on the last day of the week.

? **Essential Question** How do properties of integer exponents help you write equivalent expressions?

EXAMPLE 1 **Multiply Exponential Expressions: Same Base**

Scan for Multimedia

The weight of a juvenile alligator is shown on the right. The adult alligator weighs about 2^6 times more than the juvenile. How can you determine the weight of the adult alligator?

2^3 pounds

Look for Relationships How do the two weights relate?

ONE WAY Write the two expressions in expanded form.

$2^3 \qquad\qquad 2^6$

$\underbrace{2 \times 2 \times 2}_{\substack{2 \text{ is multiplied} \\ 3 \text{ times}}} \times \underbrace{2 \times 2 \times 2 \times 2 \times 2 \times 2}_{\substack{2 \text{ is multiplied} \\ 6 \text{ times}}}$

Join the two expressions.

$\underbrace{2 \times 2 \times 2 \times 2 \times 2 \times 2 \times 2 \times 2 \times 2}_{\substack{2 \text{ is multiplied} \\ 9 \text{ times}}} = 2^9$

ANOTHER WAY Use the Product of Powers Property.

$2^3 \times 2^6 = 2^{3+6} = 2^9$

The **Product of Powers Property** states that when multiplying two powers with the same base, add the exponents.

☑ **Try It!**

The local zoo welcomed a newborn African elephant that weighed 3^4 kg. It is expected that at adulthood, the newborn elephant will weigh approximately 3^4 times as much as its birth weight. What expression represents the expected adult weight of the newborn elephant?

Convince Me! Explain why the Product of Powers Property makes mathematical sense.

Find the volume in cubic inches of a cube with edge length of 2 feet.

$V = 2^3$ cubic feet   1 cubic foot $= 12^3$ cubic inches

$2^3 \times 12^3 = \underbrace{2 \times 2 \times 2} \times \underbrace{12 \times 12 \times 12}$

> Use the Associative and Commutative Properties.

$= (2 \times 12) \times (2 \times 12) \times (2 \times 12)$

$= (2 \times 12)^3$

$= 24^3$ cubic inches

> Use the **Power of Products Property:** when multiplying two exponential expressions with the same exponent and different bases, multiply the bases and keep the exponent the same.

1 cubic foot

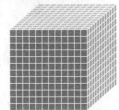

12^3 cubic inches

EXAMPLE **3** **Find the Power of a Power**

Write an equivalent expression for $(5^2)^4$.

$(5^2)^4 = \underbrace{(5^2)(5^2)(5^2)(5^2)}$
                5^2 multiplied 4 times

> Use the Product of Powers Property to add the exponents.

$= 5^{(2+2+2+2)}$

$= 5^8$

> The **Power of Powers Property** states that to find the power of a power, multiply the exponents.

EXAMPLE **4** **Divide Exponential Expressions: Same Base**

Write an equivalent expression for $6^5 \div 6^3$.

$6^5 \div 6^3 = \dfrac{6^5}{6^3}$

> Write as a fraction.

$= \dfrac{\overset{\text{6 multiplied 5 times}}{6 \times 6 \times 6 \times 6 \times 6}}{\underset{\text{6 multiplied 3 times}}{6 \times 6 \times 6}}$

> Remember, $\frac{6}{6} = 1$.

$= \dfrac{6 \times \boxed{6 \times 6 \times 6} \times 6}{\boxed{6 \times 6 \times 6}}$

$= 6 \times 6 \text{ or } 6^2$

> The **Quotient of Powers Property** states that when dividing two exponential expressions with the same base, subtract the exponents.

 **Try It!**

Write equivalent expressions using the properties of exponents.

a. $(7^3)^2$ **b.** $(4^5)^3$ **c.** $9^4 \times 8^4$ **d.** $8^9 \div 8^3$

Use these properties when simplifying expressions with exponents (when a, m, and $n \neq 0$).

Product of Powers Property

When the bases are the same, $a^m \times a^n = a^{m+n}$ add the exponents.

Power of Products Property

When the bases are different, $a^n \times b^n = (a \times b)^n$ multiply the bases and keep the exponent the same.

Power of a Power Property

To find the power of a power, $(a^m)^n = a^{m \times n}$ multiply the exponents.

Quotient of Powers Property

When the bases are the same, $a^m \div a^n = a^{m-n}$ subtract the exponents.

Do You Understand?

1. **Essential Question** How do properties of integer exponents help you write equivalent expressions?

2. **Look for Relationships** If you are writing an equivalent expression for $2^3 \cdot 2^4$, how many times would you write 2 as a factor?

3. **Construct Arguments** Kristen wrote 5^8 as an expression equivalent to $(5^2)^4$. Her math partner writes 5^6. Who is correct?

4. **Critique Reasoning** Tyler says that an equivalent expression for $2^3 \times 5^3$ is 10^9. Is he correct? Explain.

Do You Know How?

5. Write an equivalent expression for $7^{12} \cdot 7^4$.

6. Write an equivalent expression for $(8^2)^4$.

7. A billboard has the given dimensions.

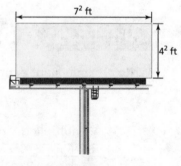

Using exponents, write two equivalent expressions for the area of the rectangle.

8. Write an equivalent expression for $18^9 \div 18^4$.

Name: _____

Practice & Problem Solving

Scan for Multimedia

Leveled Practice In 9–12, use the properties of exponents to write an equivalent expression for each given expression.

9. $2^8 \cdot 2^4$

$2^8 \cdot 2^4 = 2^8 \boxed{} 4$

$= \boxed{}^{\boxed{}}$

10. $\dfrac{8^7}{8^3}$

$\dfrac{8^7}{8^3} = 8^7 \boxed{} 3$

$= \boxed{}^{\boxed{}}$

11. $(3^4)^5$

$(3^4)^5 = 3^4 \boxed{} 5$

$= \boxed{}^{\boxed{}}$

12. $3^9 \cdot 2^9$

$3^9 \cdot 2^9 = \left(\boxed{} \cdot \boxed{} \right)^{\boxed{}}$

13. a. How do you multiply powers that have the same base?

b. How do you divide powers that have the same base?

c. How do you find the power of a power?

d. How do you multiply powers with different bases but the same exponent?

14. Which expressions are equivalent to 2^{11}? Select all that apply.

☐ $\dfrac{2^{23}}{2^{12}}$

☐ $2^7 \cdot 2^4$

☐ $\dfrac{2^9}{2^2}$

☐ $2^2 \cdot 2^9$

In 15–18, use the properties of exponents to write an equivalent expression for each given expression.

15. $(4^4)^3$

16. $\dfrac{3^{12}}{3^3}$

17. $4^5 \cdot 4^2$

18. $6^4 \cdot 2^4$

19. Critique Reasoning Alberto incorrectly stated that $\frac{5^7}{5^4} = 1^3$. What was Alberto's error? Explain your reasoning and find the correct answer.

20. Is the expression 8×8^5 equivalent to $(8 \times 8)^5$? Explain.

21. Is the expression $(3^2)^{-3}$ equivalent to $(3^3)^{-2}$? Explain.

22. Is the expression $3^2 \cdot 3^{-3}$ equivalent to $3^3 \cdot 3^{-2}$? Explain.

23. Model with Math What is the width of the rectangle written as an exponential expression?

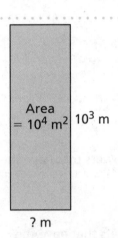

Area $= 10^4$ m^2 10^3 m

? m

24. Simplify the expression $\left(\left(\frac{1}{2} \right)^3 \right)^3$.

25. Higher Order Thinking Use a property of exponents to write $(3b)^5$ as a product of powers.

 Assessment Practice

26. Select all the expressions equivalent to $4^5 \cdot 4^{10}$.

- ☐ $4^5 + 4^{10}$
- ☐ $4^3 \cdot 4^5$
- ☐ $4^3 \cdot 4^{12}$
- ☐ $4^3 + 4^{12}$
- ☐ $4^{18} - 4^3$
- ☐ 4^{15}

27. Your teacher asks the class to evaluate the expression $(2^3)^1$. Your classmate gives an incorrect answer of 16.

PART A Evaluate the expression.

PART B What was the likely error?

Ⓐ Your classmate divided the exponents.

Ⓑ Your classmate multiplied the exponents.

Ⓒ Your classmate added the exponents.

Ⓓ Your classmate subtracted the exponents.

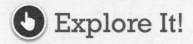 **Explore It!**

Calvin and Mike do sit-ups when they work out. They start with 64 sit-ups for the first set and do half as many each subsequent set.

Look for Relationships Determine whether the relationship shown for Set 1 is also true for Sets 2–5.

Lesson 2-7
More Properties of Integer Exponents

 Go Online

I can...
write a number with a negative or zero exponent a different way.

© **Common Core Content Standards**
8.EE.A.1

Mathematical Practices
MP.2, MP.3, MP.6

A. What representation can you use to show the relationship between the set number and the number of sit-ups?

B. What conclusion can you make about the relationship between the number of sit-ups in each set?

Focus on math practices

Use Structure How could you determine the number of sit-up sets Calvin and Mike do?

? Essential Question What do the Zero Exponent and Negative Exponent Properties mean?

  VISUAL LEARNING ASSESS

 EXAMPLE **1** **The Zero Exponent Property**

Scan for Multimedia

Marchella is playing a card-matching game with some classmates. Four matches have been made. It is Marchella's turn, and she chooses 3^0. What card would complete her match?

Organize the information in a table and look for a pattern.

Exponent Form	Simplified Form
3^4	81
3^3	27
3^2	9
3^1	3
3^0	?

÷ 3
÷ 3
÷ 3
÷ 3

As the exponent decreases by one, the product is divided by 3.

$3 \div 3 = 1$, so $3^0 = 1$.

ANOTHER WAY Use the Quotient of Powers Property.

$3^3 \div 3^3$

$= 3^{3-3} = 3^0$

When dividing two exponential expressions with the same base, subtract the exponents.

and

$\dfrac{3^3}{3^3} = \dfrac{3 \times 3 \times 3}{3 \times 3 \times 3} = 1$

so $3^0 = 1$

The **Zero Exponent Property** states that $a^0 = 1$ (assuming $a \neq 0$).

✓ **Try It!**

Evaluate.

a. $(-7)^0$ b. $(43)^0$ c. 1^0 d. $(0.5)^0$

Convince Me! Why is $2(7^0) = 2$?

EXAMPLE 2 — The Negative Exponent Property

Simplify the expression $4^3 \div 4^5$.

$$4^3 \div 4^5 = \frac{4^3}{4^5}$$

Remember, $\frac{4}{4} = 1$.

$$= \frac{\boxed{4 \times 4 \times 4}}{4 \times \boxed{4 \times 4 \times 4} \times 4} = \frac{1}{16}$$

and

$$4^3 \div 4^5 = 4^{(3-5)} = 4^{-2}$$

Use the Quotient of Powers Property.

So, $4^{-2} = \frac{1}{16}$.

The **Negative Exponent Property** states that $a^{-n} = \frac{1}{a^n}$ (assuming $a \neq 0$).

Try It!

Write each expression using positive exponents.

a. 8^{-2} b. 2^{-4} c. 3^{-5}

EXAMPLE 3 — Expressions with Negative Exponents

Write the expression $\frac{1}{7^{-3}}$ with a positive exponent.

$$\frac{1}{7^{-3}} = \frac{1}{\frac{1}{7^3}}$$

Use the Negative Exponent Property.

$$= 1 \cdot \frac{7^3}{1}$$

Multiply by the reciprocal of the denominator.

$$= 7^3$$

Try It!

Write each expression using positive exponents.

a. $\frac{1}{5^{-3}}$ b. $\frac{1}{2^{-6}}$

Use these additional properties when simplifying or generating equivalent expressions with exponents (when $a \neq 0$ and $n \neq 0$).

Zero Exponent Property	Negative Exponent Property
$a^0 = 1$	$a^{-n} = \dfrac{1}{a^n}$

Do You Understand?

1. ? **Essential Question** What do the Zero Exponent and Negative Exponent Properties mean?

2. **Reasoning** In the expression 9^{-12}, what does the negative exponent mean?

3. **Reasoning** In the expression $3(2^0)$, what is the order of operations? Explain how you would evaluate the expression.

Do You Know How?

4. Simplify $1{,}999{,}999^0$.

5. **a.** Write 7^{-6} using a positive exponent.

   b. Rewrite $\dfrac{1}{10^{-3}}$ using a positive **exponent**.

6. Evaluate $27x^0y^{-2}$ for $x = 4$ and $y = 3$.

Name: _____

Practice & Problem Solving

Scan for Multimedia

Leveled Practice In **7–8**, complete each table to find the value of a nonzero number raised to the power of 0.

7.

Exponent	Simplified
4^4	256
4^3	
4^2	
4^1	
4^0	

8.

Exponent	Simplified
$(-2)^4$	16
$(-2)^3$	
$(-2)^2$	
$(-2)^1$	
$(-2)^0$	

9. Given: $(-3.2)^0$

  a. Simplify the given expression.

  b. Write two expressions equivalent to the given expression. Explain why the three expressions are equivalent.

10. Simplify each expression for $x = 6$.

  a. $12x^0(x^{-4})$

  b. $14(x^{-2})$

In **11** and **12**, compare the values using >,<, or =.

11. 3^{-2} ☐ 1

12. $(\frac{1}{4})^0$ ☐ 1

In **13** and **14**, rewrite each expression using a positive exponent.

13. 9^{-4}

14. $\dfrac{1}{2^{-6}}$

15. Given: $9y^0$

  a. Simplify the expression for $y = 3$.

  b. Construct Arguments Will the value of the given expression vary depending on y? Explain.

16. Simplify each expression for $x = 4$.

   a. $-5x^{-4}$

   b. $7x^{-3}$

17. Evaluate each pair of expressions.

   a. $(-3)^{-8}$ and -3^{-8}

   b. $(-3)^{-9}$ and -3^{-9}

18. Be Precise To win a math game, Lamar has to pick a card with an expression that has a value greater than 1. The card Lamar chooses reads $\left(\frac{1}{2}\right)^{-4}$. Does Lamar win the game? Explain.

$\left(\frac{1}{2}\right)^{-4}$

19. Simplify the expression. Assume that x is nonzero. Your answer should have only positive exponents.

$x^{-10} \cdot x^{6}$

20. Higher Order Thinking

   a. Is the value of the expression $\left(\frac{1}{4^{-3}}\right)^{-2}$ greater than 1, equal to 1, or less than 1?

   b. If the value of the expression is greater than 1, show how you can change one sign to make the value less than 1. If the value is less than 1, show how you can change one sign to make the value greater than 1. If the value is equal to 1, show how you can make one change to make the value not equal to 1.

☑ Assessment Practice

21. Which expressions are equal to 5^{-3}? Select all that apply.

   ☐ 125

   ☐ 125^{-1}

   ☐ 5^3

   ☐ $\frac{1}{5^3}$

   ☐ $\frac{1}{125}$

22. Which expressions have a value less than 1 when $x = 4$? Select all that apply.

   ☐ $\left(\frac{3}{x^2}\right)^0$

   ☐ $\frac{x^0}{3^2}$

   ☐ $\frac{1}{6^{-x}}$

   ☐ $\frac{1}{x^{-3}}$

   ☐ $3x^{-4}$

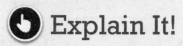 **Explain It!**

Keegan and Jeff did some research and found that there are approximately 7,492,000,000,000,000,000 grains of sand on Earth. Jeff says that it is about 7×10^{15} grains of sand. Keegan says that this is about 7×10^{18} grains of sand.

 ACTIVITY

I can...
estimate large and small quantities using a power of 10.

© **Common Core Content Standards**
8.EE.A.3

Mathematical Practices
MP.3, MP.6, MP.7

7,492,000,000,000,000,000

A. How might Jeff have determined his estimate? How might Keegan have determined his estimate?

B. Whose estimate, Jeff's or Keegan's, is more logical? Explain.

Focus on math practices

Be Precise Do you think the two estimates are close in value? Explain your reasoning.

EXAMPLE 1 👁 Estimate Very Large Quantities

Scan for
Multimedia

Janelle is comparing the estimated populations of Japan and China. The estimated population of Japan is 126,818,019. The estimated population of China is shown. How can Janelle compare the two populations more easily?

Use Structure You can estimate large quantities and write them in a format that is easier to compare.

Population (Est.)

1 4 0 2 9 4 1 4 8 7

STEP 1 Estimate each population by rounding to the greatest place value. Then write the number as a single digit times a power of 10.

Population of China

1,402,941,487

rounds to 1,000,000,000

1×10^9

Count the zeros to determine the power of 10.

Population of Japan

126,818,019

rounds to 100,000,000

1×10^8

STEP 2 Compare the estimated values.

$$10^9 > 10^8$$

$$1 \times 10^9 > 1 \times 10^8$$

Janelle can use estimates using powers of 10 to compare the populations more easily.

☑ Try It!

Light travels 299,792,458 meters per second. Sound travels at 332 meters per second. Use a power of 10 to compare the speed of light to the speed of sound.

299,792,458 rounded to the greatest place value

is ⬜.

322 rounded to the greatest place value

is ⬜.

There are ⬜ zeros in the rounded number.

The estimated speed of light

is ⬜ × 10^⬜ meters per second.

There are ⬜ zeros in the rounded number.

The estimated speed of sound

is ⬜ × 10^⬜ meters per second.

$3 \times 10^⬜ > 3 \times 10^⬜$, so the speed of light is faster than the speed of sound.

Convince Me! Country A has a population of 1,238,682,005 and Country B has a population of 1,106,487,394. How would you compare these populations?

EXAMPLE **2** **Estimate Very Small Quantities**

  ACTIVITY ASSESS

Matthias used a laser to measure the average thickness of a human hair. A sheet of paper is about 0.0013 meter thick. How do the two thicknesses compare?

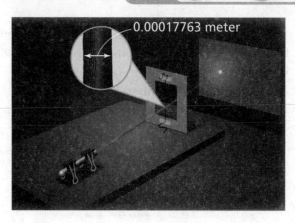

0.00017763 meter

Write the estimated thickness of a human hair using a single digit and a power of 10.	Write the estimated thickness of a sheet of paper using a single digit and a power of 10.
Round 0.00017763 to 0.0002.	Round 0.0013 to 0.001.
Write 0.0002 as 2×10^{-4}.	Write 0.001 as 1×10^{-3}.

Compare the estimates.

$2 \times 10^{-4} < 1 \times 10^{-3}$

A human hair is thinner than a sheet of paper.

EXAMPLE **3** **Find How Many Times as Much**

How does the Gross Domestic Product (GDP) of Canada compare to that of the United States?

Gross Domestic Product	
Canada	$1,785,387,000,000,000
USA	$17,348,075,000,000,000

STEP 1 Write each GDP as a single digit times a power of 10.

Canada: $1,785,387,000,000,000 \approx 2,000,000,000,000,000$
$$= 2 \times 10^{15}$$

Count the zeros to determine the power of 10.

USA: $17,348,075,000,000,000 \approx 20,000,000,000,000,000$
$$= 2 \times 10^{16}$$

STEP 2 Compare the two estimates.

$(2 \times 10^{16}) > (2 \times 10^{15})$

The U.S. GDP is about 10 times greater than that of Canada.

 **Try It!**

There are approximately 1,020,000,000 cars in the world. The number of cars in the United States is approximately 239,800,000.

Compare the number of cars in the world to that in the United States.

You can estimate a very large or very small number by rounding the number to its greatest place value, and then writing that number as a single digit times a power of 10.

Very Large Numbers

$3{,}564{,}879{,}000 \approx 4{,}000{,}000{,}000$

$\approx 4 \times 10^9$

Count the number of zeros to determine the power of 10.

Very Small Numbers

$0.000000235 \approx 0.0000002$

$\approx 2 - 10^{-7}$

The number is greater than 1, so the exponent is positive.

The number is less than 1, so the exponent is negative.

Do You Understand?

1. ? **Essential Question** When would you use powers of 10 to estimate a quantity?

2. **Construct Arguments** Kim writes an estimate for the number 0.00436 as 4×10^3. Explain why this cannot be correct.

3. **Be Precise** Raquel estimated 304,900,000,000 as 3×10^8. What error did she make?

Do You Know How?

4. Use a single digit times a power of 10 to estimate the height of Mt. Everest to the nearest ten thousand feet.

Mt. Everest is 29,035 feet tall.

5. A scientist records the mass of a proton as 0.00000000000000000000000016726231 gram. Use a single digit times a power of 10 to estimate the mass.

6. The tanks at the Georgia Aquarium hold approximately 8.4×10^6 gallons of water. The tanks at the Audubon Aquarium of the Americas hold about 400,000 gallons of water. Use a single digit times a power of 10 to estimate how many times greater the amount of water is at the Georgia Aquarium.

Practice & Problem Solving

Scan for
Multimedia

Leveled Practice In 7–9, use powers of 10 to estimate quantities.

7. A city has a population of 2,549,786 people. Estimate this population to the nearest million. Express your answer as the product of a single digit and a power of 10.

Rounded to the nearest million, the population

is about [　　　].

Written as the product of a single digit and

a power of ten, this number is [　] × 10[　].

8. Use a single digit times a power of 10 to estimate the number 0.00002468.

Rounded to the nearest hundred thousandth,

the number is about [　　　].

Written as a single digit times a power of ten,

the estimate is [　] × 10[　].

9. The approximate circumferences of Earth and Saturn are shown. How many times greater is the circumference of Saturn than the circumference of Earth?

The circumference of Saturn is

[　] × 10[　] km.

Saturn's circumference is about [　] times

greater than the circumference of Earth.

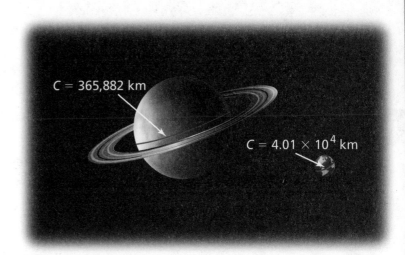

C = 365,882 km

$C = 4.01 \times 10^4$ km

10. Estimate 0.037854921 to the nearest hundredth. Express your answer as a single digit times a power of ten.

11. Compare the numbers 6×10^{-6} and 2×10^{-8}.

a. Which number has the greater value?

b. Which number has the lesser value?

c. How many times greater is the greater number?

12. Taylor made $43,785 last year. Use a single digit times a power of ten to express this value rounded to the nearest ten thousand.

13. The length of plant cell A is 8×10^{-5} meter. The length of plant cell B is 0.000004 meter. How many times greater is plant cell A's length than plant cell B's length?

14. Critique Reasoning The diameter of one species of bacteria is shown. Bonnie approximates this measure as 3×10^{-11} meter. Is she correct? Explain.

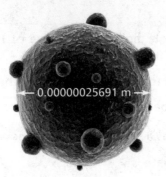

$\leftarrow$ 0.00000025691 m $\rightarrow$

15. The populations of Cities A and B are 2.6×10^5 and 1,560,000, respectively. The population of City C is twice the population of City B.

The population of City C is how many times the population of City A?

16. Earth is approximately 5×10^9 years old. For which of these ages could this be an approximation?

Ⓐ 4,762,100,000 years

Ⓑ 48,000,000,000 years

Ⓒ 4.45×10^9 years

Ⓓ 4.249999999×10^9 years

17. PART A

Express 0.000000298 as a single digit times a power of ten rounded to the nearest ten millionth.

PART B

Explain how negative powers of 10 can be helpful when writing and comparing small numbers.

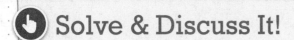 Solve & Discuss It!  ACTIVITY

Scientists often write very large or very small numbers using exponents. How might a scientist write the number shown using exponents?

I can...
use scientific notation to write very large or very small quantities.

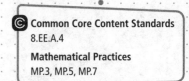 **Common Core Content Standards**
8.EE.A.4

Mathematical Practices
MP.3, MP.5, MP.7

Use Structure How can you use your knowledge of powers of 10 to rewrite the number?

Focus on math practices

Look for Relationships What does the exponent in 10^{15} tell you about the value of the number?

? Essential Question What is scientific notation and why is it used?

VISUAL LEARNING   ASSESS

EXAMPLE 1 👁 **Write Large Numbers in Scientific Notation**

Scan for Multimedia

Louisa is researching the approximate distance between Earth and the Sun. Her father told her that the distance is 9.296×10^7 miles. In an astronomy book, she found the following.

Which distance is correct?

92,960,000 miles

Louisa's father used **scientific notation** to express the approximate distance because the distance is so great. Numbers in scientific notation have two factors.

$$9.296 \times 10^7$$

The first factor is always a number greater than or equal to 1 and less than 10.

The second factor is always a power of 10.

Write the number in standard form in scientific notation.

Place the decimal point after the first nonzero digit.

7 digits

9.2,960,000

Count the number of digits after the decimal point to determine the power of 10.

$$9.296 \times 10^7$$

The two numbers represent the same distance.

☑ **Try It!**

The height of Angel Falls, the tallest waterfall in the world, is 3,212 feet. How do you write this number in scientific notation?

☐.☐☐☐ × 10☐

Convince Me! Why do very large numbers have positive exponents when written in scientific notation? Explain.

EXAMPLE 2 ▶ Write Small Numbers in Scientific Notation

What is the width of a red blood cell written in scientific notation?

Write the number as the product of two factors.

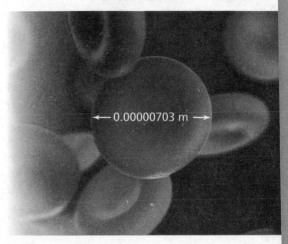

← 0.00000703 m →

Place the decimal after the first nonzero digit.	Count the number of digits before the decimal point to determine the power of 10.
0.00000703 ↪ 7.03	6 digits $\overbrace{0.000007}.03$ 10^{-6}

7.03 × 10⁻⁶

The width of the red blood cell, expressed in scientific notation, is 7.03×10^{-6} meter.

 **Try It!**

A common mechanical pencil lead measures about 0.005 meter in diameter. How can you express this measurement using scientific notation?

EXAMPLE 3 ▶ Convert Scientific Notation to Standard Form

A. Kelly used a calculator to multiply large numbers. How can she write the number on her calculator screen in standard form?

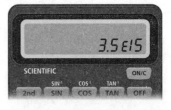

$$10^{15}$$
$$3.5 \times 10^{15} = 3,500,000,000,000,000$$

The exponent is positive so move the decimal point to the right.

B. How can Charlie write the number on the calculator screen in standard form?

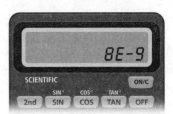

$$10^{-9}$$
$$8 \times 10^{-9} = 0.000000008$$

The exponent is negative so move the decimal point to the left.

Use Appropriate Tools Certain calculators may display scientific notation using the symbol EE or E. The number that follows is the power of 10.

 **Try It!**

Write the numbers in standard form.

a. 9.225×10^{18}

b. 6.3×10^{-8}

Scientific notation is a way to write very large numbers or very small numbers. Scientists use scientific notation as a more efficient and convenient way of writing such numbers.

A number in scientific notation is the product of two factors. The first factor must be greater than or equal to 1 and less than 10. The second factor is a power of 10.

> Count the number of digits **after** the decimal point. The exponent is positive.

7 digits

$6.5,000,000 \rightarrow 6.5 \times 10^7$

> Place the decimal point after the first nonzero digit.

> Count the number of digits **before** the decimal point. The exponent is negative.

5 digits

$0.00009.87 \rightarrow 9.87 \times 10^{-5}$

> Place the decimal point after the first nonzero digit.

To write a number in scientific notation in standard form, multiply the decimal number by the power of 10.

Do You Understand?

1. **? Essential Question** What is scientific notation and why is it used?

2. **Critique Reasoning** Taylor states that 2,800,000 in scientific notation is 2.8×10^{-6} because the number has six places to the right of the 2. Is Taylor's reasoning correct?

3. **Construct Arguments** Sam will write 0.000032 in scientific notation. Sam thinks that the exponent of 10 will be positive. Do you agree? Construct an argument to support your response.

Do You Know How?

4. Express 586,400,000 in scientific notation.

5. The genetic information of almost every living thing is stored in a tiny strand called DNA. Human DNA is 3.4×10^{-8} meter long. Write the length in standard form.

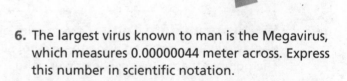

6. The largest virus known to man is the Megavirus, which measures 0.00000044 meter across. Express this number in scientific notation.

7. How would you write the number displayed on the calculator screen in standard form?

7.6 E12

Practice & Problem Solving

Scan for
Multimedia

Leveled Practice In **8** and **9**, write the numbers in the correct format.

8. The Sun is 1.5×10^8 kilometers from Earth.

   1.5×10^8 is written as [   ] in standard form.

9. Brenna wants an easier way to write 0.0000000000000000587.

   0.0000000000000000587 is written as [   ] $\times$ 10[   ] in scientific notation.

10. Is 23×10^{-8} written in scientific notation? Justify your response.

11. Is 8.6×10^7 written in scientific notation? Justify your response.

12. Simone evaluates an expression using her calculator. The calculator display is shown at the right. Express the number in standard form.

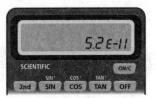

13. Express the number 0.00001038 in scientific notation.

14. Express the number 80,000 in scientific notation.

15. Peter evaluates an expression using his calculator. The calculator display is shown at the right. Express the number in standard form.

16. a. What should you do first to write 5.871×10^{-7} in standard form?

b. Express the number in standard form.

17. Express 2.58×10^{-2} in standard form.

18. At a certain point, the Grand Canyon is approximately 1,600,000 centimeters across. Express this number in scientific notation.

1,600,000 cm

19. The length of a bacterial cell is 5.2×10^{-6} meter. Express the length of the cell in standard form.

20. Higher Order Thinking Express the distance 4,300,000 meters using scientific notation in meters, and then in millimeters.

✓ Assessment Practice

21. Which of the following numbers are written in scientific notation?

☐ 12×10^6

☐ 12

☐ 6.89×10^6

☐ 6.89

☐ 0.4

☐ 4×10^{-1}

22. Jeana's calculator display shows the number to the right.

PART A

Express this number in scientific notation.

PART B

Express this number in standard form.

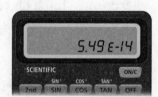

3-ACT MATH ▶ ▶ ▶

Hard-Working
Organs

3-Act Mathematical Modeling:
Hard-Working Organs

📶 Go Online

ⓒ **Common Core Content Standards**
8.EE.A.1, 8.EE.A.3
Mathematical Practices
MP.4, MP.1, MP.2, MP.3, MP.7, MP.8

ACT 1

1. After watching the video, what is the first question that comes to mind?

2. Write the Main Question you will answer.

3. Construct Arguments Predict an answer to this Main Question. Explain your prediction.

4. On the number line below, write a number that is too small to be the answer. Write a number that is too large.

Too small   Too large

⟵————————————————⟶

5. Plot your prediction on the same number line.

6. What information in this situation would be helpful to know?
How would you use that information?

7. Use Appropriate Tools What tools can you use to solve the problem?
Explain how you would use them strategically.

8. Model with Math Represent the situation using mathematics.
Use your representation to answer the Main Question.

9. What is your answer to the Main Question? Is it greater or less than your
prediction? Explain why.

10. Write the answer you saw in the video.

11. Reasoning Does your answer match the answer in the video? If not, what are some reasons that would explain the difference?

12. Make Sense and Persevere Would you change your model now that you know the answer? Explain.

Reflect

13. Model with Math Explain how you used a mathematical model to represent the situation. How did the model help you answer the Main Question?

14. Generalize What pattern did you notice in your calculations? How did that pattern help you solve the problem?

SEQUEL

15. Use Structure How many times does a heart beat in a lifetime? Use your solution to the Main Question to help you solve.

Solve & Discuss It!  ACTIVITY

The homecoming committee wants to fly an aerial banner over the football game. The banner is 1,280 inches long and 780 inches tall. How many different ways can the area of the banner be expressed?

I can...
perform operations with numbers in scientific notation.

© **Common Core Content Standards**
8.EE.A.4

Mathematical Practices
MP.3, MP.6, MP.7

Focus on math practices

Be Precise Which of the solutions is easiest to manipulate?

? Essential Question How does using scientific notation help when computing with very large or very small numbers?

 VISUAL LEARNING ASSESS

 EXAMPLE 1 **Add or Subtract Numbers in Scientific Notation**

Scan for Multimedia

The mass of Earth and the mass of the Moon are shown. How much greater is the mass of Earth than that of the Moon?

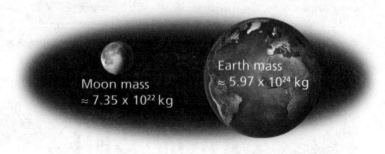

Moon mass ≈ 7.35×10^{22} kg

Earth mass ≈ 5.97×10^{24} kg

Use Structure What does the exponent tell you about the magnitude of the number?

ONE WAY Write the masses in standard form and then subtract.

$5.97 \times 10^{24} = 5{,}970{,}000{,}000{,}000{,}000{,}000{,}000{,}000$

$7.35 \times 10^{22} = 73{,}500{,}000{,}000{,}000{,}000{,}000{,}000$

$$\begin{array}{r} 5{,}970{,}000{,}000{,}000{,}000{,}000{,}000{,}000 \\ -\ \ \ 73{,}500{,}000{,}000{,}000{,}000{,}000{,}000 \\ \hline 5{,}896{,}500{,}000{,}000{,}000{,}000{,}000{,}000 \end{array}$$

The difference is about 5.8965×10^{24} kilograms.

ANOTHER WAY Write the masses using the same power of 10. Then subtract.

5.97×10^{24}

$= (5.97 \times 10^2) \times 10^{22}$ — Use a property of exponents to write 10^{24} as $10^2 \times 10^{22}$.

$= 597 \times 10^{22}$

$(597 \times 10^{22}) - (7.35 \times 10^{22})$

$= (597 - 7.35) \times 10^{22}$ — Remember, the first factor must be greater than or equal to 1 and less than 10.

$= 589.65 \times 10^{22}$

$= 5.8965 \times 10^{24}$

The difference is about 5.8965×10^{24} kilograms.

☑ Try It!

The planet Venus is on average 2.5×10^7 kilometers from Earth. The planet Mars is on average 2.25×10^8 kilometers from Earth. When Venus, Earth, and Mars are aligned, what is the average distance from Venus to Mars?

$2.25 \times 108 = (2.25 \times \boxed{} \times \boxed{})$

$\qquad = \boxed{} \times 10^7$

$2.5 \times 10^7 + \boxed{} \times 10^7 = (2.5 + \boxed{}) \times 10^7$

$\qquad = \boxed{} \times 10^7$

$\qquad = \boxed{} \times \boxed{}$

Convince Me! In Example 1 and the Try It, why did you move the decimal point to get the final answer?

EXAMPLE 2 **Multiply Numbers in Scientific Notation**

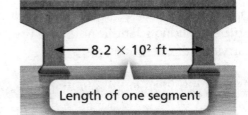

The Confederation Bridge connects New Brunswick to Prince Edward Island. The main part of the bridge rests on piers that form 43 segments. What is the approximate length of the main part of the bridge? Express your answer in scientific notation.

8.2×10^2 ft

Length of one segment

STEP 1 Write an expression to represent the problem situation.

$(8.2 \times 10^2) \times 43$

$= (8.2 \times 10^2) \times (4.3 \times 10^1)$

> Express both numbers in scientific notation.

STEP 2 Multiply.

$(8.2 \times 10^2) \times (4.3 \times 10^1)$

$= (8.2 \times 4.3) \times (10^2 \times 10^1)$

> Remember: The Product of Powers Property states that when multiplying powers with the same base, you add the exponents.

$= 35.26 \times (10)^{2+1}$

$= 35.26 \times 10^3$

$= 3.526 \times 10^4$

> The first factor must be less than 10 and greater than or equal to 1.

The length of the main part of the bridge is approximately 3.5×10^4 feet.

EXAMPLE 3 **Divide Numbers in Scientific Notation**

A queen ant lays 1.83×10^6 eggs over a period of 30 days. Assuming she lays the same number of eggs each day, about how many eggs does she lay in one day? Express your answer in scientific notation.

First, write 30 in scientific notation: 3.0×10^1

Then, divide.

$(1.83 \times 10^6) \div (3.0 \times 10^1)$

$\dfrac{1.83 \times 10^6}{3.0 \times 10^1}$

$\dfrac{1.83}{3.0} \times \dfrac{10^6}{10^1}$

$(1.83 \div 3.0) \times (10^6 \div 10^1)$

> The Quotient of Powers Property states that when dividing powers with the same base, you subtract the exponents.

0.61×10^5

6.1×10^4

The queen ant lays about 6.1×10^4 eggs per day.

☑ Try It!

There are 1×10^{14} good bacteria in the human body. There are 2.6×10^{18} good bacteria among the spectators in a soccer stadium. About how many spectators are in the stadium? Express your answer in scientific notation.

Operations with very large or very small numbers can be carried out more efficiently using scientific notation. The properties of exponents apply when carrying out operations.

Addition or Subtraction	Multiplication	Division
$(2.3 \times 10^6) + (1.6 \times 10^9)$	$(2.3 \times 10^6) \times (1.6 \times 10^9)$	$(2.3 \times 10^6) \div (1.6 \times 10^9)$
$(2.3 \times 10^6) + (1.6 \times 10^3) \times 10^6$	$(2.3 \times 1.6) \times (10^6 \times 10^9)$	$(2.3 \div 1.6) \times (10^6 \div 10^9)$
$(2.3 \times 10^6) + (1,600 \times 10^6)$	$3.68 \times 10^{6+9}$	$1.4375 \times 10^{6-9}$
$(2.3 + 1,600) \times 10^6$ Use the	3.68×10^{15} Use the	1.4375×10^{-3} Use the
$1,602.3 \times 10^6$ Product	Product	Quotient
1.6023×10^9 of Powers Property.	of Powers Property.	of Powers Property.

Do You Understand?

1. **? Essential Question** How does using scientific notation help when computing with very small or very large numbers?

2. **Use Structure** When multiplying and dividing two numbers in scientific notation, why do you sometimes have to rewrite one factor?

3. **Use Structure** For the sum of (5.2×10^4) and (6.95×10^4) in scientific notation, why will the power of 10 be 10^5?

Do You Know How?

4. A bacteriologist estimates that there are 5.2×10^4 bacteria growing in each of 20 petri dishes. About how many bacteria in total are growing in the petri dishes? Express your answer in scientific notation.

5. The distance from Earth to the Moon is approximately 1.2×10^9 feet. The Apollo 11 spacecraft was approximately 360 feet long. About how many spacecraft of that length would fit end to end from Earth to the Moon? Express your answer in scientific notation.

6. The mass of Mars is 6.42×10^{23} kilograms. The mass of Mercury is 3.3×10^{23} kilograms.

   a. What is the combined mass of Mars and Mercury expressed in scientific notation?

   b. What is the difference in the mass of the two planets expressed in scientific notation?

Practice & Problem Solving

Leveled Practice In **7** and **8**, perform the operation and express your answer in scientific notation.

7. $(7 \times 10^{-6})(7 \times 10^{-6})$

$(\boxed{} \cdot \boxed{}) \times (10^{\boxed{}} \cdot 10^{\boxed{}})$

$\boxed{} \times 10^{\boxed{}}$

$4.9 \times 10^{\boxed{}}$

8. $(3.76 \times 10^5) + (7.44 \times 10^5)$

$(\boxed{} + \boxed{}) \times (10^{\boxed{}})$

$\boxed{} \times \boxed{}$

$1.12 \times 10^{\boxed{}}$

9. What is the value of n in the equation $1.9 \times 10^7 = (1 \times 10^5)(1.9 \times 10^n)$?

10. Find $(5.3 \times 10^3) - (8 \times 10^2)$. Express your answer in scientific notation.

11. What is the mass of 30,000 molecules? Express your answer in scientific notation.

Mass of one molecule of oxygen $= 5.3 \times 10^{-23}$ gram

12. Critique Reasoning Your friend says that the product of 4.8×10^8 and 2×10^{-3} is 9.6×10^{-5}. Is this answer correct? Explain.

13. Find $\frac{7.2 \times 10^{-8}}{3 \times 10^{-2}}$. Write your answer in scientific notation.

14. A certain star is 4.3×10^2 light years from Earth. One light year is about 5.9×10^{12} miles. How far from Earth (in miles) is the star? Express your answer in scientific notation.

15. The total consumption of fruit juice in a particular country in 2006 was about 2.28×10^9 gallons. The population of that country that year was 3×10^8. What was the average number of gallons consumed per person in the country in 2006?

16. The greatest distance between the Sun and Jupiter is about 8.166×10^8 kilometers. The greatest distance between the Sun and Saturn is about 1.515×10^9 kilometers. What is the difference between these two distances?

17. What was the approximate number of pounds of garbage produced per person in the country in one year? Express your answer in scientific notation.

Garbage generated in country:
6.958×10^{10} pounds
Population of country:
4.57×10^6 people

18. Higher Order Thinking

a. What is the value of n in the equation $1.5 \times 10^{12} = (5 \times 10^5)(3 \times 10^n)$?

b. Explain why the exponent on the left side of the equation is not equal to the sum of the exponents on the right side.

✓ Assessment Practice

19. Find $(2.2 \times 10^5) \div (4.4 \times 10^{-3})$. When you regroup the factors, what do you notice about the quotient of the decimal factors? How does this affect the exponent of the quotient?

20. Which expression has the least value?

Ⓐ $(4.7 \times 10^4) + (8 \times 10^4)$

Ⓑ $(7.08 \times 10^3) + (2.21 \times 10^3)$

Ⓒ $(5.43 \times 10^8) - (2.33 \times 10^8)$

Ⓓ $(9.35 \times 10^6) - (6.7 \times 10^6)$

? Topic Essential Question

What are real numbers? How are real numbers used to solve problems?

Vocabulary Review

Draw lines to connect each vocabulary word with its definition.

Vocabulary Word	Definition
1. cube root	a number that cannot be written in the form $\frac{a}{b}$, where a and b are integers and $b \neq 0$
2. irrational number	a way to express a number as the product of two factors, one greater than or equal to 1 and less than 10, and the other a power of 10
3. Product of Powers Property	a number that when multiplied by itself equals the original number
4. perfect cube	the cube of an integer
5. perfect square	a number whose cube equals the original number
6. Power of Powers Property	To multiply two powers with the same base, keep the common base and add the exponents.
7. Powers of Products Property	To multiply two powers with the same exponent and different bases, multiply the bases and keep the exponent.
8. scientific notation	a number that is the square of an integer
9. square root	When you have an exponent raised to a power, keep the base and multiply the exponents.

Use Vocabulary in Writing

Use vocabulary words to explain how to find the length of each side of a square garden with an area of 196 square inches.

Concepts and Skills Review

Rational Numbers as Decimals

Quick Review

You can write repeating decimals in fraction form by writing two equations. You multiply each side of one equation by a power of 10. Then you subtract the equations to eliminate the repeating decimal.

Example

Write 1.0505... as a mixed number.

$x = 1.\overline{05}$

$100 \cdot x = 100 \cdot 1.\overline{05}$

$100x = 105.\overline{05}$

$100x - x = 105.\overline{05} - 1.\overline{05}$

$99x = 104$

$x = \dfrac{104}{99}$ or $1\dfrac{5}{99}$

Practice

Write each number as a fraction or a mixed number.

1. $0.\overline{7}$

2. $.0.0\overline{4}$

3. $4.\overline{45}$

4. $2.191919...$

Understand Irrational Numbers

Quick Review

An **irrational number** is a number that cannot be written in the form $\dfrac{a}{b}$, where a and b are integers and $b \neq 0$. Rational and irrational numbers together make up the real number system.

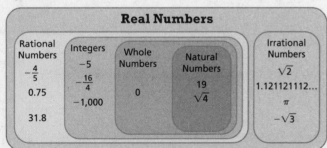

Example

Classify $-\sqrt{50}$ as rational or irrational.

The number $-\sqrt{50}$ is irrational because 50 is not the square of any integer.

Practice

1. Determine which numbers are irrational. Select all that apply.

- ☐ $\sqrt{36}$
- ☐ $\sqrt{23}$
- ☐ $-4.232323...$
- ☐ $0.151551555...$
- ☐ $0.3\overline{5}$
- ☐ π

2. Classify $-0.\overline{25}$ as rational or irrational. Explain.

LESSON 2-3 · Compare and Order Real Numbers

Quick Review

To compare and order real numbers, it helps to first write each number in decimal form.

Example

Compare and order the following numbers. Locate each number on a number line.

$7.\overline{8}$, $7\frac{4}{5}$, $\sqrt{56}$

Write each number in decimal form.

$7.\overline{8} = 7.8888...$

$7\frac{4}{5} = 7.8$

$\sqrt{56} \approx 7.5$

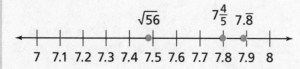

So, $\sqrt{56} < 7\frac{4}{5} < 7.\overline{8}$.

Practice

1. Between which two whole numbers does $\sqrt{89}$ lie?

$\sqrt{89}$ is between $\boxed{}$ and $\boxed{}$.

2. Compare and order the following numbers. Locate each number on a number line.

$2.\overline{3}$, $\sqrt{8}$, 2.5, $2\frac{1}{4}$

LESSON 2-4 · Evaluate Square Roots and Cube Roots

Quick Review

Remember that a perfect square is the square of an integer. A square root of a number is a number that when multiplied by itself is equal to the original number. Similarly, a **perfect cube** is the cube of an integer. A **cube root** of a number is a number that when cubed is equal to the original number.

Example

A monument has a cube shape with a volume of 729 cubic meters. What is the length of each edge of the monument?

$\sqrt[3]{729} = \sqrt[3]{9 \cdot 9 \cdot 9}$

$\qquad = \sqrt[3]{9^3}$

$\qquad = 9$

So, the length of each edge is 9 meters.

Practice

Classify each number as a perfect square, a perfect cube, both, or neither.

1. 27

2. 100

3. 64

4. 24

5. A gift box is a cube with a volume of 512 cubic inches. What is the length of each edge of the box?

Quick Review

You can use square roots to solve equations involving squares. You can use cube roots to solve equations involving cubes. Equations with square roots often have two solutions. Look at the context to see whether both solutions are valid.

Example

Mattie wants to build a square deck to make a kiddie play area of 144 square feet. What will be the length of each side of the deck?

Use the formula $A = s^2$ to find each side length.

$144 = s2$

$\sqrt{144} = \sqrt{s^2}$

$\pm 12 = s$

Length cannot be negative, so the length of each side of the deck will be 12 feet.

Practice

Solve for x.

1. $x^3 = 64$

2. $x^2 = 49$

3. $x^3 = 25$

4. $x^2 = 125$

5. A container has a cube shape. It has a volume of 216 cubic inches. What are the dimensions of one face of the container?

Quick Review

These properties can help you write equivalent expressions that contain exponents.

Product of Powers Property

$a^m \cdot a^n = a^{m+n}$

Power of Powers Property

$(a^m)^n = a^{mn}$

Power of Products Property

$a^n \cdot b^n = (a \cdot b)^n$

Quotient of Powers Property

$a^m \div a^n = a^{m-n}$, when $a \neq 0$

Example

Write an equivalent expression for $(4^3)^2$.

$(4^3)^2 = (4^3)(4^3)$

$= (4 \cdot 4 \cdot 4)(4 \cdot 4 \cdot 4)$

$= 4^6$

Practice

Use the properties of exponents to write an equivalent expression for each given expression.

1. $6^4 \cdot 6^3$

2. $(3^6)^{-2}$

3. $7^3 \cdot 2^3$

4. $4^{10} \div 4^4$

Quick Review

The Zero Exponent Property states that any nonzero number raised to the power of 0 is equal to 1. The Negative Exponent Property states that for any nonzero rational number a and integer n, $a^{-n} = \frac{1}{a^n}$.

Example

Evaluate the expression for $x = 2$ and $y = 4$.

$$\frac{2}{y^{-2}} + 5x^0 = \frac{2}{(4)^{-2}} + 5(2)^0$$

$$= \frac{2(4^2)}{1} + 5(1)$$

$$= 2(16) + 5(1)$$

$$= 32 + 5$$

$$= 37$$

Practice

Write each expression using positive exponents.

1. 9^{-4}

2. $\frac{1}{3^{-5}}$

Evaluate each expression for $x = 2$ and $y = 5$

3. $-4x^{-2} + 3y^0$

4. $2x^0y^{-2}$

Quick Review

You can estimate very large and very small quantities by writing the number as a single digit times a power of 10.

Example

Keisha is about 1,823,933 minutes old. Write this age as a single digit times a power of 10.

First round to the greatest place value. 1,823,933 is about 2,000,000.

Write the rounded number as a single digit times a power of 10.

$$2{,}000{,}000 = 2 \times 10^6$$
6 5 4 3 2 1

Keisha is about 2×10^6 minutes old.

Practice

1. In the year 2013 the population of California was about 38,332,521 people. Write the estimated population as a single digit times a power of 10.

2. The wavelength of green light is about 0.00000051 meter. What is this estimated wavelength as a single digit times a power of 10?

3. The land area of Connecticut is about 12,549,000,000 square meters. The land area of Rhode Island is about 2,707,000,000 square meters. How many times greater is the land area of Connecticut than the land area of Rhode Island?

Quick Review

A number in **scientific notation** is written as a product of two factors, one greater than or equal to 1 and less than 10, and the other a power of 10.

Example

Write 65,700,000 in scientific notation.

First, place the decimal point to the right of the first nonzero digit.

Then, count the number of digits to the right of the decimal point to determine the power of 10.

65,700,000 in scientific notation is 6.57×10^7.

Practice

1. Write 803,000,000 in scientific notation.

2. Write 0.0000000068 in scientific notation.

3. Write 1.359×10^5 in standard form.

4. The radius of a hydrogen atom is 0.000000000025 meter. How would you express this radius in scientific notation?

Quick Review

When multiplying and dividing numbers in scientific notation, multiply or divide the first factors. Then multiply or divide the powers of 10. When adding and subtracting numbers in scientific notation, first write the numbers with the same power of 10. Then add or subtract the first factors, and keep the same power of 10.

If the decimal part of the result is not greater than or equal to 1 and less than 10, move the decimal point and adjust the exponent.

Example

Multiply $(4.2 \times 10^5) \times (2.5 \times 10^3)$.

$(4.2 \times 10^5) \times (2.5 \times 10^3)$

$= (4.2 \times 2.5) \times (10^5 \times 10^3)$

$= 10.5 \times 10^8$

$= 1.05 \times 10^9$

Practice

Perform each operation. Express your answers in scientific notation.

1. $(2.8 \times 10^4) \times (4 \times 10^5)$

2. $(6 \times 10^9) \div (2.4 \times 10^3)$

3. $(4.1 \times 10^4) + (5.6 \times 10^6)$

4. The population of Town A is 1.26×10^5 people. The population of Town B is 2.8×10^4 people. How many times greater is the population of Town A than the population of Town B?

Crisscrossed

Solve each equation. Write your answers in the cross-number puzzle below. Each digit, negative sign, and decimal point of your answer goes in its own box.

I can...
solve one-step equations, including those involving square roots and cube roots. © 8.EE.C.7b

Across

A $-377 = x - 1{,}000$

B $x^3 = 1{,}000$

C $x^3 = -8$

D $x + 7 = -209$

F $x + 19 = -9$

J $14 + x = -19$

L $m - 2.02 = -0.58$

M $-3.09 + x = -0.7$

N $-2.49 = -5 + x$

Q $x - 3.5 = -3.1$

T $q - 0.63 = 1.16$

V $8.3 + x = 12.1$

Down

A $y - 11 = 49$

B $x + 8 = 20$

C $z^3 = -1{,}331$

D $11 + x = 3$

E $x - 14 = -7.96$

F $14 + x = -9$

G $d + 200 = 95$

H $x^2 = 144$

K $-12 = t - 15.95$

P $0.3 + x = 11$

R $x - 3 = -21$

S $-7 = -70 + y$

ANALYZE AND USE PROPORTIONAL RELATIONSHIPS

? Topic Essential Question

How can you recognize and represent proportional relationships and use them to solve problems?

Topic Overview

3-1 Connect Ratios, Rates, and Unit Rates

3-2 Determine Unit Rates with Ratios of Fractions

3-3 Understand Proportional Relationships: Equivalent Ratios

3-4 Describe Proportional Relationships: Constant of Proportionality

3-Act Mathematical Modeling: Mixin' It Up

3-5 Graph Proportional Relationships

3-6 Apply Proportional Reasoning to Solve Problems

Topic Vocabulary

- constant of proportionality
- proportion
- proportional relationship

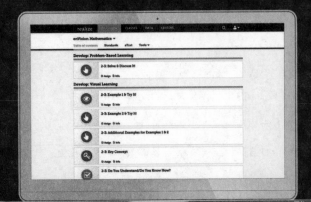

Lesson Digital Resources

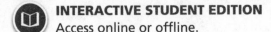

INTERACTIVE STUDENT EDITION
Access online or offline.

VISUAL LEARNING ANIMATION
Interact with visual learning animations.

ACTIVITY Use with *Solve & Discuss It, Explore It,* and *Explain It* activities, and to explore Examples.

VIDEOS Watch clips to support *3-Act Mathematical Modeling Lessons* and *STEM Projects.*

Go online

Mixin' It Up

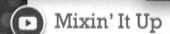

▶ Mixin' It Up

Drinking plenty of water each day is important. Water is necessary for everything your body does. Not drinking enough water can lead to health problems. It's even easier to drink enough water if you like the taste.

There are many ways to make water more exciting. You can drink seltzer or filtered water. You can add fruit, vegetables, herbs, or flavor enhancers. You can add more or less based on what you like. Think about this during the 3-Act Mathematical Modeling lesson.

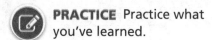 **PRACTICE** Practice what you've learned.

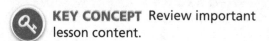 **KEY CONCEPT** Review important lesson content.

TUTORIALS Get help from *Virtual Nerd*, right when you need it.

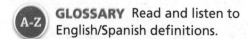 **GLOSSARY** Read and listen to English/Spanish definitions.

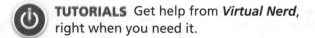 **MATH TOOLS** Explore math with digital tools.

 **ASSESSMENT** Show what you've learned.

 **GAMES** Play Math Games to help you learn.

Did You Know?

There are more than **326 million trillion gallons** of water on Earth.

Only a **small percentage** of all this water is fresh water...

...and **much of that fresh water** is locked up in ice caps and glaciers.

71% Water

29% Land

The United Nations says that each person needs about **50 liters** of water each day.

Each person in Africa has access to less than **20 liters** of water each day.

Many doctors recommend that each person drinks eight 8-ounce glasses of water each day.

Each person in the United States uses on average about **35–40 gallons** of water each day.

Your Task: An Essential Resource

Access to fresh, clean water is important for human survival. You and your classmates will determine how much fresh water is available on Earth for people to use. You will also explore ways in which people have developed access to clean water.

Review What You Know!

Vocabulary

Choose the best term from the box to complete each definition.

complex fraction
equivalent ratios
rate
ratio
terms

1. The quantities x and y in the ratio $\frac{x}{y}$ are called _____.

2. $\frac{2 \text{ dogs}}{3 \text{ cats}}$ and $\frac{10 \text{ dogs}}{15 \text{ cats}}$ are an example of _____.

3. A(n) _____ is a type of ratio that has both terms expressed in different units.

4. A(n) _____ has a fraction in its numerator, denominator, or both.

Equivalent Ratios

Complete each equivalent ratio.

5. $\dfrac{4 \text{ boys}}{7 \text{ girls}} = \dfrac{8 \text{ boys}}{\boxed{} \text{ girls}}$

6. $\dfrac{16 \text{ tires}}{4 \text{ cars}} = \dfrac{\boxed{} \text{ tires}}{1 \text{ car}}$

7. $\dfrac{8 \text{ correct}}{10 \text{ total}} = \dfrac{\boxed{} \text{ correct}}{50 \text{ total}}$

8. $\dfrac{16 \text{ pearls}}{20 \text{ opals}} = \dfrac{8 \text{ pearls}}{\boxed{} \text{ opals}}$

9. $\dfrac{32 \text{ pencils}}{8 \text{ erasers}} = \dfrac{8 \text{ pencils}}{\boxed{} \text{ erasers}}$

10. $\dfrac{7 \text{ balls}}{9 \text{ bats}} = \dfrac{\boxed{} \text{ balls}}{27 \text{ bats}}$

Rates

Write each situation as a rate.

11. John travels 150 miles in 3 hours.

12. Cameron ate 5 apples in 2 days.

Equations

Write an equation that represents the pattern in the table.

13.

x	4	5	6	7	8
y	12	15	18	21	24

Language Development

Complete the graphic organizer to help you understand new vocabulary terms.

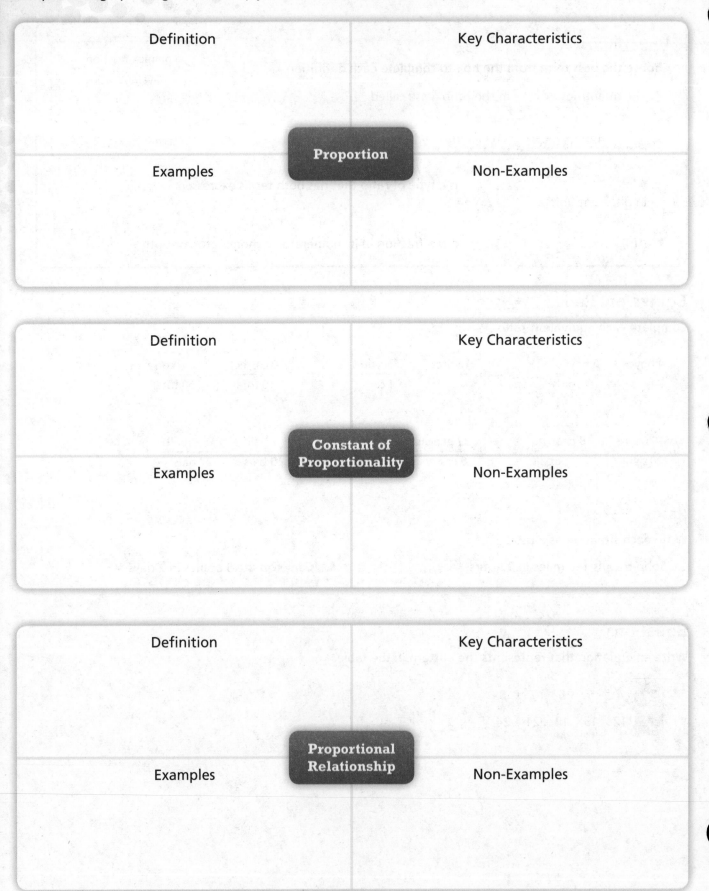

Definition	Key Characteristics

Proportion

Examples	Non-Examples

Definition	Key Characteristics

Constant of Proportionality

Examples	Non-Examples

Definition	Key Characteristics

Proportional Relationship

Examples	Non-Examples

PROJECT
3A

Who do you think would win a race involving different types of animals?

PROJECT: PREDICT RACE RESULTS

PROJECT
3B

What would it be like to travel to another planet?

PROJECT: CALCULATE THE WEIGHT OF YOUR PACK

PROJECT 3C

What stories can you tell?

PROJECT: WRITE A SHORT STORY

PROJECT 3D

If you could play any musical instrument, what would you play? Why?

PROJECT: PLAY MUSIC

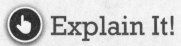 **Explain It!**

 ACTIVITY

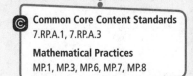
In a basketball contest, Elizabeth made 9 out of 25 free throw attempts. Alex made 8 out of 20 free throw attempts. Janie said that Elizabeth had a better free-throw record because she made more free throws than Alex.

I can...
use ratio concepts and reasoning to solve multi-step problems.

© **Common Core Content Standards**
7.RP.A.1, 7.RP.A.3
Mathematical Practices
MP.1, MP.3, MP.6, MP.7, MP.8

A. Critique Reasoning Do you agree with Janie's reasoning? Explain.

B. Construct Arguments Decide who had the better free-throw record. Justify your reasoning using mathematical arguments.

Focus on math practices

Construct Arguments What mathematical model did you use to justify your reasoning? Are there other models you could use to represent the situation?

EXAMPLE 1 👁 Find Unit Rates

Scan for Multimedia

Nathan and Dan were both hired as lifeguards for the summer. They receive their paychecks for the first week. Who earns more per hour?

Make Sense and Persevere
You can use a ratio to relate the number of hours worked and the amount earned.

LIFEGUARD SERVICES INC.	EARNINGS STATEMENT
EMPLOYEE	Dan Jones
HOURS	9
TOTAL EARNINGS	$78.75

LIFEGUARD SERVICES INC.	EARNINGS STATEMENT
EMPLOYEE	Nathan Smith
HOURS	5
TOTAL EARNINGS	$46.25

Draw a model to show how the quantities are related.

Nathan's Pay

Dan's Pay

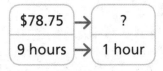

Find unit rates to determine how much each lifeguard earns each hour.

$$\overset{\div 5}{\underset{\div 5}{\frac{46.25}{5} = \frac{9.25}{1}}}$$

$$\overset{\div 9}{\underset{\div 9}{\frac{78.75}{9} = \frac{8.75}{1}}}$$

Nathan earns 50¢ more per hour.

☑ Try It!

Jennifer is a lifeguard at the same pool. She earns $137.25 for 15 hours of lifeguarding. How much does Jennifer earn per hour?

Jennifer earns $ [ ] per hour.

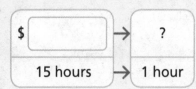

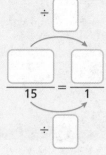

$$\frac{\boxed{}}{15} = \frac{\boxed{}}{1}$$

Convince Me! What do you notice about the models used to find how much each lifeguard earns per hour?

EXAMPLE 2 **Use Unit Rates**

Brian agrees to watch his neighbor's dogs for 7 days. His neighbor provided a 128-ounce bag of dog food. Does Brian have enough food to feed the dogs all 7 days? Explain.

20.5 ounces in **2** days

22.5 ounces in **3** days

Buster   Roxy

STEP 1 Use unit rates to find how much each dog eats in 7 days.

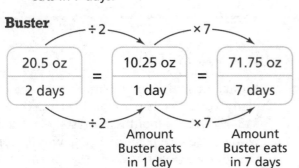
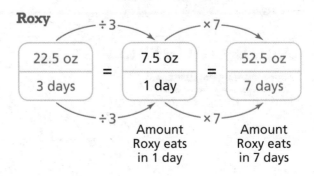

STEP 2 Find the total amount of dog food needed for 7 days. Then compare.

71.75 + 52.5 = 124.25 and 124.25 < 128, so Brian has enough dog food.

EXAMPLE 3 **Compare Using Rates**

Suppose that each jump covers the same distance. How many jumps does it take each animal to cover the same distance?

Rabbit

8 meters

Kangaroo Rat

12 meters

Make tables of equivalent ratios until the distance jumped is the same.

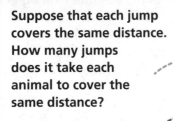

Rabbit

Jumps	Meters
3	8
6	16
9	24

×3

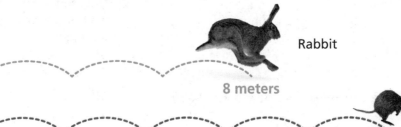

Kangaroo Rat

Jumps	Meters
5	12
10	24

×2

The rabbit jumps 24 meters in 9 jumps.

The kangaroo rat jumps 24 meters in 10 jumps.

Try It!

A kitchen sink faucet streams 0.5 gallon of water in 10 seconds.
A bathroom sink faucet streams 0.75 gallon of water in 18 seconds.
Which faucet will fill a 3-gallon container faster?

You can use equivalent ratios and rates, including unit rates, to compare ratios and to solve problems.

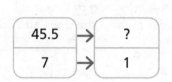

Do You Understand?

1. **Essential Question** How are ratios, rates, and unit rates used to solve problems?

2. **Use Structure** Dorian buys 2 pounds of almonds for $21.98 and 3 pounds of dried apricots for $26.25. Which is less expensive per pound? How much less expensive?

   Complete the tables of equivalent ratios to help you solve.

   Almonds

Cost	Weight (lb)
	2

   Dried Apricots

Cost	Weight (lb)
$26.25	

3. **Generalize** How are unit rates and equivalent ratios related?

Do You Know How?

4. Krystal is comparing two Internet service plans. Plan 1 costs $34.99 per month. Plan 2 costs $134.97 every 3 months. If Krystal plans to stay with one service plan for 1 year, which should she choose? How much will she save?

5. Pam read 126 pages of her summer reading book in 3 hours. Zack read 180 pages of his summer reading book in 4 hours. If they continue to read at the same speeds, will they both finish the 215-page book after 5 total hours of reading? Explain.

6. Nora and Eli are making homemade spring rolls for a party. Nora can make 8 spring rolls in 10 minutes. Eli can make 10 spring rolls in 12 minutes. If they each make 40 spring rolls, who will finish first?

Practice & Problem Solving

Leveled Practice In 7–8, complete the tables of equivalent ratios to solve.

7. After Megan walked 5 miles, her activity tracker had counted 9,780 steps. David's activity tracker had counted 11,928 steps after he walked 6 miles. Suppose each person's step covers about the same distance. Who takes more steps to walk 1 mile? How many more steps?

[   ] takes more steps to walk 1 mile.

[   ] – [   ] = [   ] more steps for 1 mile

Meghan's Steps

Steps	Miles
9,780	
	1

David's Steps

Steps	Miles
	6
	1

8. A package of 5 pairs of insulated gloves costs $29.45. What is the cost of a single pair of gloves?

One pair of gloves

costs [   ].

Price	Pairs of Gloves
	5
	1

9. Which package has the lowest cost per ounce of rice?

10. A nursery owner buys 5 panes of glass to fix some damage to her greenhouse. The 5 panes cost $14.25. Unfortunately, she breaks 2 more panes while repairing the damage. What is the cost of another 2 panes of glass?

11. Be Precise An arts academy requires there to be 3 teachers for every 75 students and 6 tutors for every 72 students. How many tutors does the academy need if it has 120 students?

12. Make Sense and Persevere In large cities, people often take taxis to get from one place to another. What is the cost per mile of a taxi ride? How much is a 47-mile taxi ride?

13. The Largo Middle School track team needs new uniforms. The students plan to sell plush toy tigers (the school mascot) for $5. The students find three companies online that sell stuffed mascots.

Company A
12 tigers for
$33.24

Company C
15 tigers for
$41.10

Company B
16 tigers for
$44.80

a. Which company has the lowest cost per tiger?

b. If they use that company, how much profit will the students make for each tiger sold?

14. A contractor purchases 7 dozen pairs of padded work gloves for $103.32. He incorrectly calculates the unit price at $14.76 per pair.

a. What is the correct unit price?

b. **Critique Reasoning** What error did the contractor likely make?

15. **Higher Order Thinking** A warehouse store sells 5.5-ounce cans of tuna in packages of 6. A package of 6 cans costs $9.24. The store also sells 6.5-ounce cans of the same tuna in packages of 3 cans for $4.68. It also sells 3.5-ounce cans in packages of 4 cans for $4.48. Which package has the lowest cost per ounce of tuna?

Assessment Practice

16. Lena is making two dishes for an event. Each batch of her mac-and-cheese recipe calls for 6 ounces of cheese and 2 tablespoons of basil. For every two pizzas, she needs 16 ounces of cheese and 5 tablespoons of basil.

PART A

Lena buys a 32-oz package of cheese. Does she have enough cheese to make 2 batches of mac-and-cheese and 3 pizzas? Explain.

PART B

Lena decides to make 1 batch of mac-and-cheese and 3 pizzas. How many tablespoons of basil does she need? Explain your answer.

17. It cost Irene $58.90 to fill her car's gas tank with $15\frac{1}{2}$ gallons of gas.
Select all the rates that are equivalent to $58.90 for $15\frac{1}{2}$ gallons of gas.

☐ $41.80 for 11 gallons of gas

☐ $28.80 for 8 gallons of gas

☐ $26.60 for 7 gallons of gas

☐ $8.55 for 2 gallons of gas

☐ $3.80 for 1 gallon of gas

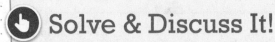 Solve & Discuss It!  ACTIVITY

Allison and her classmates planted bean seeds at the same time as Yuki and her classmates in Tokyo did. Allison is video-chatting with Yuki about their class seedlings. Assume that both plants will continue to grow at the same rate. Who should expect to have the taller plant at the end of the school year?

Allison's Class
2.5 inches in **5 days**

Yuki's Class
5.5 centimeters in **4 days**

I can...
find unit rates with ratios of fractions and use them to solve problems.

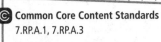 **Common Core Content Standards**
7.RP.A.1, 7.RP.A.3
Mathematical Practices MP.2, MP.3, MP.6, MP.7

Look for Relationships
How can you compare the growth rates of the seedlings?

Focus on math practices

Be Precise What must the students do before they can compare the heights of the plants?

175

Essential Question > Why is it useful to write a ratio of fractions as a unit rate?

VISUAL LEARNING   ASSESS

EXAMPLE 1 > Find a Unit Rate Involving Unit Fractions

Scan for Multimedia

Sergio is training for a triathlon. His target speed is 25 miles per hour. Did he achieve his target speed for the first 7 miles of his ride?

> **Reasoning** You can use a unit rate to describe Sergio's cycling speed.

7 miles

15 minutes

You know that 15 minutes is equal to $\frac{1}{4}$ hour. Draw a diagram to show how the distance Sergio bikes is related to the time he bikes.

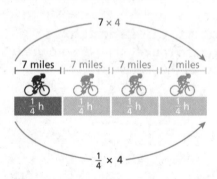

7 × 4

| 7 miles | 7 miles | 7 miles | 7 miles |
| $\frac{1}{4}$ h | $\frac{1}{4}$ h | $\frac{1}{4}$ h | $\frac{1}{4}$ h |

$\frac{1}{4}$ × 4

Make a table of equivalent ratios to find the unit rate.

× 4

Miles	7	28
Hour	$\frac{1}{4}$	1

× 4

Sergio bikes $\frac{28 \text{ miles}}{1 \text{ hour}}$, or 28 miles per hour, so he has achieved, and exceeded, his target speed.

☑ Try It!

Sergio increases his target speed to 30 miles per hour. How many more miles does Sergio need to ride in $\frac{1}{4}$ hour to achieve this target speed?

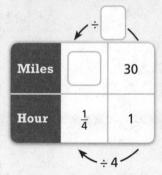

÷ □

Miles	□	30
Hour	$\frac{1}{4}$	1

÷ 4

Sergio must ride □ miles in $\frac{1}{4}$ hour to achieve this target speed, so he needs to ride an additional □ mile per $\frac{1}{4}$ hour.

Convince Me! How does the unit rate describe Sergio's cycling speed? How is the unit rate helpful in determining how much farther Sergio must cycle in a given amount of time each time he increases his target speed?

EXAMPLE 2 Find and Apply a Unit Rate Involving Fractions

Bronwyn mows the lawn every other weekend. She can mow 12,000 ft² in $\frac{2}{3}$ hour. The lawn is 36,000 ft².

How long does it take her to mow the entire lawn?

$$\frac{12,000}{\frac{2}{3}} = \frac{12,000 \times \frac{3}{2}}{\frac{2}{3} \times \frac{3}{2}} = \frac{18,000 \text{ ft}^2}{1 \text{ h}}$$

$$\frac{18,000 \times 2}{1 \times 2} = \frac{36,000}{2}$$

> Multiply each term by 2 for the area of the entire lawn.

Bronwyn mows at a rate of 18,000 ft² per hour. It takes her 2 hours to mow the entire lawn.

Look for Relationships How do the operations used in the table relate to the operations used in the equations at the left?

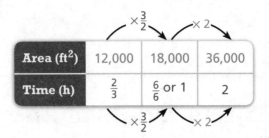

Area (ft²)	12,000	18,000	36,000
Time (h)	$\frac{2}{3}$	$\frac{6}{6}$ or 1	2

 Try It!

Every other weekend, Bronwyn's brother Daniel mows the lawn. He can mow 15,000 ft² in $\frac{3}{4}$ hour. Who mows the lawn in less time? Explain.

EXAMPLE 3 **Solve Problems Using Unit Rates**

Omar knows that his friend Chris lives $\frac{3}{5}$ mile away. **How far is the school from his house?**

$$\frac{\frac{3}{5} \text{ mi}}{\frac{3}{4} \text{ in.}} = \frac{\frac{3}{5} \times \frac{4}{3}}{\frac{3}{4} \times \frac{4}{3}} = \frac{\frac{4}{5} \text{ mi}}{1 \text{ in.}}$$

> Divide both terms by $\frac{3}{4}$ to find the unit rate.

$$\frac{\frac{4}{5} \text{ mi} \times 2}{1 \text{ in.} \times 2} = \frac{\frac{8}{5} \text{ mi}}{2 \text{ in.}} = \frac{1\frac{3}{5} \text{ mi}}{2 \text{ in.}}$$

> Multiply both terms of the unit rate by 2 to find an equivalent rate.

Omar's school is $1\frac{3}{5}$ miles from his house.

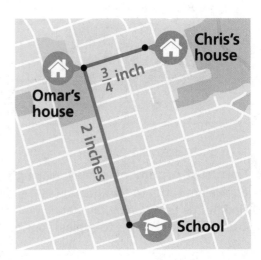

 Try It!

Sonoma bikes 5 miles to Paige's house. On a map, they measure that distance as $\frac{5}{6}$ cm. The same map shows that the mall is $3\frac{1}{2}$ cm from Paige's house. What is the actual distance between Paige's house and the mall?

You can use what you know about equivalent ratios and operations with fractions to write a ratio of fractions as a unit rate.

Tia skateboards $\frac{2}{3}$ mile for every $\frac{1}{6}$ hour.

$$\frac{\frac{2}{3}}{\frac{1}{6}} = \frac{\frac{2}{3} \times \frac{6}{1}}{\frac{1}{6} \times \frac{6}{1}} = \frac{4}{1} = 4$$

		$\times \frac{6}{1}$
Miles	$\frac{2}{3}$	4
Hours	$\frac{1}{6}$	1

$\times \frac{6}{1}$

She skateboards 4 miles per hour.

Do You Understand?

1. **? Essential Question** Why is it useful to write a ratio of fractions as a unit rate?

2. **Use Structure** Jacob mixes $\frac{1}{3}$ cup of yellow paint for every $\frac{1}{5}$ cup of blue paint to make green paint. How many cups of yellow paint are needed for 1 cup of blue paint? Complete the table below.

Cups of Yellow Paint	$\frac{1}{3}$	
Cups of Blue Paint	$\frac{1}{5}$	1

3. **Construct Arguments** How is making a table of equivalent ratios to find the unit rate similar to finding the unit rate by calculating with fractions? Use a specific example to explain your reasoning.

Do You Know How?

4. Claire boarded an airplane in Richmond, VA, and flew 414 miles directly to Charleston, SC. The total flight time was $\frac{3}{4}$ hour. How fast did Claire's airplane fly, in miles per hour?

5. Brad buys two packages of mushrooms. Which mushrooms cost less per pound? Explain.

Cremini $11.25 for $\frac{2}{3}$ lb

Chanterelle $7.99 for $\frac{1}{2}$ lb

6. Jed is baking shortbread for a bake sale. The recipe calls for $1\frac{1}{4}$ cups of flour and $\frac{1}{2}$ stick of butter. How many cups of flour will Jed need if he uses 3 sticks of butter?

Practice & Problem Solving

Leveled Practice In **7–10**, fill in the boxes to find the unit rate.

7.

| Cups of Sugar | $\frac{3}{4}$ | |
| Cups of Butter | $\frac{1}{8}$ | |

☐ cups of sugar for each cup of butter

8.

| Miles | $\frac{3}{5}$ | |
| Hours | $\frac{1}{3}$ | |

☐ miles in 1 hour

9.

$$\frac{7 \text{ mi}}{\frac{1}{3}\text{ gal}} = \frac{7 \div \boxed{}}{\boxed{} \div \boxed{}} = \frac{7 \times \boxed{}}{\boxed{} \times \boxed{}} = \frac{\boxed{}}{\boxed{}}$$

☐ miles per gallon

10. $\dfrac{\frac{3}{4}\text{ page}}{2 \text{ minutes}}$

☐ page in 1 minute

11. Hadley paddled a canoe $\frac{2}{3}$ mile in $\frac{1}{4}$ hour. How fast did Hadley paddle, in miles per hour?

12. A box of cereal states that there are 90 Calories in a $\frac{3}{4}$-cup serving. How many Calories are there in 4 cups of the cereal?

13. A robot can complete 8 tasks in $\frac{5}{6}$ hour. Each task takes the same amount of time.

a. How long does it take the robot to complete one task?

b. How many tasks can the robot complete in one hour?

14. You are running a fuel economy study. You want to find out which car can travel a greater distance on 1 gallon of gas.

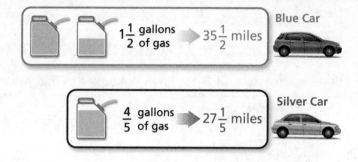
Blue Car
$1\frac{1}{2}$ gallons of gas → $35\frac{1}{2}$ miles

Silver Car
$\frac{4}{5}$ gallons of gas → $27\frac{1}{5}$ miles

   a. What is the gas mileage, in miles per gallon, for the blue car?

   b. What is the gas mileage, in miles per gallon, for the silver car?

   c. Which car could travel the greater distance on 1 gallon of gas?

---

15. Henry incorrectly said the rate $\dfrac{\frac{1}{5} \text{ pound}}{\frac{1}{20} \text{ quart}}$ can be written as the unit rate $\frac{1}{100}$ pound per quart.

   a. What is the correct unit rate?

   b. Critique Reasoning What error did Henry likely make?

16. Higher Order Thinking Ari walked $2\frac{3}{4}$ miles at a constant speed of $2\frac{1}{2}$ miles per hour. Beth walked $1\frac{3}{4}$ miles at a constant speed of $1\frac{1}{4}$ miles per hour. Cindy walked for 1 hour and 21 minutes at a constant speed of $1\frac{1}{8}$ miles per hour. List the three people in order of the times they spent walking from least time to greatest time.

Assessment Practice

17. A blueprint shows a house with two fences. Fence A is $1\frac{4}{5}$ inches long on the blueprint and is to be $1\frac{1}{2}$ feet long. How long is Fence B on the blueprint?

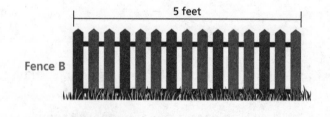
5 feet

Fence B

18. Leo reads 13 pages in $\frac{1}{3}$ hour. Use the table to find how many pages he reads in one hour.

Leo reads ⬚ pages in one hour.

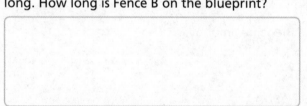

Pages		
Hours	$\frac{1}{3}$	

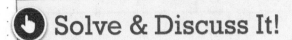 Solve & Discuss It!  ACTIVITY

Go Online

Weight is a measure of force affected by gravity. The Moon's gravity is less than Earth's gravity, so objects weigh less on the Moon than on Earth.

Using the information provided, how much do you think a cat will weigh on the Moon? Explain your reasoning.

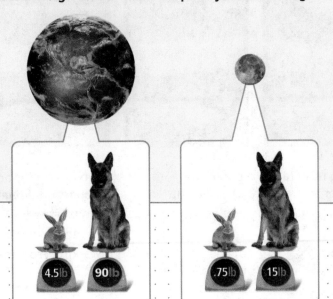

I can...
test for equivalent ratios to decide whether quantities are in a proportional relationship.

Ⓒ **Common Core Content Standards**
7.RP.A.2a

Mathematical Practices
MP.1, MP.2, MP.3, MP.7, MP.8

Make Sense and Persevere
About how much does a cat weigh on Earth?

Focus on math practices
Generalize How could you find the approximate weight of any object on the Moon? Explain your reasoning.

EXAMPLE 1 Recognize a Proportional Relationship

Scan for Multimedia

On Sarah's favorite mobile game, she is awarded game lives when she finds gold coins. How is the number of game lives awarded related to the number of gold coins found? Explain.

Write ratios that relate the gold coins found and the game lives awarded.

$$\frac{💰\ 💰\ 💰}{❤❤\ ❤❤\ ❤❤} = \frac{3}{9}$$

$$\frac{💰\ 💰}{❤❤\ ❤❤} = \frac{2}{6}$$

$$\frac{💰\ 💰\ 💰\ 💰\ 💰}{❤❤\ ❤❤\ ❤❤\ ❤❤\ ❤❤} = \frac{5}{15}$$

Make a ratio table to determine whether the ratios are equivalent.

Coins	3	2	5
Game Lives	9	6	15
Coins / Game Lives	$\frac{3}{9} = \frac{1}{3}$	$\frac{2}{6} = \frac{1}{3}$	$\frac{5}{15} = \frac{1}{3}$

Two quantities are in a **proportional relationship** if all of the ratios that relate the quantities are equivalent.

Each ratio $\frac{\text{coins}}{\text{game lives}}$ is equivalent to $\frac{1}{3}$. The number of game lives awarded is proportional to the number of gold coins found.

☑ Try It!

Miles records the time it takes to download a variety of file types. How is the download time related to the file size? Explain.

The ratios for each pair of data are [ ],

so the download time and the file size are

[ ].

Convince Me! How can you show that two quantities have a proportional relationship?

Type of Media	File Size (MB)	Download Time (s)	Download Time / File Size
Document	1.25	25	$\frac{25}{\boxed{}} = 20$
Song	3.6	72	$\frac{\boxed{}}{3.6} = 20$
Video	6.25	125	$\frac{125}{6.25} = \boxed{}$

EXAMPLE 2 Decide Whether Quantities are Proportional

Is the relationship between the area and the side length of the squares proportional? Explain your reasoning.

2 in.   3 in.   4 in.

STEP 1 Make a table to organize the data. Find the ratio of area to side length for each data pair.

STEP 2 Compare the ratios by finding the unit rates.

$$\frac{2}{1} \neq \frac{3}{1} \qquad \frac{3}{1} \neq \frac{4}{1} \qquad \frac{2}{1} \neq \frac{4}{1}$$

The ratios are not equivalent so the relationship between the area and side length is NOT proportional.

Side Length (x)	Area (y)	Area (y) / Side Length (x)
2	4	$\frac{4}{2} = \frac{2}{1}$
3	9	$\frac{9}{3} = \frac{3}{1}$
4	16	$\frac{16}{4} = \frac{4}{1}$

 Try It!

The table at the right shows information about regular hexagons. Is the relationship between the perimeter and the side length of the hexagons proportional? Explain.

Side Length (x)	Perimeter (y)
2	12
3	18

EXAMPLE 3 Use Proportions to Solve Problems

A proportion is an equation that represents equal ratios. Use the table at the right. How many times will a hummingbird beat its wings in 60 seconds?

Hummingbird Wing Beats

Seconds (x)	2	7	10
Wing Beats (y)	160	560	800

wing beat

STEP 1 Verify that the quantities are proportional.

$$\frac{160}{2} = \frac{80}{1} \qquad \frac{560}{7} = \frac{80}{1} \qquad \frac{800}{10} = \frac{80}{1}$$

The ratios are equivalent, so the quantities are proportional.

STEP 2 Write and solve a proportion.

$$\frac{80}{1} = \frac{y}{60}$$

$$\frac{80}{1} \cdot 60 = \frac{y}{60} \cdot 60$$

Multiply both sides by 60 to solve for y.

$$4{,}800 = y$$

A hummingbird beats its wings 4,800 times in 60 seconds.

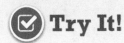 Try It!

Ginny's favorite cookie recipe requires $1\frac{1}{2}$ cups of sugar to make 24 cookies. How much sugar does Ginny need to make 36 of these cookies?

Two quantities x and y have a proportional relationship if all the ratios $\frac{y}{x}$ for related pairs of x and y are equivalent.

A proportion is an equation that states that two ratios are equivalent.

$$\frac{3}{120} = \frac{5}{200}$$

x	y	$\frac{y}{x}$
120	3	$\frac{3}{120} = 0.025$
200	5	$\frac{5}{200} = 0.025$

Do You Understand?

1. **? Essential Question** How are proportional quantities described by equivalent ratios?

2. **Look for Relationships** How do you know if a relationship between two quantities is NOT proportional?

3. **Reasoning** If the ratio $\frac{y}{x}$ is the same for all related pairs of x and y, what does that mean about the relationship between x and y?

Do You Know How?

4. Use the table below. Do x and y have a proportional relationship? Explain.

x	2	3	5	8
y	5	7.5	12.5	18

5. Each triangle is equilateral. Is the relationship between the perimeter and the side length of the equilateral triangles proportional? Explain.

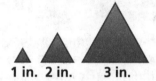

1 in. 2 in.   3 in.

6. Is the relationship between the number of tickets sold and the number of hours proportional? If so, how many tickets were sold in 8 hours?

Hours (h)	Tickets Sold (t)
3	240
5	400
9	720

Name: _____

Practice & Problem Solving

Scan for Multimedia

7. The amount of seed a landscaper uses and the area of lawn covered have a proportional relationship. Complete the table.

Lawn Seed

Seed (oz)	2	3	4
Area Covered (ft^2)	50	75	100
$\dfrac{\text{Area Covered}}{\text{Seed}}$	$\dfrac{50}{2} = \dfrac{25}{1}$		

8. Construct Arguments Is the relationship between the number of slices of salami in a sandwich and the number of Calories proportional? Explain.

Calories in a Sandwich

Slices of Salami	Calories
1	66
2	96
3	126
4	156

9. Look for Relationships A wholesale club sells eggs by the dozen. Does the table show a proportional relationship between the number of dozens of eggs and the cost? Explain.

Cost of Dozens of Eggs

Dozen	Cost ($)
6	21
8	28
10	35
14	49

10. Does the table show a proportional relationship? If so, what is the value of y when x is 11?

x	4	5	6	10
y	64	125	216	1,000

11. Does the table show a proportional relationship? If so, what is the value of y when x is 10?

x	5	6	7	8
y	$1\frac{2}{3}$	2	$2\frac{1}{3}$	$2\frac{2}{3}$

12. The height of a building is proportional to the number of floors. The figure shows the height of a building with 9 floors.

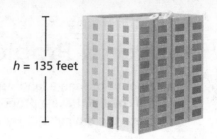

h = 135 feet

a. **Reasoning** Write the ratio of height of the building to the number of floors. Then find the unit rate, and explain what it means in this situation.

b. How tall would the building be if it had 15 floors?

13. **Higher Order Thinking** Do the two tables show the same proportional relationship between x and y? Explain how you know.

x	160	500	1,200
y	360	1,125	2,700

x	2	5	7
y	4.5	11.25	15.75

✓ Assessment Practice

14. The table shows the number of cell phone towers a company will build as the number of its customers increases.

PART A

Is the relationship between number of towers and number of customers proportional? Explain.

Cell Phone Towers

Customers (thousands)	Towers
5.25	252
6.25	300
7.25	348
9.25	444

PART B

If there are 576 towers, how many customers does the company have? Write a proportion you can use to solve.

15. Select all true statements about the table at the right.

☐ The table shows a proportional relationship.

☐ When x is 20, y is 2.55.

☐ All the ratios $\frac{y}{x}$ for related pairs of x and y are equivalent to 8.

☐ The unit rate of $\frac{y}{x}$ for related pairs of x and y is $\frac{1}{8}$.

☐ If the table continued, when x is 30, y would be 3.75.

x	12	18	22	26
y	1.5	2.25	2.75	3.25

Solve & Discuss It!

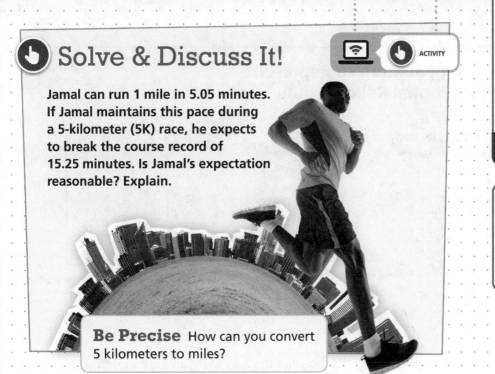

Jamal can run 1 mile in 5.05 minutes. If Jamal maintains this pace during a 5-kilometer (5K) race, he expects to break the course record of 15.25 minutes. Is Jamal's expectation reasonable? Explain.

Be Precise How can you convert 5 kilometers to miles?

I can...
use the constant of proportionality in an equation to represent a proportional relationship.

 Common Core Content Standards
7.RP.A.2b, 7.RP.A.2c

Mathematical Practices
MP.2, MP.3, MP.4, MP.6, MP.8

Focus on math practices

Reasoning Assuming that Jamal runs at a constant rate, how does his pace describe the time it takes him to finish a race of any length?

VISUAL LEARNING   ASSESS

EXAMPLE 1 Write an Equation to Represent a Proportional Relationship

Scan for Multimedia

A sponge is an example of a *filter feeder*. It takes in food by filtering water through its body. The sponge maintains a constant flow of water through its body.

What is an equation that represents the proportional relationship between the time and the amount of water filtered?

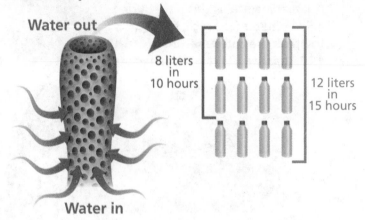

Water out

8 liters in 10 hours

12 liters in 15 hours

Water in

The **constant of proportionality** is the constant multiple that relates proportional quantities x and y. It is the value of the ratio $\frac{y}{x}$ and is represented by k.

Make a table to find the constant of proportionality.

Hours (x)	Liters (y)	Liters/Hours $\left(\frac{y}{x}\right)$
10	8	$\frac{8}{10} = 0.8$
15	12	$\frac{12}{15} = 0.8$

The constant of proportionality, k, is 0.8.

You can use k to write an equation that represents a proportional relationship.

$$k = \frac{y}{x}$$

$$kx = y$$

$$y = kx$$

You can use an equation in the form y = kx to represent any proportional relationship.

Use the equation to represent the relationship between time and the amount of water filtered.

$$y = 0.8x$$

☑ Try It!

Maria made two batches of fruit punch. The table at the right shows how many quarts of juice she used for each batch. Write an equation that relates the proportional quantities.

Apple Juice (x)	Grape Juice (y)	Grape Juice/Apple Juice $\left(\frac{y}{x}\right)$
5	8	
10	16	

Convince Me! How does the equation change if the amount of grape juice is the independent variable, x, and the amount of apple juice is the dependent variable, y?

The constant of proportionality is ☐.

An equation that represents this proportional relationship is y = ☐ x.

EXAMPLE 2 Solve Problems Using an Equation ACTIVITY ASSESS

1 inch = 2.54 centimeters. How many centimeters long is an 18-inch ruler?

2.54 cm

STEP 1 Write an equation to represent this relationship.

centimeters   inches

$$y = kx$$

constant multiple or constant of proportionality

$$y = 2.54x$$

STEP 2 Use the equation to find the length of the ruler in centimeters.

$$y = 2.54x$$

$$y = 2.54(18)$$

$$y = 45.72$$

The ruler is 45.72 centimeters long.

 Try It!

A florist sells a dozen roses for $35.40. She sells individual roses for the same unit cost. Write an equation to represent the relationship between the number of roses, x, and the total cost of the roses, y. How much would 18 roses cost?

EXAMPLE 3 **Determine Whether $y = kx$ Describes a Situation**

WELCOME TO
FUN FAIR
ADMISSION: $20
EACH RIDE: $5

Can you represent the total cost, y, for admission and x rides at the amusement park using an equation in the form $y = kx$? Explain.

STEP 1 Make a table that shows the total cost.

Rides	Cost
1	$25
2	$30
3	$35

STEP 2 Compare the ratios to determine whether the relationship is proportional.

$$\frac{\$25}{1} = \$25$$

$$\frac{\$30}{2} = \$15$$

$$\frac{\$35}{3} = \$11.67$$

This relationship is not proportional, so it cannot be represented with an equation of the form $y = kx$.

 Try It!

Balloon A is released 5 feet above the ground. Balloon B is released at ground level. Both balloons rise at a constant rate.

Which situation can you represent using an equation of the form $y = kx$? Explain.

Balloon A

Time (s)	Height (ft)
1	9
2	13
3	17

Balloon B

Time (s)	Height (ft)
1	4
2	8
3	12

Two proportional quantities x and y are related by a constant multiple, or the constant of proportionality, k.

You can represent a proportional relationship using the equation $y = kx$.

Do You Understand?

1. **Essential Question** How can you represent a proportional relationship with an equation?

2. **Generalize** How can you use an equation to find an unknown value in a proportional relationship?

3. **Reasoning** Why does the equation $y = 3x + 5$ NOT represent a proportional relationship?

Do You Know How?

4. Determine whether each equation represents a proportional relationship. If it does, identify the constant of proportionality.

   a. $y = 0.5x - 2$

   b. $y = 1,000x$

   c. $y = x + 1$

5. The manager of a concession stand estimates that she needs 3 hot dogs for every 5 people who attend a baseball game. If 1,200 people attend the game, how many hot dogs should the manager order?

6. A half dozen cupcakes cost $15. What constant of proportionality relates the number of cupcakes and total cost? Write an equation that represents this relationship.

Name: _____

Practice & Problem Solving

 PRACTICE TUTORIAL

7. What is the constant of proportionality in the equation $y = 5x$?

8. What is the constant of proportionality in the equation $y = 0.41x$?

9. The equation $P = 3s$ represents the perimeter P of an equilateral triangle with side length s. Is there a proportional relationship between the perimeter and the side length of an equilateral triangle? Explain.

10. Model with Math In a chemical compound, there are 3 parts zinc for every 16 parts copper, by mass. A piece of the compound contains 320 grams of copper. Write and solve an equation to determine the amount of zinc in the chemical compound.

11. The weight of 3 eggs is shown. Assuming the three eggs are all the same weight, find the constant of proportionality.

12. The height of a stack of DVD cases is proportional to the number of cases in the stack. The height of 6 DVD cases is 114 mm.

   a. Write an equation that relates the height, y, of a stack of DVD cases and the number of cases, x, in the stack.

   b. What would be the height of 13 DVD cases?

13. Ann's car can travel 228 miles on 6 gallons of gas.

   a. Write an equation to represent the distance, y, in miles Ann's car can travel on x gallons of gas.

   b. Ann's car used 7 gallons of gas during a trip. How far did Ann drive?

14. The value of a baseball player's rookie card began to increase once the player retired in 1996. The value has increased by $2.52 each year since then.

1996

Value: $7.46

   a. How much was the baseball card worth in 1997? In 1998? In 1999?

   b. Construct Arguments Why is there not a proportional relationship between the years since the player retired and the card value? Explain.

15. Higher Order Thinking A car travels $2\frac{1}{3}$ miles in $3\frac{1}{2}$ minutes at a constant speed.

   a. Write an equation to represent the distance the car travels, d, in miles for m minutes.

   b. Write an equation to represent the distance the car travels, d, in miles for h hours.

✓ Assessment Practice

16. For every ten sheets of stickers you buy at a craft store, the total cost increases $20.50.

An equation that relates the number of sheets purchased, x, and the total cost, y, of the stickers is $y = \boxed{}\,x$.

Use the equation you wrote to complete the table.

Cost of Stickers

Number of Sheets (x)	3			19
Total Cost (y)		$10.25	$26.65	

17. 600,000 gallons of water pass through a given point along a river every minute. Which equation represents the amount of water, y, that passes through the point in x minutes?

   Ⓐ $x = 10{,}000y$

   Ⓑ $y = 600{,}000x$

   Ⓒ $y = 10{,}000x$

   Ⓓ $y = 600{,}000 + x$

1. **Vocabulary** How do you know if a situation represents a proportional relationship? *Lesson 3-3*

2. Ana runs $\frac{3}{4}$ mile in 6 minutes. Assuming she runs at a constant rate, what is her speed, in miles per hour? *Lessons 3-1 and 3-2*

Miles	$\frac{3}{4}$	
Hour		

3. A trail mix recipe includes granola, oats, and almonds. There are 135 Calories in a $\frac{1}{4}$-cup serving of the trail mix. How many Calories are in 2 cups of trail mix? *Lesson 3-2*

4. Does this table show a proportional relationship? If so, what is the constant of proportionality? *Lessons 3-3 and 3-4*

x	40	50	60	70
y	8	10	12	14

Ⓐ Yes; $\frac{1}{5}$

Ⓑ Yes; 5

Ⓒ Yes; 10

Ⓓ The quantities are not proportional.

5. Janet, Rosi, and Tanya buy postcards from their favorite souvenir shop. Janet buys 3 postcards for $1.05. Rosi buys 5 postcards for $1.75. Tanya buys 8 postcards for $2.80. Are the cost, y, in dollars and the number of postcards, x, proportional? Explain your answer. Write an equation to represent this relationship, if possible. *Lesson 3-4*

6. Four movie tickets cost $30.00. Five concert tickets cost $36.50. Does the movie or the concert cost less per ticket? How much less? *Lesson 3-1*

How well did you do on the mid-topic checkpoint? Fill in the stars. ☆☆☆

MID-TOPIC PERFORMANCE TASK

The school's theater club is building sets that will make ordinary students look like giants. The actors need a door, a table, and a stool that will make them look almost twice as tall.

PART A

The heights of objects in the set are proportional to the actual heights of objects. Complete the table.

The constant of proportionality is ☐ .

	Actual Height	Height on Set
Door	80 in.	44 in.
Table	28 in.	☐
Stool	18 in.	☐

PART B

How can the stage manager use the constant of proportionality to find the dimensions of any new props the director requires?

PART C

What should the height of a can of fruit juice used as a prop be if its actual height is 7 inches? Show your work.

3-ACT MATH ▷ ▷ ▷

Mixin' It Up

3-Act Mathematical Modeling:
Mixin' It Up

📶 Go Online

ⓒ **Common Core Content Standards**
7.RP.A.1, 7.RP.A.2a

Mathematical Practices
MP.4, MP.1, MP.2, MP.3, MP.5, MP.7, MP.8

ACT 1

1. After watching the video, what is the first question that comes to mind?

2. Write the Main Question you will answer.

3. Construct Arguments Predict an answer to this Main Question. Explain your prediction.

4. On the number line below, write a number that is too small to be the answer. Write a number that is too large.

Too small   Too large

5. Plot your prediction on the same number line.

6. What information in this situation would be helpful to know? How would you use that information?

7. Use Appropriate Tools What tools can you use to solve the problem? Explain how you would use them strategically.

8. Model with Math Represent the situation using mathematics. Use your representation to answer the Main Question.

9. What is your answer to the Main Question? Is it higher or lower than your prediction? Explain why.

10. Write the answer you saw in the video.

11. Reasoning Does your answer match the answer in the video? If not, what are some reasons that would explain the difference?

12. Make Sense and Persevere Would you change your model now that you know the answer? Explain.

Reflect

13. Model with Math Explain how you used a mathematical model to represent the situation. How did the model help you answer the Main Question?

14. Critique Reasoning Choose a classmate's model. How would you adjust that model?

15. Use Structure A classmate usually adds 6 drops to 16 ounces of water. Use your updated model to predict the number of drops she would use for the large container.

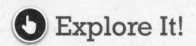 **Explore It!**

The graph shows the time it takes Jacey to print T-shirts for her school's math club.

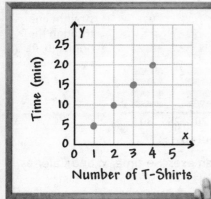

I can...
use a graph to determine whether two quantities are proportional.

© **Common Core Content Standards**
7.RP.A.2a, 7.RP.A.2b, 7.RP.A.2d

Mathematical Practices
MP.2, MP.3, MP.4, MP.7

A. Use the points on the graph to complete the table. Are the quantities proportional? Explain.

Number of T-Shirts (x)				
Time in Minutes (y)				

B. Start at (1, 5). As you move from one point to the next on the graph, how does the x-coordinate change? How does the y-coordinate change?

C. Write the points for 0 T-shirts and for 5 T-shirts as ordered pairs. Graph the points and draw the line that passes through all six points.

Focus on math practices

Reasoning Suppose that after printing 4 T-shirts it takes Jacey 4 minutes to change the ink cartridge. Would this point for 5 T-shirts lie on the line you drew in Part C? Explain.

? Essential Question What does the graph of a proportional relationship look like?

EXAMPLE 1 Graph to Recognize a Proportional Relationship

Scan for Multimedia

Tanya exercised for 30 minutes. She noted the Calories burned at three times during her workout. How can Tanya use this information to find how many Calories she burned after 15 minutes of exercise?

STEP 1 Use a graph to display the data.

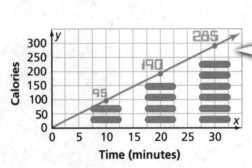

The graph is a straight line through the origin, (0, 0).

The relationship between exercise time, x, and Calories burned, y, is proportional.

STEP 2 Use the graph to find the constant of proportionality.

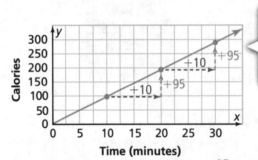

Find the differences between the coordinates of any two ordered pairs.

The constant of proportionality is $\frac{95}{10}$ or 9.5.

Tanya can use the graph and the constant of proportionality to determine that she burned 142.5 Calories in 15 minutes.

Model with Math You can represent the situation on the coordinate plane.

Try It!

Each $\frac{1}{4}$-cup serving of cereal has 3 grams of protein. How can you use the graph at the right to determine whether the quantities are proportional and to find how many grams of protein are in 1 cup of the cereal?

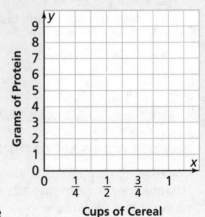

Convince Me! How can you find the constant of proportionality from the coordinates of one point on the graph?

EXAMPLE 2 **Interpret the Graph of a Proportional Relationship**

The graph shows a proportional relationship between the distance and the amount of time Mr. Brown drives.

a. What does each of these points represent in this situation: (0, 0), (1, 55), and (5, 275)?

(0, 0): Mr. Brown drives 0 miles in 0 hours.
(1, 55): Mr. Brown drives 55 miles in 1 hour.
(5, 275): Mr. Brown drives 275 miles in 5 hours.

b. What is the constant of proportionality?

Find the y-coordinate when x is 1.
The constant of proportionality is 55.

c. What equation relates the distance, y, and the time, x?

$y = 55x$

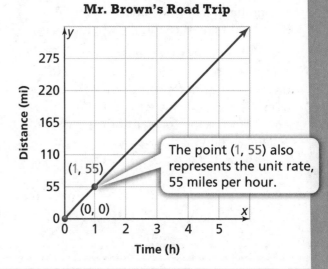

Mr. Brown's Road Trip

The point (1, 55) also represents the unit rate, 55 miles per hour.

 Try It!

Suppose the graph of Mr. Brown's Road Trip is extended. Find the ordered pair with an x-coordinate of 7. What does this point represent in the situation?

If the graph is extended, it will pass through the point (7, ⬚). This means

Mr. Brown drives ⬚ miles in ⬚ hours.

EXAMPLE 3 **Recognize Graphs of Proportional Relationships**

Explain why each graph does or does not show a proportional relationship.

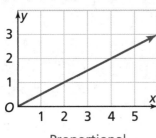

Proportional

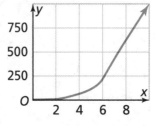

NOT Proportional

NOT Proportional

The graph is a straight line that passes through the origin.

The graph is a straight line but does not pass through the origin.

The graph passes through the origin but is not a straight line.

 Try It!

Draw two graphs that pass through the point (2, 3), one that represents a proportional relationship and one that does not. Label your graphs as *Proportional* or *NOT Proportional*.

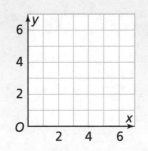

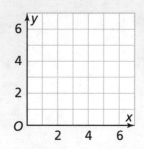

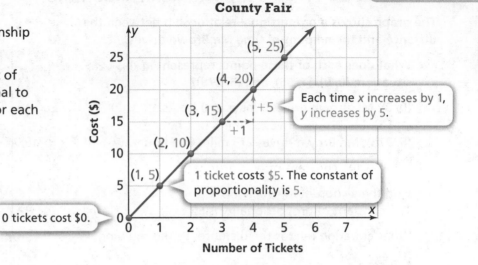

County Fair

The graph of a proportional relationship is a straight line through the origin.

This graph shows that the total cost of tickets at a county fair is proportional to the number of tickets purchased. For each point (x, y) on the line except $(0, 0)$, $\frac{y}{x} = 5$, which is the constant of proportionality.

Each time x increases by 1, y increases by 5.

1 ticket costs $5. The constant of proportionality is 5.

0 tickets cost $0.

Do You Understand?

1. **? Essential Question** What does the graph of a proportional relationship look like?

2. **Reasoning** Why will the graph of every proportional relationship include the point $(0, 0)$?

3. **Construct Arguments** Makayla plotted two points, $(0, 0)$ and $(3, 33)$, on a coordinate grid. Noah says that she is graphing a proportional relationship. Is Noah correct? Explain.

Do You Know How?

For 4–7, use the information below.

Martin and Isabelle go bowling. Each game costs $10, and they split that cost. Martin has his own bowling shoes, but Isabelle pays $3 to rent shoes.

4. Complete the graphs below.

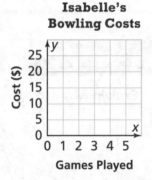

Martin's Bowling Costs

Isabelle's Bowling Costs

5. Which graph shows a proportional relationship? Explain why.

6. Choose one point on the graph of the proportional relationship and explain what this point means in terms of the situation.

7. What equation represents the proportional relationship?

Practice & Problem Solving

Scan for Multimedia

8. For each graph shown, tell whether it shows a proportional relationship. Explain your reasoning.

a.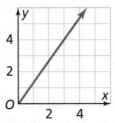

b.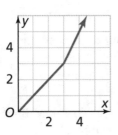

c.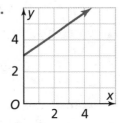

9. The graph shows the number of boxes a machine packages over time. Is the relationship proportional? How many boxes does the machine package in 4 minutes?

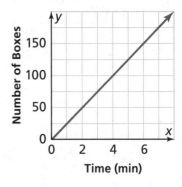

10. Does the graph show a proportional relationship? If so, use the graph to find the constant of proportionality.

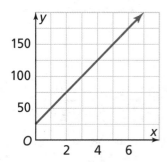

11. The graph shows a proportional relationship between the cups of flour a baker uses and the number of cookies made.

a. Use Structure What does the point (0, 0) represent in the situation?

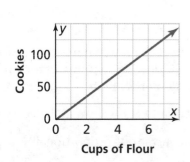

b. What does the point (1, 18) represent?

12. The points $\left(0.5, \frac{1}{10}\right)$ and $\left(7, 1\frac{2}{5}\right)$ are on the graph of a proportional relationship.

  a. What is the constant of proportionality?

  b. Name one more point on the graph.

  c. Write an equation that represents the proportional relationship.

....

13. Higher Order Thinking Denmark uses the kroner as its currency. Before a trip to Denmark, Mia wants to exchange $1,700 for kroner.

  a. Does Bank A or Bank B have the better exchange rate? Explain.

  b. How many more kroner would Mia get if she exchanged her $1,700 at the bank with the better exchange rate?

Bank A

Dollars ($)	Kroner
80	408
100	510
120	612

Bank B

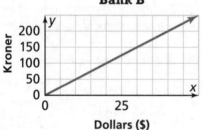

✅ Assessment Practice

14. Does the graph at the right show a proportional relationship between *x* and *y*? Explain.

15. The graph at the right shows the relationship between rainfall during the growing season and the growth of a type of plant. Which statements about the graph are true?

  ☐ The point (1, 10) shows the constant of proportionality.

  ☐ The constant of proportionality is $\frac{5}{7}$.

  ☐ The graph does not show a proportional relationship.

  ☐ The graph is a straight line through the origin.

  ☐ The point (28, 20) means the type of plant grows 20 mm when it rains 28 cm.

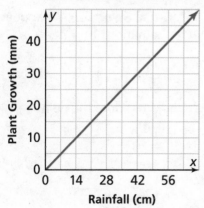

Rainfall and Plant Growth

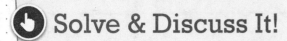 Solve & Discuss It!  ACTIVITY

Xander and Pedro are at an ice cream social. For every scoop of ice cream, Xander uses $\frac{1}{8}$ cup of fruit topping. Pedro uses one more tablespoon of fruit topping than the number of scoops. If Xander and Pedro each use the same amount of fruit topping, how many scoops of ice cream does each use?

Look for Relationships
There are 2 tablespoons in $\frac{1}{8}$ cup.

I can...
determine whether a relationship is proportional and use representations to solve problems.

© **Common Core Content Standards**
7.RP.A.2, 7.RP.A.3

Mathematical Practices
MP.1, MP.2, MP.5, MP.7

Focus on math practices

Reasoning For which person, Xander or Pedro, is the relationship between the quantities of ice cream and fruit topping proportional? Explain.

EXAMPLE 1 Use Proportional Reasoning to Solve a Problem

Scan for Multimedia

The ratio of collectible cards DeShawn owns to cards that Stephanie owns is 5:2. Stephanie has 36 cards. How will the ratio of DeShawn's cards to Stephanie's cards change if they both sell half their cards? Explain.

DeShawn's Cards

Make Sense and Persevere
How can you use proportional reasoning to compare the quantities of cards?

Stephanie's Cards

STEP 1 Draw a diagram that represents the ratio of DeShawn's cards to Stephanie's cards. You can use the diagram to find the number of cards DeShawn owns.

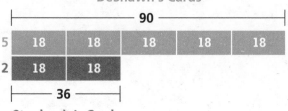

$$\overset{\times 18}{\overset{\frown}{\frac{5}{2}} = \frac{90}{36}}$$
$$\underset{\times 18}{\smile}$$

DeShawn owns 90 cards.

STEP 2 Find the ratio after they sell half their cards.

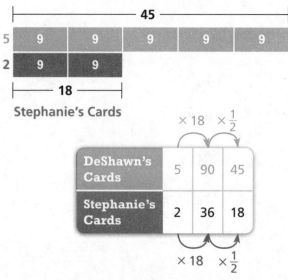

After they both sell half their cards, the ratio is $\frac{45}{18}$, or $\frac{5}{2}$. If the numbers of cards change by the same multiple, the ratio that relates them is equivalent, so it does not change.

☑ Try It!

After selling half their card collections, DeShawn and Stephanie each buy 9 new cards. What is the ratio of the number of cards DeShawn has to the number Stephanie has?

Convince Me! Why did the ratio stay the same in the Example but change in the Try It?

EXAMPLE **2** **Recognize When to Use Proportional Reasoning**

Martin is 6 years old when his sister Cassandra is 3 years old. How old will Martin be when Cassandra is 6 years old?

Make a table to find Martin's age.

> **Use Structure** Look for a constant multiple to determine whether you can use proportional reasoning to solve this problem.

$\times 1.5$

Martin's Age	Cassandra's Age
6	3
7	4
8	5
9	6

$\times 2$

There is no constant multiple so you cannot use proportional reasoning. In 3 years when Cassandra is 6 years old, Martin will also be 3 years older, or 9 years old.

EXAMPLE **3** **Apply Proportional Reasoning**

A video streaming service charged Bryan $143.84 for a full year of access. Bryan thinks he was not charged the correct amount. What should Bryan say when he calls customer service?

STEP 1 Write an equation to represent the situation.

The rate is $8.99 per month. So an equation that represents the cost y after x months is $y = 8.99x$.

STEP 2 Substitute the given information into the equation and solve.

VIDEO STREAMING
Only $8.99 a month!

Option 1

$y = 8.99x$

$\quad = 8.99(12)$

$\quad = 107.88$

Bryan should have been charged $107.88. He should ask customer service for a credit of $143.84 - $107.88 = $35.96.

Option 2

$y = 8.99x$

$143.84 = 8.99x$

$\dfrac{143.84}{8.99} = \dfrac{8.99x}{8.99}$

$16 = x$

Bryan was charged for 16 months, so he should ask customer service to give him 4 months of free online service.

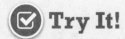 **Try It!**

A florist makes bouquets that include 50 white flowers and 7 red flowers. If the florist orders 1,050 white flowers and 140 red flowers, there will be leftover flowers. How can the florist adjust the order so there are no leftover flowers?

Think about how two quantities are related before you decide to use proportional reasoning to solve a problem.

When Evie is 2 years old, Josh is 6 years old.

Josh is 4 years older than Evie.
Josh is 3 times as old as Evie.

In 2 years

When Evie is 4 years old, Josh is 8 years old.

Josh is still 4 years older than Evie.
Josh is now 2 times as old as Evie.

You cannot use proportional reasoning to solve this problem because Josh's age is not a constant multiple of Evie's age.

Do You Understand?

1. **? Essential Question** How can proportional reasoning help solve a problem?

2. **Use Appropriate Tools** How can knowing how to represent proportional relationships in different ways be useful in solving problems?

3. **Reasoning** How many ways are there to adjust two quantities so that they are in a given proportional relationship? Explain your reasoning.

Do You Know How?

4. A recipe calls for 15 oz of flour for every 8 oz of milk.

   a. Is the relationship between ounces of flour and ounces of milk proportional? Explain.

   b. If you use 15 oz of milk, how much flour should you use?

5. A food packing company makes a popular fruit cocktail. To ensure a good mixture of fruit, there are 3 cherry halves for every 8 white grapes in a jar. An inspector notices that one jar has 12 cherry halves and 20 white grapes. What can be done to fix the error?

Practice & Problem Solving

In 6 and 7, determine whether you can use proportional reasoning and then solve.

6. If Hector is 8 years old and Mary is 3 years old, how old will Mary be when Hector is 16?

7. Marco needs to buy some cat food. At the nearest store, 3 bags of cat food cost $15.75. How much would Marco spend on 5 bags of cat food?

8. An architect makes a model of a new house with a patio made with pavers. In the model, each paver in the patio is $\frac{1}{3}$ in. long and $\frac{1}{6}$ in. wide. The actual dimensions of the pavers are shown.

   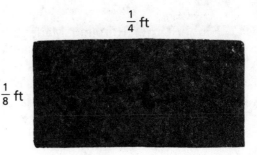

   $\frac{1}{4}$ ft

   $\frac{1}{8}$ ft

   a. What is the constant of proportionality that relates the length of a paver in the model and the length of an actual paver?

   b. What is the constant of proportionality that relates the area of a paver in the model and the area of an actual paver? Explain your reasoning.

9. **Reasoning** The table lists recommended amounts of food to order for 25 guests. Nathan is hosting a graduation party for 40 guests. There will also be guests stopping by for a short time. For ordering purposes, Nathan will count each of the 45 "drop-in" guests as half a guest. How much of each food item should Nathan order?

Party Food

Item	Amount
Fried Chicken	24 pieces
Deli Meats	$3\frac{2}{3}$ pounds
Lasagna	$10\frac{3}{4}$ pounds

10. Emily and Andy each go to a hardware store to buy wire. The table shows the relationship between the cost and the length of wire.

   a. Emily needs 24 feet of wire. How much will she spend on wire?

   b. Andy needs 13 yards of wire. How much will he spend on wire?

Cost of Wire

Length in Inches (x)	Cost in Dollars (y)
120	4.80
135	5.40
150	6.00
175	7.00

11. **Make Sense and Persevere** The weights of Michael's and Brittney's new puppies are shown in the table and graph. Whose dog gains weight more quickly? Explain.

Weight of Michael's Puppy

Age (months)	1	2	3
Weight (pounds)	8.6	17.2	25.8

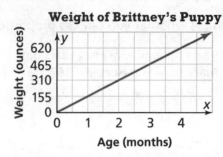

Weight of Brittney's Puppy

12. **Higher Order Thinking** Marielle's painting has the dimensions shown. The school asks her to paint a larger version that will hang in the cafeteria. The larger version will be twice the width and twice the height. Is the area of the original painting proportional to the area of the larger painting? If so, what is the constant of proportionality?

18 in.

24 in.

☑ Assessment Practice

13. The ratio of orange juice concentrate to water that Zoe used to make orange juice yesterday was 3 : 7. She used 14 ounces of water in the juice yesterday. Today she wants to make twice as much orange juice.

PART A

Is the relationship between the amount of orange juice concentrate c and the amount of water w proportional? Explain.

PART B

How much orange juice concentrate does she need?

Ⓐ 6 ounces

Ⓑ 12 ounces

Ⓒ 18 ounces

Ⓓ 28 ounces

? Topic Essential Question

How can you recognize and represent proportional relationships and use them to solve problems?

Vocabulary Review

Complete each definition and then provide an example of each vocabulary word.

Vocabulary constant of proportionality   ratio   proportion
proportional relationship   rate   unit rate

Definition	Example
1. For two quantities x and y, if y is always a constant multiple of x, they have a(n) _____ .	
2. The value of the ratio $\frac{y}{x}$ of two proportional quantities x and y is called the _____ .	
3. An equation that shows that two ratios are equal is a(n) _____ .	

Use Vocabulary in Writing

A sunflower grows 8 feet in 92 days. Assuming that it grows at a constant rate, explain how you could use this information to find the number of days it took for the sunflower to grow 6 feet. Use vocabulary words in your explanation.

Concepts and Skills Review

Connect Ratios, Rates, and Unit Rates |
Determine Unit Rates with Ratios of Fractions

Quick Review

A **ratio** is a relationship in which for every
x units of one quantity there are *y* units of
another quantity. A **rate** is a ratio that relates
two quantities with different units. A **unit
rate** relates a quantity to 1 unit of another
quantity. You can use what you know about
equivalent fractions and calculating with fractions
to write a ratio of fractions as a unit rate.

Example

In 3 days, a typical robin can eat up to
42.6 feet of earthworms. Write a rate to
relate the number of feet of earthworms to
the number of days. Then find the unit rate.

$$\frac{42.6 \text{ feet}}{3 \text{ days}} = \frac{14.2 \text{ feet}}{1 \text{ day}}$$

A robin eats 14.2 feet of earthworms per day.

Practice

1. Mealworms are a healthy food for wild
   songbirds. Adam buys a 3.5-oz container of
   mealworms for $8.75. Marco buys a 3.75-oz
   container of mealworms for $9.75. Which
   container is the better deal?

2. A painter mixes $2\frac{1}{2}$ pints of yellow paint with
   4 pints of red paint to make a certain shade of
   orange paint. How many pints of yellow paint
   should be mixed with 10 pints of red paint to
   make this shade of orange?

Understand Proportional Relationships: Equivalent Ratios

Quick Review

Two quantities *x* and *y* have a proportional
relationship if the ratios $\frac{y}{x}$ for every related
pair of *x* and *y* are equivalent. You can write
a proportion to show that two ratios have
the same value.

Example

Does the table show a proportional
relationship between *x* and *y*? Explain.

x	200	400	500
y	600	1,200	1,500

$$\frac{600}{200} = \frac{3}{1} \qquad \frac{1,200}{400} = \frac{3}{1} \qquad \frac{1,500}{500} = \frac{3}{1}$$

Because every ratio is equivalent, there is a
proportional relationship between *x* and *y*.

Practice

In **1** and **2**, use the table below that shows
information about squares.

Side Length (cm)	2	4	6
Perimeter (cm)	8	16	24

1. Are the perimeter and the side length of
   squares proportional? Explain.

2. Write and solve a proportion to find the
   perimeter of a square when its side length is 12.

Quick Review

The equation $y = kx$ describes a proportional relationship between two quantities x and y, where k is the constant of proportionality. $k = \frac{y}{x}$ for any related pair of x and y except when $x = 0$.

Example

The table shows the wages Roger earned for the hours he worked. What equation relates the wages, w, and the number of hours, h?

Time (h)	Wages (w)
3	$27.00
5	$45.00
6	$54.00

Find the constant of proportionality, k.

$$\frac{27}{3} = 9 \qquad \frac{45}{5} = 9 \qquad \frac{54}{6} = 9$$

Write the equation in the form $y = kx$.

$$w = 9h$$

Practice

1. Sally is going on vacation with her family. In 2 hours they travel 90.5 miles. If they travel at the same speed, write an equation that represents how far they will travel, d, in h hours.

2. The table shows the weights of bunches of bananas and the price of each bunch. Identify the constant of proportionality. Write an equation to relate weight, w, to the price, p.

Weight (w)	Price (p)
3 pounds	$1.35
3.8 pounds	$1.71
5.2 pounds	$2.34

Quick Review

The graph of a proportional relationship is a straight line through the origin. You can identify the constant of proportionality, k, from the point $(1, k)$ or by dividing $\frac{y}{x}$ for any point (x, y) except the origin.

Example

Is the number of sunny days proportional to the number of rainy days? If so, find the constant of proportionality, and explain its meaning in this situation.

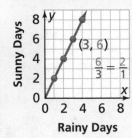

The graph is a straight line through the origin, so it shows a proportional relationship. The constant of proportionality is 2, which means for every 1 rainy day, there were 2 sunny days.

$$\frac{6}{3} = \frac{2}{1}$$

Practice

1. Does the graph show a proportional relationship? Explain.

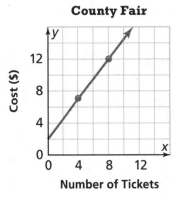

County Fair

2. Sketch a graph that represents a proportional relationship.

Quick Review

Think about how two quantities are related before you decide to use proportional reasoning to solve a problem.

Example

Ann-Marie makes gift baskets that each contain 3 pounds of gourmet cheese with every 2 boxes of crackers. She ordered 80 pounds of cheese and 50 boxes of crackers. How can she adjust her order to make 25 gift baskets, with no leftover items?

$$\frac{3 \times 25}{2 \times 25} = \frac{75}{50}$$

Ann-Marie can order 5 fewer pounds of cheese so that her order of 75 pounds of cheese and 50 boxes of crackers will make exactly 25 gift baskets.

Practice

Decide which problems can be solved by using proportional reasoning. Select all that apply.

☐ Yani buys 4 dozen flyers for $7.25. What is the cost of 12 dozen?

☐ First-class letters cost $0.49 for the first ounce and $0.22 for each additional ounce. What is the cost of a 5-oz letter?

☐
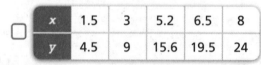

x	1	2	3	4	5
y	3	4	5	6	7

What is the value of y when x = 8?

☐

x	1.5	3	5.2	6.5	8
y	4.5	9	15.6	19.5	24

What is the value of y when x = 5?

Pathfinder

Shade a path from START to FINISH. Follow the solutions from the least value to the greatest value. You can only move up, down, right, or left.

START

$3 - 24$	$3 \times (-13)$	-3×14	$44 - 49$	$-48 \div 16$
$-26 + 7$	$-7 - 27$	$13 \times (-4)$	$8 - 19$	$-18 \div (-6)$
$3 \times (-5)$	$28 \div (-2)$	$(-35) \div 2$	$4 + (-25)$	$-68 \div 17$
$23 - 46$	$-2 - 11$	$15 + (-26)$	$17 - 23$	$29 - 38$
$-12 \div (-3)$	$18 + (-32)$	$11 - 29$	$-60 \div 12$	$-3 \times (-2)$

FINISH

ANALYZE AND SOLVE PERCENT PROBLEMS

? Topic Essential Question

How can percents show proportional relationships between quantities and be used to solve problems?

Topic Overview

4-1 Analyze Percents of Numbers

4-2 Connect Percent and Proportion

4-3 Represent and Use the Percent Equation

4-4 Solve Percent Change and Percent Error Problems

3-Act Mathematical Modeling: The Smart Shopper

4-5 Solve Markup and Markdown Problems

4-6 Solve Simple Interest Problems

Topic Vocabulary

- interest rate
- markdown
- markup
- percent change
- percent equation
- percent error
- percent markdown
- percent markup
- principal
- simple interest

Lesson Digital Resources

INTERACTIVE STUDENT EDITION
Access online or offline.

VISUAL LEARNING ANIMATION
Interact with visual learning animations.

ACTIVITY Use with *Solve & Discuss It, Explore It*, and *Explain It* activities, and to explore Examples.

VIDEOS Watch clips to support *3-Act Mathematical Modeling Lessons* and *STEM Projects*.

 Go online

THE Smart Shopper

▶ The Smart Shopper

Why do stores and manufacturers print coupons? It seems like they lose money every time you use one. Well, some coupons are designed to steer you toward a specific brand and gain your loyalty. Stores also offer coupons to get you into the store, counting on you buying other items while you are there. If you're clever, you can use multiple coupons. Think about this during the 3-Act Mathematical Modeling lesson.

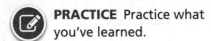
PRACTICE Practice what you've learned.

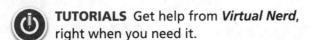
TUTORIALS Get help from *Virtual Nerd*, right when you need it.

MATH TOOLS Explore math with digital tools.

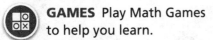
GAMES Play Math Games to help you learn.

KEY CONCEPT Review important lesson content.

GLOSSARY Read and listen to English/Spanish definitions.

ASSESSMENT Show what you've learned.

enVision® STEM Project

Did You Know?

One of the first popular activity trackers was a pedometer, which measures number of steps taken. Some sources trace the history of the pedometer back to Leonardo da Vinci.

A pedometer called *Manpo-kei* (10,000 steps meter) was introduced in Japan in the mid-1960s. Research led by Dr. Yoshiro Hatano indicated that 10,000 steps a day is the ideal energy output to maintain health.

Today, most activity trackers are electronic devices that can sync to a computer or a smartphone.

Many activity trackers are *wearable technology*. Some common places to wear activity trackers are on the wrist, arm, or chest. There are even collar-mounted activity trackers for dogs.

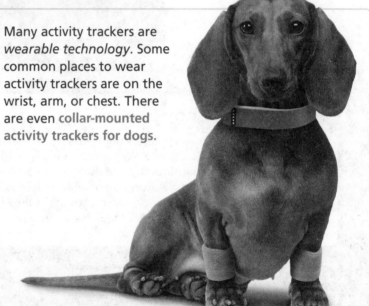

Your Task: Analyze Activity Tracker Data

Activity trackers, also called fitness trackers, have become quite popular in recent years. But is the data collected actually helpful to the user? You and your classmates will explore the types of data that an activity tracker collects, and how that data can help users reach their activity and fitness goals.

Review What You Know!

Vocabulary

Choose the best term from the box. Write it on the blank.

percent
proportion
rate
ratio

1. A _____ is a ratio in which the first term is compared to 100.

2. A ratio that relates two quantities with different units of measure is

   a _____.

3. A statement that two ratios are equal is called a _____.

4. The relationship "3 students out of 5 students" is an example of a _____.

Fractions, Decimals, and Percents

Write each number in two equivalent forms as a fraction, decimal, or percent.

5. 0.29

6. 35%

7. $\frac{2}{5}$

Proportions

Find the unknown number in each proportion.

8. $\dfrac{x \text{ days}}{4 \text{ years}} = \dfrac{365.25 \text{ days}}{1 \text{ year}}$

9. $\dfrac{33{,}264 \text{ feet}}{x \text{ miles}} = \dfrac{5{,}280 \text{ feet}}{1 \text{ mile}}$

10. A cooking magazine shows a photo of a main dish on the front cover of 5 out of the 12 issues it publishes each year. Write and solve a proportion to determine how many times a photo of a main dish will be on the front cover during the next 5 years.

Language Development

Fill in the spider map by writing new vocabulary terms on each diagonal and related ideas.

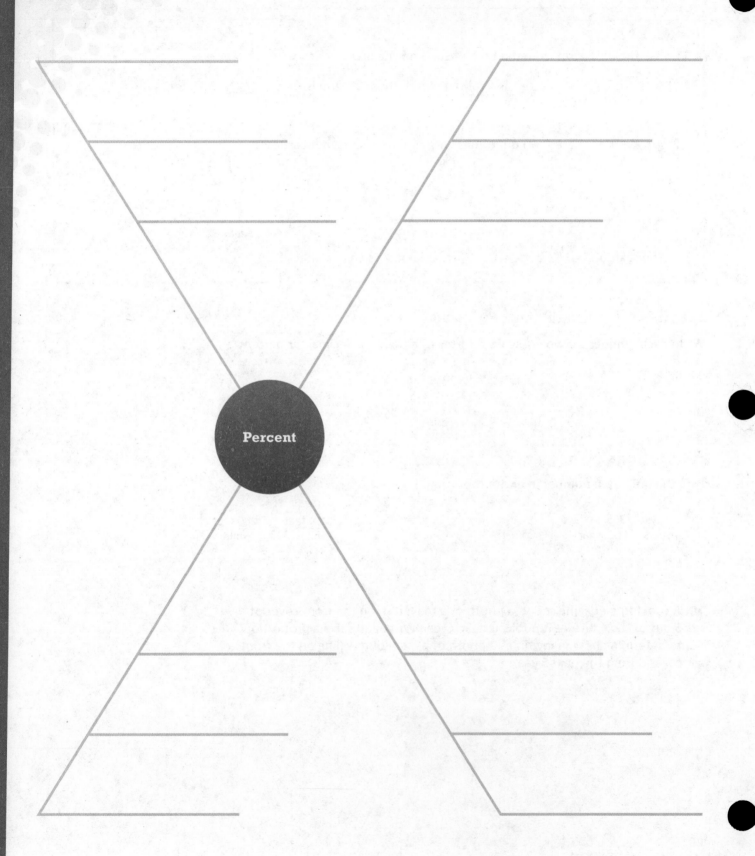

PROJECT 4A

How can you make sure you are getting the best deal?

PROJECT: SEARCH FOR BARGAINS

PROJECT 4B

What makes a song's lyrics easy to remember?

PROJECT: WRITE AND PERFORM A CHEER OR A RAP

PROJECT 4C

If you were to play basketball, what strategies would you practice?

PROJECT: ESTIMATE BASKETS

PROJECT 4D

What are some elements of your favorite app?

PROJECT: DESIGN AN APP ICON

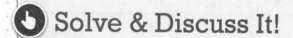 Solve & Discuss It!  ACTIVITY

Jaime's older brother and his three friends want to split the cost of lunch. They also want to leave a 15%–20% tip. How much should each person pay?

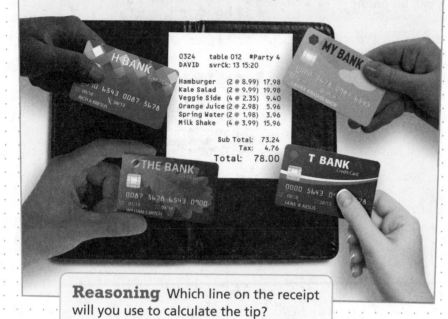

```
0324      table 012  #Party 4
DAVID    svrCk: 13 15:20

Hamburger    (2 @ 8.99) 17.98
Kale Salad   (2 @ 9.99) 19.98
Veggie Side  (4 @ 2.35)  9.40
Orange Juice (2 @ 2.98)  5.96
Spring Water (2 @ 1.98)  3.96
Milk Shake   (4 @ 3.99) 15.96

      Sub Total: 73.24
           Tax:   4.76
      Total:     78.00
```

Reasoning Which line on the receipt will you use to calculate the tip?

I can...
understand, find, and analyze percents of numbers.

© **Common Core Content Standards**
7.RP.A.3

Mathematical Practices
MP.1, MP.2, MP.3, MP.7

Focus on math practices
Reasoning How would the amount each person pays change if the tip is determined before or after the bill is split?

VISUAL LEARNING   ASSESS

EXAMPLE 1   👁 **Find Percents of Numbers**

Scan for Multimedia

Diego starts a 12-hour road trip with his phone's battery charge at 75%. Given his normal usage, will his phone last the whole trip? Explain.

> **Look for Relationships** How many hours will the phone last when the battery charge is at 75%?

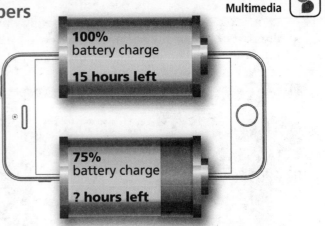

100% battery charge

15 hours left

75% battery charge

? hours left

STEP 1 Draw a bar diagram and write equivalent ratios to represent the hours remaining and the battery charge.

15 hours of use

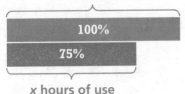

100%

75%

x hours of use

$\frac{75}{100} = \frac{x}{15}$

STEP 2 Use the equivalent ratios to find 75% of 15.

$\frac{75}{100} = \frac{x}{15}$ Solve for x.

$\frac{75}{100} \cdot 15 = \frac{x}{15} \cdot 15$

$11.25 = x$

75% of 15 is 11.25 hours.

The remaining battery life is 11.25 hours, so the phone will not last the whole 12-hour trip.

☑ **Try It!**

Kita's phone had a fully charged battery. With normal usage, her phone will last 18 hours. How much time is left on Kita's phone battery with 12% charge remaining?

$\frac{\boxed{}}{100} = \frac{x}{\boxed{}}$

$\frac{\boxed{}}{100} \cdot \boxed{} = \frac{x}{\boxed{}} \cdot \boxed{}$

$\boxed{} = x$

Kita's phone battery has $\boxed{}$ hours remaining.

? hours of use

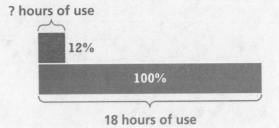

12%

100%

18 hours of use

Convince Me! Why is 51% of a number more than half of the number?

EXAMPLE 2 **Use Percents Greater than 100%**

  ACTIVITY ASSESS

A full set of adult teeth includes 160% as many teeth as a full set of baby teeth. How many teeth are there in a full set of adult teeth?

Use the bar diagram to write equivalent ratios. Then solve for t to find the number of adult teeth.

t adult teeth

| 160% |
| 100% |

20 baby teeth

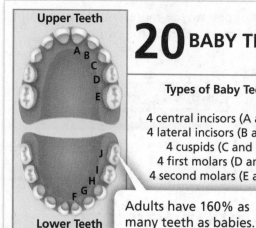

Upper Teeth

20 BABY TEETH

Types of Baby Teeth

4 central incisors (A and F)
4 lateral incisors (B and G)
4 cuspids (C and H)
4 first molars (D and I)
4 second molars (E and J)

Adults have 160% as many teeth as babies.

Lower Teeth

$$\frac{160}{100} = \frac{t}{20}$$

$$\frac{160}{100} \cdot 20 = \frac{t}{20} \cdot 20$$

$$32 = t$$

A full set of adult teeth includes 32 teeth.

EXAMPLE 3 **Use Percents Less than 1%**

What is the approximate distance in miles from Earth to the Moon?

STEP 1 Draw a bar diagram and write equivalent ratios.

x miles

0.27%

| 100% |

93 million miles

93,000,000 miles

0.27% of the distance between the Sun and Earth

$$\frac{x}{93,000,000} = \frac{0.27}{100}$$

STEP 2 Solve for x.

$$\frac{0.27}{100} \cdot 93,000,000 = \frac{x}{93,000,000} \cdot 93,000,000$$

$$251,100 = x$$

The distance from Earth to the Moon is about 251,100 miles.

Check Your Answer Use compatible numbers to estimate the solution. 93,000,000 is approximately 100,000,000. 1% of 100,000,000 miles is 1,000,000 miles.

0.27% is about $\frac{1}{4}$ of 1%, so the distance is about $\frac{1}{4}$ of 1,000,000, or 250,000 miles.

Reasoning The exact distance is close to the estimated distance, so the answer is reasonable.

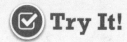 **Try It!**

a. Find 0.08% of 720.   **b.** Find 162.5% of 200.   **c.** Find 0.3% of 60.

A percent is one way to represent the relationship between two quantities, generally that of a part to the whole.

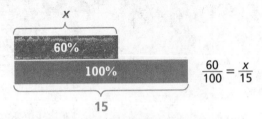

$$\frac{60}{100} = \frac{x}{15}$$

Do You Understand?

1. **Essential Question** How do percents show the relationship between quantities?

2. **Reasoning** How does a value that is greater than 100% of the original value or less than 1% of the original value compare to the original value?

3. **Construct Arguments** Gene stated that finding 25% of a number is the same as dividing the number by $\frac{1}{4}$. Is Gene correct? Explain.

Do You Know How?

4. An 8-ounce serving of apples contains 8% of your daily vitamin C. How many ounces of apples would you need to get 100% of your daily vitamin C?

5. Find the percent of each number.

   a. 59% of 640

   b. 0.20% of 3,542

   c. 195% of 568

   d. 74% of 920

6. Water is 2 parts hydrogen and 1 part oxygen (H_2O). For one molecule of water, each atom has the atomic mass unit, u, shown. What percent of the mass of a water molecule is hydrogen?

   16.00 u

   H 1.01 u

   H 1.01 u

Name: _____

Practice & Problem Solving

Leveled Practice In 7–8, fill in the boxes to solve.

7. A local Little League has a total of 60 players, 80% of whom are right-handed. How many right-handed players are there?

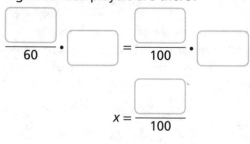

$$\frac{\boxed{}}{60} \cdot \boxed{} = \frac{\boxed{}}{100} \cdot \boxed{}$$

$$x = \frac{\boxed{}}{100}$$

$$x = \boxed{} \text{ right-handed players}$$

8. Sandra's volleyball team has a total of 20 uniforms. 20% are medium-sized uniforms. How many uniforms are medium-sized?

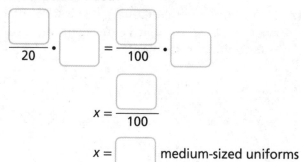

$$\frac{\boxed{}}{20} \cdot \boxed{} = \frac{\boxed{}}{100} \cdot \boxed{}$$

$$x = \frac{\boxed{}}{100}$$

$$x = \boxed{} \text{ medium-sized uniforms}$$

9. Meg is a veterinarian. In a given week, 50% of the 16 dogs she saw were Boxers. Steve is also a veterinarian. In the same week, 7 of the 35 dogs he saw this week were Boxers. Each wants to record the part, the whole, and the percent.

   a. Does Meg need to find the part, the whole, or the percent?

   b. Does Steve need to find the part, the whole, or the percent?

10. Olivia is a stockbroker. She makes 4% of her sales in commission. Last week, she sold $7,200 worth of stocks.

    a. How much commission did she make last week?

    b. If she were to average that same commission each week, how much would she make in commissions in a year, treating a year as having exactly 52 weeks?

11. The registration fee for a used car is 0.8% of the sale price of $5,700. How much is the fee?

12. The total cost of an item is the price plus the sales tax.

    Find the sales tax to complete the table. Then find the total cost of the item.

    Sales Tax

Selling Price	Rate of Sales Tax	Sales Tax
$40.00	4%	

13. Is 700% of 5 less than 10, greater than 10 but less than 100, or greater than 100? Explain your reasoning.

14. Is 250% of 44 less than 100, greater than 100 but less than 150, or greater than 150? Explain your reasoning.

15. The seed and skin of a typical avocado is about 30%–40% of the avocado's weight. For an 8-ounce avocado, how many ounces of edible fruit does it have?

16. A new health drink has 130% of the recommended daily allowance (RDA) for a certain vitamin. The RDA for this vitamin is 45 mg. How many milligrams of the vitamin are in the drink?

17. Make Sense and Persevere 153 is 0.9% of what number? Tell which equivalent ratios you used to find the solution.

18. Construct Arguments Brad says that if a second number is 125% of the first number, then the first number must be 75% of the second number. Is he correct? Justify your answer.

19. Higher-Order Thinking Mark and Joe work as jewelers. Mark has an hourly wage of $24 and gets overtime for every hour he works over 40 hours. The overtime pay rate is 150% of the normal rate. Joe makes 5% commission on all jewelry he sells. Who earns more money in a week if Mark works 60 hours and Joe sells $21,000 worth of jewelry? Explain.

☑ Assessment Practice

20. Pamela and John work as tutors at two different test-prep companies. Pamela earns $20 per hour. John earns $65 per pupil. Pamela works 40 hours each week. John has 11 pupils. Who earns more money in a week? Explain.

21. An Olympic-sized pool, which holds 660,000 gallons of water, is only 63% full. The pool maintenance company adds more water, filling the pool to 90% full. How many gallons of water did they add?

Ⓐ 244,200

Ⓒ 178,200

Ⓑ 594,000

Ⓓ 415,800

Solve & Discuss It!

 ACTIVITY

A florist is making flower arrangements for a party. He uses purple and white flowers in a ratio of 3 purple flowers to 1 white flower. How many flowers will he need in order to make 30 identical arrangements?

I can...
use proportions to solve percent problems.

© **Common Core Content Standards**
7.RP.A.3, 7.RP.A.2c

Mathematical Practices
MP.1, MP.2, MP.3, MP.7

Look for Relationships
How are the number of purple flowers related to the number of white flowers?

Focus on math practices

Make Sense and Persevere If the florist can only buy white flowers in groups of flowers that have 3 white flowers and 2 red flowers, how many red flowers will the florist have to purchase? Explain your answer.

EXAMPLE 1 **Use a Proportion to Find the Percent**

Scan for Multimedia

The basketball team statistician tracked the shots Emily made and the shots she missed during the last game. What percent of attempted shots did she make?

Legend
● Shots made
● Shots missed

Draw a bar diagram and write a proportion to represent the number of shots made and the total number of shots.

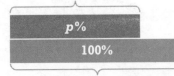

9 shots made

$p\%$

100%

12 attempted shots

$$\frac{9}{12} = \frac{p}{100}$$

Solve the proportion to find the percent of shots made during the last game.

$$\frac{9}{12} = \frac{p}{100}$$

$$\frac{9}{12} \cdot 100 = \frac{p}{100} \cdot 100$$

$$75 = p$$

Reasoning The ratio of part to whole describes a proportional relationship.

Emily made 75% of her shots.

☑ **Try It!**

Camila makes 2 of her 5 shots attempted. Is the percent of shots she made more than, less than, or the same as Emily's percent of shots?

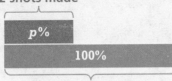

2 shots made

$p\%$

100%

5 attempted shots

$$\frac{\boxed{}}{\boxed{}} = \frac{p}{\boxed{}}$$

$$\frac{\boxed{}}{} = \frac{p}{\boxed{}}$$

$$\boxed{} = p$$

Camila made $\boxed{}$ % of her shots.

Camila's percent of the shots made is $\boxed{}$ Emily's.

Convince Me! A hockey goalie stops 37 out of 40 shots. What percent of attempted goals did she stop?

EXAMPLE **2** Use a Proportion to Find the Part

  ACTIVITY ASSESS

A plan to expand Megan's room will make the length of the room 175% of the current length. What will be the new length of her room?

Draw a bar diagram to represent the problem and then write a percent proportion to find the new length.

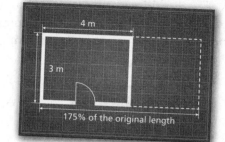

4 m

3 m

175% of the original length

n meters

175%

100%

4 meters

$$\frac{\text{new length}}{\text{old length}} = \frac{p}{100}$$

$$\frac{n}{4} = \frac{175}{100}$$

$$\frac{n}{4} \cdot 4 = \frac{175}{100} \cdot 4$$

$$n = 7$$

The new length of the room will be 7 meters.

EXAMPLE **3** Use a Proportion to Find the Whole

The nutrition label shows the percents of the recommended daily intake for nutrients found in a serving of a soy milk. How many milligrams of calcium should you consume each day?

Write a percent proportion to find the amount of calcium.

$$\frac{\text{calcium per serving}}{\text{daily value}} = \frac{p}{100}$$

$$\frac{260}{w} = \frac{20}{100}$$

$$\frac{260}{w} \cdot w = \frac{20}{100} \cdot w \qquad \boxed{\text{Multiply both sides by the variable.}}$$

$$260 = \frac{20w}{100}$$

$$260 \cdot \frac{100}{20} = \frac{20w}{100} \cdot \frac{100}{20} \qquad \boxed{\text{Multiply both sides by the reciprocal.}}$$

$$1{,}300 = w$$

The daily value for calcium is 1,300 mg.

Organic

SOY MILK

SOY MILK

Nutrition Facts
Serving Size 5 oz.
Servings Per Container 8

Amount Per Serving
Calories 90   Calories from Fat 30

10%	Vitamin D 2mcg
20%	Calcium 260mg
45%	Iron 8mg
5%	Potassium 8mg

Percent Daily Values are based on a 2,000 calorie diet. Your daily may be higher or lower

---

 Try It!

a. Megan's room is expanded so the width is 150% of 3 meters. What is the new width?

b. Use the soy milk label in Example 3. What is the recommended amount of iron needed each day? Round your answer to the nearest mg.

Percent problems represent a kind of proportional relationship. You can use proportional reasoning to solve percent problems.

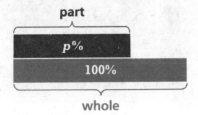

part

p%

100%

whole

$$\frac{part}{whole} = \frac{p}{100}$$

Do You Understand?

1. **Essential Question** How does proportional reasoning relate to percent?

2. **Reasoning** Why does one of the ratios in a percent proportion always have a denominator of 100?

3. **Construct Arguments** The proportion $\frac{75}{w} = \frac{150}{100}$ can be used to find the whole, w. Use the language of percent to explain whether w is less than or greater than 75.

Do You Know How?

4. Write a percent proportion for the bar diagram shown.

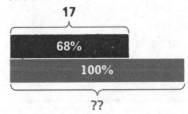

17

68%

100%

??

5. Use a proportion to find each value.
   a. 2% of 180

   $$\frac{n}{\boxed{}} = \frac{2}{\boxed{}}$$

   b. What percent is 17 out of 40?

   $$\frac{\boxed{}}{\boxed{}} = \frac{p}{\boxed{}}$$

6. **Construct Arguments** Gia researches online that her car is worth $3,000. She hopes to sell it for 85% of that value, but she wants to get at least 70%. She ends up selling it for $1,800. Did she get what she wanted? Justify your answer.

Practice & Problem Solving

Leveled Practice In 7–8, fill in the boxes to solve.

7. The rabbit population in a certain area is 200% of last year's population. There are 1,100 rabbits this year. How many were there last year?

$$\frac{1,100}{w} = \frac{\boxed{}}{\boxed{}}$$

There were $\boxed{}$ rabbits last year.

8. A company that makes hair-care products had 3,000 people try a new shampoo. Of the 3,000 people, 9 had a mild allergic reaction. What percent of the people had a mild allergic reaction?

$$\frac{9}{3,000} = \frac{p}{\boxed{}}$$

Percent = $\boxed{}$ %

9. A survey was given to people who owned a certain type of car. What percent of the people surveyed were completely satisfied with the car?

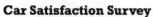

Car Satisfaction Survey

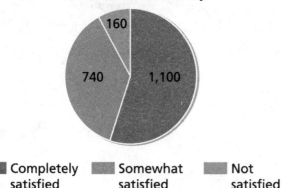

160

740   1,100

■ Completely   ■ Somewhat   ■ Not
  satisfied   satisfied   satisfied

10. The Washingtons buy a studio apartment for $240,000. They pay a down payment of $60,000.

a. Their down payment is what percent of the purchase price?

b. What percent of the purchase price would a $12,000 down payment be?

11. A restaurant customer left $3.50 as a tip. The tax on the meal was 7% and the tip was 20% of the cost including tax.

a. What piece of information is not needed to compute the bill after tax and tip?

b. **Make Sense and Persevere** What was the total bill?

12. **Reasoning** What is a good estimate for 380% of 60? Explain.

13. **Critique Reasoning** Marna thinks that about 35% of her mail is junk mail. She gets about twice as much regular mail as junk mail. Is she correct? Explain.

14. Hypatia has read 13 chapters of a 22-chapter book. What percent of the chapters has she read?

15. A school year has 4 quarters. What percent of a school year is 7 quarters?

16. **Construct Arguments** A survey found that 27% of high school students and 94% of teachers and school employees drive to school. The ratio of students to employees is about 10 to 1. Roger states that the number of students who drive to school is greater than the number of teachers and employees who drive to school. Explain how Roger's statement could be correct.

17. **Higher Order Thinking** Stefan sells Jin a bicycle for $114 and a helmet for $18. The total cost for Jin is 120% of what Stefan spent originally to buy the bike and helmet. How much did Stefan spend originally? How much money did he make by selling the bicycle and helmet to Jin?

✓ Assessment Practice

18. Last month Nicole spent $30. This month she spent 140% of what she spent last month.

    Write a proportional equation to represent the situation. How much did Nicole spend this month?

19. Mr. Jones, the owner of a small store buys kayak paddles for $50.00 each, and sells them for 180% of the purchase price.

    PART A

    A customer buys a paddle for $97.65, which includes the selling price and sales tax. What is the sales tax rate?

    Ⓐ 7.65%

    Ⓑ 4.7%

    Ⓒ 9.75%

    Ⓓ 8.5%

    PART B

    If Mr. Jones buys paddles for $35 instead of $50, and uses the same percent increase on price, how many paddles must Mr. Jones sell for the total paddle sales, before tax, to be at least $250? Explain your answer.

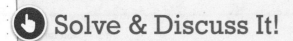 Solve & Discuss It!

ACTIVITY

Fran is shopping for a new pair of shoes. She did some research and has narrowed the options to the two pairs she likes the most. Based on buyers' reviews, which pair do you recommend that she buy? Explain your thinking.

Compare Styles

19 OUT OF **25**
positive reviews

Add to Cart 🛒

99 OUT OF **132**
positive reviews

Add to Cart 🛒

Model with Math How can you use what you know about ratios to compare the reviews?

I can...
represent and solve percent problems using equations.

© **Common Core Content Standards**
7.RP.A.2c, 7.RP.A.3

Mathematical Practices
MP.1, MP.2, MP.3, MP.4, MP.6, MP.7

Focus on math practices

Model with Math Describe another situation in which you could use ratios to make a decision.

VISUAL LEARNING ASSESS

EXAMPLE 1 **Find the Percent**

Scan for Multimedia

In science class, students compared their vertical reach and height to see if they are proportional. Maria is 60 inches tall and can reach 75 inches high. What percent of her total vertical reach is her height?

Vertical Reach
75 in.

Height
60 in.

Use proportional reasoning to develop the **percent equation**.

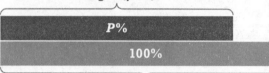

height (part)

P%

100%

vertical reach (whole)

$$\frac{part}{whole} = \frac{p}{100}$$

$$\frac{part}{whole} = percent$$

$$\frac{part}{whole} \cdot whole = percent \cdot whole$$

$$part = percent \cdot whole$$

Use Structure The percent is a constant of proportionality that relates a *part* to the *whole*. The equation has the same form as $y = mx$.

The percent equation is part = percent • whole.

height = percent • vertical reach

$$60 = \quad P \quad \cdot \quad 75$$

$$\frac{60}{75} = \frac{P \cdot 75}{75}$$

$$0.80 = P$$

To represent a decimal as a percent, multiply by 100 and add the percent symbol.

Maria's height is 80% of her total vertical reach.

☑ **Try It!**

An elephant weighs 15,000 pounds on Earth and 2,500 pounds on the Moon. Assuming the weights are proportional, what percent of its weight on Earth is its weight on the Moon?

Convince Me! How does the percent describe how the weights are related?

$$\boxed{} = P \cdot 15,000$$

$$\frac{\boxed{}}{\boxed{}} = \frac{P \cdot 15,000}{\boxed{}}$$

$$\boxed{} \approx P$$

The elephant's weight on the Moon is about

$\boxed{}$ % of its weight on Earth.

EXAMPLE 2 **Find the Part**

Many states have a meal tax that is proportional to the total spent on food and beverages. In one state, the meal tax is 8.44%. How much tax will a customer pay if the food and beverages total $54?

Tax ($)

8.44%	
	100%

Total food and beverage ($)

part = percent • whole

tax = percent • bill

> Use *t* for the tax and *b* for the food and beverages bill.

$t = 8.44\% \cdot b$

$t = 0.0844 \cdot 54$

> Express the percent as a decimal.

$t = 4.5576$

> **Reasoning** What does 4.5576 mean in this situation?

The customer will pay $4.56 in tax.

EXAMPLE 3 **Find the Whole**

Jane earns a 5.5% commission on the selling price of each home she sells. She earned $9,020 in commission on the sale of a home. What was the selling price of the home?

Commission ($)

5.5%	
	100%

Selling price ($)

> **Be Precise** Instead of a salary, some workers earn a percent of the value of a transaction, called a *commission*.

part = percent • whole

$c = 5.5\% \cdot h$

> Use *c* for the commission and *h* for the selling price of the home.

$9,020 = 0.055h$

$$\frac{9,020}{0.055} = \frac{0.055h}{0.055}$$

$164,000 = h$

Jane sold the home for $164,000.

 Try It!

To make a profit, a clothing store sells board shorts at 115% of the amount they paid for them. How much did the store pay for the board shorts shown?

$28

The percent equation shows how a percent relates proportional quantities. The percent is a constant of proportionality and the equation has the same form as $y = mx$.

$$\frac{\text{part}}{\text{whole}} = \text{percent}$$

$$\text{part} = \text{percent} \cdot \text{whole}$$

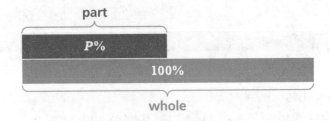

Do You Understand?

1. **Essential Question** How are percent problems related to proportional reasoning?

2. **Reasoning** A waiter at a restaurant receives $11 as a tip on a $47.20 bill. He usually receives tips that are 20% of the total bill. Is the tip amount what the waiter typically receives? Explain.

3. **Construct Arguments** Sara used an equation to solve the problem below. Justify each step of her work.

   About 11% of people are left-handed. How many people would you expect to be left-handed in a class of 30 students?

   $\ell = 0.11 \cdot 30$
   $\ell = 3.3$
   about 3 students

Do You Know How?

4. An auto insurance company pays 12% commission to its agents for each new insurance policy they sell. How much commission does an agent make on a $1,000 policy?

5. Curt and Melanie are mixing blue and yellow paint to make seafoam green paint. Use the percent equation to find how much yellow paint they should use.

6. Bill paid $35.99 in tax on a laptop that cost $449.99. About what percent sales tax did Bill pay?

Name: _____

Practice & Problem Solving

Scan for
Multimedia

Leveled Practice In **7** and **8**, solve each percent problem.

7. In a survey of 500 voters, 430 said they would vote for the same candidate again. What percent of the voters would vote the same way again?

part = percent • whole

$\boxed{}$ = P% • $\boxed{}$

$\boxed{}$ = P%

8. The local newspaper has letters to the editor from 40 people. If this number represents 5% of all of the newspaper's readers, how many readers, r, does the newspaper have?

part = percent • whole

$\boxed{}$ = $\boxed{}$ • r

$\boxed{}$ = r

---

9. Make Sense and Persevere What percent of the 16-gigabyte hard drive shown is used for photos?

3.32 GB

| Music | Photos | Apps | Other | Free Space |

├───────────── **16 GB** ─────────────┤

---

10. A shirt that normally costs $30 is on sale for $21.75. What percent of the regular price is the sale price?

11. Complete the table.

Earning Commission

Sales	Commission Rate	Commission
$768	4%	$\boxed{}$

---

12. Complete the table.

Sales Tax

Selling Price	Tax Rate	Sales Tax
$39.98	4.5%	$\boxed{}$

13. A restaurant automatically charges a 20% gratuity if a party has 6 or more people. How much gratuity is added to a party of 6 on a $141 bill?

14. Make Sense and Persevere A large university accepts 70% of the students who apply. Of the students the university accepts, 25% actually enroll. If 20,000 students apply, how many enroll?

15. Model with Math There are 4,000 books in the town's library. Of these, 2,600 are fiction. Write a percent equation that you can use to find the percent of the books that are fiction. Then solve your equation.

16. A salesperson earns 4% commission on furnace sales.

a. What is the commission that the salesperson earns on the sale of $33,000 worth of furnaces?

b. Suppose the salesperson doubles his sales of furnaces. What would be true about the commission? Explain without using any calculations.

17. Heidi earns 3% commission on the jewelry she sells each week. Last week, she sold the pieces of jewelry shown.

a. How much did she make in commission?

b. Reasoning How much did the jewelry store take in from her sales? How do you know?

$110
$275
$200
$145

18. Higher Order Thinking In a company, 60% of the workers are men. If 1,380 women work for the company, how many workers are there in all? Show two different ways that you can solve this problem.

19. A salesperson starts working 40 hours per week at a job with two options for being paid. Option A is an hourly wage of $19. Option B is a commission rate of 8% on weekly sales.

How much does the salesperson need to sell in a given week to earn the same amount with each option?

Ⓐ $9,500   Ⓑ $4,750   Ⓒ $760   Ⓓ $320

20. At a real estate agency, an agent sold a house for $382,000. The commission rate is 5.5% for the real estate agency. The commission for the agent is 30% of the amount the real estate agency gets. How much did the agent earn in commission? Explain your answer.

1. **Vocabulary** Explain how the percent equation relates proportional quantities. *Lesson 4-3*

2. Colleen buys a movie for $20 and pays 7% sales tax. Her cousin, Brad, lives in another state. Brad buys the same movie for $22 and pays 6% sales tax. Who pays more sales tax? How much more? *Lessons 4-1 and 4-3*

3. Kamesh and Paolo each read 40 books in one year. Kamesh read 12 nonfiction books. Thirty-five percent of the books Paolo read were nonfiction. Who read more nonfiction books? How many more?
Lesson 4-2

4. Val buys a computer for $920. If this is 115% of what the store paid for the same computer, how much did the store earn on the sale? *Lesson 4-3*

5. For each situation, select the percent to answer the question.
Lessons 4-1, 4-2, and 4-3

	5%	15%	20%	25%
At an auto repair shop, 14 of the 56 cars received oil changes. What percent of the cars received oil changes?	☐	☐	☐	☐
Harry pays $3.50 sales tax on a $70 item. What is the sales tax rate?	☐	☐	☐	☐
In a box of 250 paperclips, 50 are red. What percent of the paperclips are red?	☐	☐	☐	☐
Rylee saved $9 on a $60 pair of shoes. What percent did she save?	☐	☐	☐	☐

6. Explain how you can use proportional reasoning to determine the whole if you know that 21 is 60% of the whole. *Lesson 4-2*

How well did you do on the mid-topic checkpoint? Fill in the stars.

MID-TOPIC PERFORMANCE TASK

The coach of a women's basketball team wants each of her starting players to make at least 75% of the free throws attempted during regular season games. The table shows the statistics for the starting players after the first 15 games.

Player	Free Throws Attempted	Free Throws Made	Percent
Wilson	36	24	
Bartholdi	42	37	
Johnson	22	15	
Garcia	29	16	
O'Malley	14	12	

PART A

Use the table. Find the percentage of free throws made by each player. Round to the nearest whole percent.

PART B

Choose one of the players with a free-throw percentage less than 75%. Determine a number of free throws the player could attempt and make during the next 10 games to increase her free-throw percentage to at least 75%.

PART C

Choose one of the players with a free-throw percentage greater than 75%. Determine the number of free throws that the player could miss during the next 10 games and still maintain an overall percentage of at least 75%.

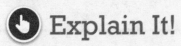 Explain It!

 ACTIVITY

Nadia lives in the town of Preston. Quinn lives in the town of Elm Ridge. Nadia and Quinn each claim that her respective town's population is growing more rapidly.

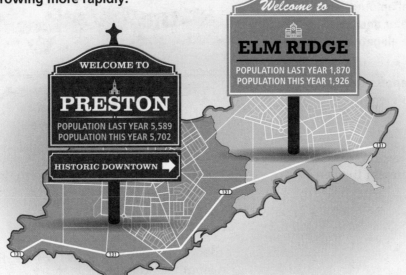

Welcome to
ELM RIDGE
POPULATION LAST YEAR 1,870
POPULATION THIS YEAR 1,926

WELCOME TO
PRESTON
POPULATION LAST YEAR 5,589
POPULATION THIS YEAR 5,702

HISTORIC DOWNTOWN ➡

I can...
solve problems involving percent change and percent error.

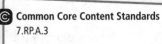

Common Core Content Standards
7.RP.A.3

Mathematical Practices
MP.1, MP.3, MP.4, MP.6

A. Write an argument to support Nadia. Why might she argue that Preston's population is growing more rapidly?

B. Write an argument to support Quinn. Why might she argue that Elm Ridge's population is growing more rapidly?

C. Whose reasoning is more logical? Explain why.

Focus on math practices

Critique Reasoning Suppose Preston's population is expected to grow 3% next year. Nadia says that means the population will increase by 300 people. Is Nadia's reasoning correct? Explain.

? **Essential Question** How is finding percent error similar to finding percent change?

 VISUAL LEARNING ASSESS

EXAMPLE 1 Find Percent Increase

Scan for Multimedia

The **percent change** describes how much a quantity has changed relative to its original amount. The percent change can be an increase or decrease. What is the percent change of the alligator's length?

Model with Math What representation can show the change in the alligator's length?

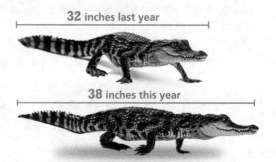

32 inches last year

38 inches this year

STEP 1 Draw a bar diagram to represent the percent change from last year to this year.

The percent change is a *percent increase* because the alligator's length increased.

% change

| 32 inches | 6 in. |
| 32 inches |

100%

The change in length is 6 inches.

STEP 2 Use the percent equation to find the percent change.

part = percent • whole

$$\frac{\text{change}}{\text{in length}} = \frac{\text{percent}}{\text{change}} \cdot \frac{\text{original}}{\text{length}}$$

$$6 = P \cdot 32$$

$$\frac{6}{32} = P$$

$$0.1875 = P$$

Express the decimal as a percent by multiplying by 100.

The alligator's length increased by 18.75% this year.

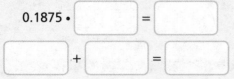 **Try It!**

What will be the length of the alligator next year if its length changes by the same percent as it changed this year?

18.75%

| 38 inches | ? in. |
| 38 inches |

100%

percent change • length this year = change in length

$$0.1875 \cdot \boxed{} = \boxed{}$$

$$\boxed{} + \boxed{} = \boxed{}$$

Next year, the length of the alligator will be $\boxed{}$ inches long.

Convince Me! Why is the increase in the alligator's length different from year to year, even though the percent change stayed the same?

EXAMPLE **2** **Find Percent Decrease**

  ACTIVITY ASSESS

Last year, a website had 40,000 visitors and this year, it had 37,000 visitors. What is the percent change in the number of visitors to the website from last year to this year?

Find the decrease in the number of visitors. Then use the percent equation to find the percent change.

> The percent change is a *percent decrease* because the number of visitors decreased.

% change

| 37,000 visitors |
| 40,000 visitors |

> The change in attendance is 3,000.

100%

change in number of visitors = **percent change** • number of visitors last year

$$3,000 = P \cdot 40,000$$

$$\frac{3,000}{40,000} = P$$

$$0.075 = P$$

The number of visitors decreased by 7.5% this year.

EXAMPLE **3** **Find Percent Error**

Shaun estimated that the attendance at a college lacrosse game was 3,000. The actual attendance was 3,296. What is the percent error of Shaun's estimate? Round to the nearest whole percent.

> **Percent error** describes the accuracy of a measured or estimated value compared to an actual value. It is always a positive percent.

Use absolute value to find the positive difference between the estimated and actual attendance. Then use the percent equation to find the percent error.

$$|3,000 - 3,296| = 296$$

difference in attendance = **percent error** • actual attendance

$$296 = P \cdot 3,296$$

$$\frac{296}{3,296} = P$$

$$0.0898 \approx P$$

> Remember to express the decimal value as a percent.

Shaun's attendance estimate has a percent error of about 9%.

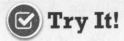 **Try It!**

The specification for the length of a bolt is 4.75 inches.
A machinist makes a bolt that is 4.769 inches long.
What is the percent error of the bolt's length?

← 4.769 in. →

Percent change and percent error problems are kinds of percent problems. You can use the percent equation to solve them.

$$\text{amount of change} = \text{percent change} \cdot \text{original amount}$$

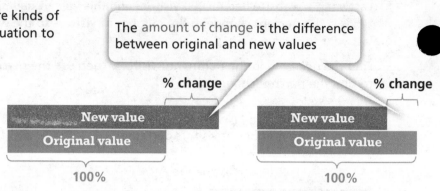

The amount of change is the difference between original and new values

Do You Understand?

1. **Essential Question** How is finding percent error similar to finding percent change?

2. **Reasoning** Give an example of a problem in which the percent error is greater than 20%, but less than 50%. Explain how you determined the percent error.

3. **Construct Arguments** A store manager marked up a $10 flash drive by 20%. She then marked it down by 20%. Explain why the new price of the flash drive is not $10.

Do You Know How?

4. Lita's softball team won 8 games last month and 10 this month. What was the percent change in games the team won? Was it an increase or decrease?

5. What is the percent change in the price of a gallon of gas, to the nearest whole percent? Is it an increase or a decrease?

6. Several students measured a 25-mm-long nail and wrote the measurements shown in the table below. Whose measurement had the greatest percent error? Round to the nearest percent.

Student	Measurement (mm)	Percent Error
Layne	26	____ %
Tenicia	23	____ %
Juan	25	____ %

Name: _____

Practice & Problem Solving

Leveled Practice In 7–8, use the bar diagram and fill in the boxes to solve.

7. The original quantity is 10 and the new quantity is 13. What is the percent change? Is it an increase or decrease?

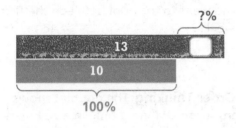

$\boxed{} = p \cdot \boxed{}$

$\boxed{} = p$

The percent increase is $\boxed{}$%.

8. The original quantity is 5 and the new quantity is 3. What is the percent change? Is it an increase or decrease?

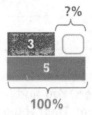

$\boxed{} = p \cdot \boxed{}$

$\boxed{} = p$

The percent decrease is $\boxed{}$%.

---

9. At noon, a tank contained 10 cm of water. After several hours, it contained 7 cm of water. What is the percent decrease of water in the tank?

10. Craig likes to collect vinyl records. Last year he had 10 records in his collection. Now he has 12 records. What is the percent increase of his collection?

---

11. Carl bought an airline ticket. Two weeks ago, the cost of this flight was $300.

What is the percent increase?

12. On Monday, a museum had 150 visitors. On Tuesday, it had 260 visitors.

   a. Estimate the percent change in the number of visitors to the museum.

   b. About how many people would have to visit the museum on Wednesday to have the same percent change from Tuesday to Wednesday as from Monday to Tuesday? Explain your answer.

---

13. Rihanna has a container with a volume of 1.5 liters. She estimates the volume to be 2.1 liters. What is the percent error?

14. The label on a package of bolts says each bolt has a diameter of 0.35 inch. To be in the package, the percent error of the diameter must be less than 5%. One bolt has a diameter of 0.33 inch. Should it go in the package? Why or why not?

15. A band expects to have 16 songs on their next album. The band writes and records 62.5% more songs than they expect to have in the album. During the editing process, 50% of the songs are removed. How many songs will there be in the final album?

16. Make Sense and Persevere In the first week of July, a record 1,060 people went to the local swimming pool. In the second week, 105 fewer people went to the pool. In the third week, 135 more people went to the pool than in the second week. In the fourth week, 136 fewer people went to the pool than in the third week.

What is the percent change in the number of people who went to the pool between the first and last weeks?

17. Be Precise You have 20 quarters. You find 40% more quarters in your room. Then you go shopping and spend 50% of the total number of quarters.

a. Write an expression that represents the total number of quarters you take with you when you go shopping.

b. How much money do you have left?

18. Higher Order Thinking The dot plot shows predictions for the winning time in a 200-meter sprint. The winner finished the race in 22.3 seconds. Find the greatest percent error for a prediction to the nearest tenth of a percent. Justify your answer.

Race Times

Seconds

Assessment Practice

19. The amount of money in a savings account increases from $250 to $270 in one month. If the percent increase is the same for every month, how much money will be in the account at the end of the next month?

Ⓐ $291.60   Ⓑ $295   Ⓒ $289.60   Ⓓ $300

20. A meteorologist predicted that there would be 1.0 inches of rainfall from a storm. Instead, there were 2.2 inches of rainfall.

Which statements are true?

☐ The prediction was off by 35%.

☐ If the percent error should be less than 60%, the prediction was acceptable.

☐ The percent error of the prediction was about 55%.

☐ If the percent error should be less than 20%, the prediction was acceptable.

☐ The difference between the predicted and actual rainfall was 1.2 inches.

THE **Smart** Shopper

Go Online

© **Common Core Content Standards**
7.RP.A.3

Mathematical Practices
MP.4, MP.1, MP.2, MP.3, MP.5, MP.6, MP.7, MP.8

ACT 1

1. After watching the video, what is the first question that comes to mind?

2. Write the Main Question you will answer.

3. Construct Arguments Make a prediction to answer this Main Question. Explain how you arrived at your prediction.

4. On the number line below, write a number that is too small to be the answer. Write a number that is too large.

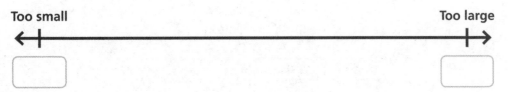

Too small   Too large

5. Plot your prediction on the same number line.

6. What information in this situation would be helpful to know? How would you use that information?

7. Use Appropriate Tools What tools can you use to solve the problem? Explain how you would use them strategically.

8. Model with Math Represent the situation using mathematics. Use your representation to answer the Main Question.

9. What is your answer to the Main Question? Is it higher or lower than your prediction? Explain why.

10. Write the answer you saw in the video.

11. Reasoning Does your answer match the answer in the video? If not, what are some reasons that wouldexplain the difference?

12. Make Sense and Persevere Would you change your model now that you know the answer? Explain.

Reflect

13. Model with Math Explain how you used a mathematical model to represent the situation. How did the model help you answer the Main Question?

14. Be Precise Describe how you would tell the friends to use their coupons.

SEQUEL

15. Make Sense and Persevere Suppose the $20 coupon requires a purchase of $100 or more. How would that affect your solution?

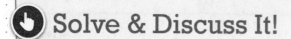 Solve & Discuss It!  ACTIVITY

Clare subscribes to an online music streaming service for a yearly fee of $96. Starting next month, there will be a 12% increase in the fee.

The ad for another music streaming service is shown below. Should Clare switch? Explain.

Welcome to our *Music* site

DIGITAL STREAMING OF MUSIC

$**8**.75 per month

Home | About Us | Services | FAQ | Contact Us

I can...
solve problems involving percent markup and markdown.

© **Common Core Content Standards**
7.RP.A.3

Mathematical Practices
MP.1, MP.2, MP.4, MP.8

Model with Math
You can use the percent equation to determine the percent increase.

Focus on math practices

Make Sense and Persevere What is another problem-solving method you could use to check that your solution makes sense?

? Essential Question How are the concepts of percent markup and percent markdown related to the percent equation?

VISUAL LEARNING   ASSESS

Scan for
Multimedia

EXAMPLE 1 Find the Percent Markup

Marty buys plain cell phone cases and then decorates them to resell online at a higher price. What is the percent markup on each phone case?

Markup is the amount of increase from the cost of an item to its selling price. The markup as a percent increase from the original cost is the **percent markup**.

$7.20 → Selling price: $11.25 each

STEP 1 Draw a bar diagram to represent the problem and to find the markup.

% markup

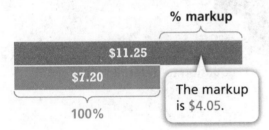

$11.25

$7.20

100%

The markup is $4.05.

STEP 2 Use the percent equation to find the percent markup.

markup = percent markup • cost

$$4.05 = P \cdot 7.20$$

$$\frac{4.05}{7.20} = P$$

$$0.5625 = P$$

Remember to express the decimal value as a percent.

The percent markup on each cell phone case is about 56%.

☑ Try It!

What is the percent markup on a $300 phone sold for $465?

markup = percent markup • cost

$$\boxed{} = P \cdot 300$$

$$\boxed{} = P$$

The percent markup on the phone is $\boxed{}$ %.

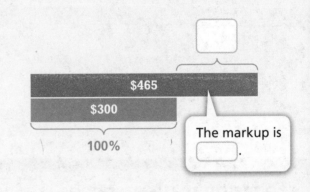

$465

$300

100%

The markup is $\boxed{}$.

Convince Me! How does the percent equation help solve markup problems?

EXAMPLE 2 Find the Selling Price

The local furniture store pays $110 for a chest of drawers and sells it with a 40% markup. What is the selling price of the chest of drawers?

STEP 1 Draw a bar diagram to represent the problem.

40% markup

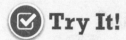

selling price

$110

100%

Amount of the markup

STEP 2 Use the percent equation to find the markup and the selling price.

$$markup = percent\ markup \cdot cost$$
$$a = 0.40 \cdot 110$$
$$a = 44$$

The markup is $44.

$$110 + 44 = 154$$

The selling price of the chest of drawers is $100 + $44 or $154.

Try It!

What is the selling price for a $45 pair of shoes with a 15% markup?

EXAMPLE 3 Find Markdown and Sales Tax

Edward wants to buy a snowboard that is on sale. If the sales tax in Edward's state is 7.5%, how much will he pay for the snowboard?

Markdown is the decrease from the original price of an item to its sale price. The markdown as a percent decrease of the original price is the **percent markdown**.

$180
30% OFF

STEP 1 Use the percent equation to find the marked down price of the snowboard.

$$markdown = percent\ markdown \cdot original\ price$$
$$m = 0.30 \cdot 180$$
$$m = 54$$

The sale price is $180 − $54, or $126.

STEP 2 Use the percent equation to find the sales tax.

$$sales\ tax = percent \cdot sale\ price$$
$$s = 0.075 \cdot 126$$
$$s = 9.45$$

Edward will pay 126 + 9.45, or $135.45, for the snowboard.

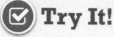 Try It!

Find the percent markdown for an $80 jacket that is on sale for $48.

You can solve markup and markdown problems using the percent equation.

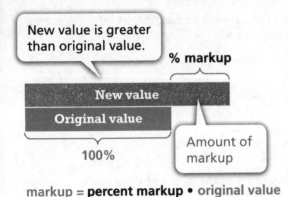

New value is greater than original value.

% markup

New value

Original value

Amount of markup

100%

markup = **percent markup** • original value

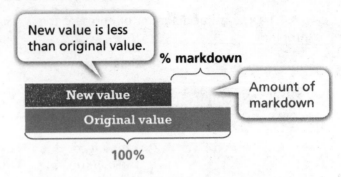

New value is less than original value.

% markdown

New value

Original value

Amount of markdown

100%

markdown = **percent markdown** • original value

Do You Understand?

1. **Essential Question** How are the concepts of markup and markdown related to the percent equation?

2. **Reasoning** What does the amount of the markup or markdown represent in the percent equation?

3. **Generalize** When an item is marked up by a certain percent and then marked down by the same percent, is the sale price equal to the price before the markup and markdown?

Do You Know How?

4. An item costs $4 before tax and $4.32 after sales tax. What is the sales tax rate?

$4

5. Sheila buys two concert tickets from her friend. She pays $90 for the two tickets. She looks at the tickets and sees that each ticket has a face value of $52.50.

   a. How much of a markdown did her friend give Sheila? Explain how you know.

   b. What was the percent markdown, rounded to the nearest whole percent?

6. Find the sale prices.

   a. $4,200 with a 35% markdown

   b. $5,000 with a 44% markdown

Name: _____

Practice & Problem Solving

Leveled Practice In 7–8, fill in the boxes to solve.

7. A $300 suit is marked down by 20%. Find the sale price rounded to the nearest dollar.

markdown = percent markdown • original price

markdown = ☐ % • $ ☐

markdown = $ ☐

original price − markdown = sale price

$ ☐ − $ ☐

sale price = $ ☐

8. The selling price of an item is $650 marked up from the wholesale cost of $450. Find the percent markup from wholesale cost to selling price.

selling price − markup = wholesale cost

$ ☐ − $ ☐ = $ ☐ .

markup = percent markup × wholesale cost

☐ = ☐ × ☐

The percent markup is about ☐ .

9. Karen purchased the DVD player shown in the sign on the right. Find the percent markdown rounded to the nearest percent.

10. A store manager instructs his employees to mark up all items by 30%. A store clerk puts a price tag of $30 on an item that the store bought for $27. As an employee, you notice that this selling price is incorrect.

a. Find the correct selling price. Round to the nearest dollar.

b. What was the clerk's likely error?

11. Nate has $50 to spend at the grocery store. He fills his shopping cart with items totaling $46. At checkout he will have to pay 6% sales tax on all items in the cart. Does he have enough money to buy everything in his cart? Explain.

12. A department store buys 300 shirts at a cost of $1,800 and sells them for $10 each. Find the percent markup rounded to the nearest percent.

13. **Make Sense and Persevere** A computer store buys a computer system at a cost of $465.60. The selling price was first at $776, but then the store advertised a 30% markdown on the system.

   a. Find the current sale price. Round to the nearest cent if necessary.

   b. Members of the store's loyalty club get an additional 10% off their computer purchases. How much do club members pay for the computer with their discount?

14. **Higher Order Thinking** A sporting goods store manager was selling a kayak set for a certain price. The manager offered the markdowns shown on the right, making the one-day sale price of the kayak set $328. Find the original selling price of the kayak set.

✓ Assessment Practice

15. Eliza cannot decide which of two bicycles to buy. The original price of each is $380. The first is marked down by 50%. The second is marked down by 30% with an additional 20% off. Which bicycle should Eliza buy if the bicycles are the same except for the selling price? Explain your answer.

16. A shoe store uses a 50% markup for all of the shoes it sells. The store also charges a 10% sales tax on all purchases. What would be the purchase price, including sales tax, of a pair of shoes that has a wholesale cost of $57?

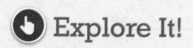 **Explore It!**

ACTIVITY

Gerard compares the offers at two different banks to decide where he should open a savings account.

Open a savings account - we'll add

$100

to your first deposit!

MY BANK

When you open a savings account with us, we'll add 5% of your first deposit to the account!

N New Bank

I can...
apply percent reasoning to solve simple interest problems.

© **Common Core Content Standards**
7.RP.A.3

Mathematical Practices
MP.1, MP.2, MP.3

A. Draw a representation to show how much would be in the first savings account if Gerard's initial deposit were *d* dollars.

B. Draw a representation to show how much would be in the second savings account if Gerard's initial deposit were *d* dollars.

C. Use the two representations you drew to explain how the offers at the two banks are similar and how they are different.

Focus on math practices

Construct Arguments Gerard's first deposit is $500. Which bank should he choose? Explain.

259

? Essential Question How does simple interest show proportional reasoning and relate to the percent equation?

EXAMPLE 1 Find Simple Interest

Victoria opens a savings account with a deposit of $300. She will earn 1.6% simple interest each year on her money. How much interest will she earn over 5 years (assuming she does not add or take out any money)?

> Interest that is applied to the initial amount only is called **simple interest**.

> The initial amount is called the **principal**.

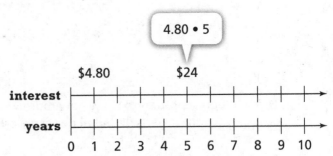

0 years   1 year   2 years   3 years   4 years   5 years

STEP 1 Use the percent equation to find the amount of interest earned in one year, *s*.

> An **interest rate** is a percent used to calculate interest on the principal.

interest amount = interest rate • principal

$$s = 0.016 \cdot 300$$

$$s = 4.80$$

The simple interest earned on the principal in one year is $4.80.

STEP 2 Multiply the interest earned in one year by 5 to calculate the total interest Victoria will earn over 5 years.

> 4.80 • 5

$4.80 $24

interest

years

0   1   2   3   4   5   6   7   8   9   10

Victoria will earn $24 in interest over 5 years.

☑ Try It!

Victoria has another account at the bank that pays $2\frac{1}{2}$% simple interest. How much interest will she earn in 8 years on an initial deposit of $250 assuming she neither adds to nor withdraws from the account?

$2\frac{1}{2}$% interest expressed as a decimal is [ ].

Interest after 1 year: $s = $ [ ] • $ [ ]

= $ [ ]

Interest after 8 years: $ [ ] • [ ]

= $ [ ]

Victoria will earn $ [ ] in interest over 8 years.

Convince Me! Would the interest for the second year be the same if it were calculated on the total after the first year? Why or why not?

EXAMPLE 2  ACTIVITY ASSESS

EXAMPLE 2 — Find the Percent of Interest

Maya's older sister got a loan to buy a used car for $3,400. What is the interest rate on the loan?

STEP 1 Multiply the interest amount by 12 to find the interest for 1 year.

$$8.50 \cdot 12 = 102$$

STEP 2 Use the percent equation to find the interest rate.

interest amount = **interest rate** · loan amount

$$102 = P \cdot 3{,}400$$
$$\frac{102}{3{,}400} = P \cdot \frac{3{,}400}{3{,}400}$$
$$0.03 = P$$

The simple interest rate is 3% for 1 year.

WE LEND IT!

Borrow **$3,400** for this car today.. and pay only **$8.50** interest

...every month!!!

JIM'S USED CARS   1-555-JIM-CARS

 Try It!

Another company will lend Maya's older sister $4,000. Every month, she will pay $11.88 in interest. What is the interest rate, rounded to the nearest tenth of a percent, for 1 year?

EXAMPLE 3 Find the Principal

Jake opened a savings account that earns 1.5% interest. Jake estimates that, assuming he neither adds to nor withdraws from his account, he will earn $240 in interest after 10 years. How much did Jake deposit when he opened the account?

First, find the amount of interest for 1 year.

$$240 \div 10 = 24$$

Then, use the percent equation to find the initial deposit or principal, d.

interest amount = **interest rate** · initial deposit

$$24 = 0.015 \cdot d$$

$$\frac{24}{0.015} = d \cdot \frac{0.015}{0.015}$$

$$1{,}600 = d$$

Jake deposited $1,600.

> Calculating simple interest is a good way to estimate how much interest Jake will have in the bank after 10 years.

Make Sense and Persevere
How can using an equation help make sense of the problem situation?

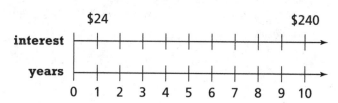

Try It!

Katelyn's older brother borrowed money for school. He took out a loan that charges 6% simple interest. He will end up paying $720 in interest after 6 years. How much did Katelyn's brother borrow for school?

Simple interest represents a proportional relationship between the yearly interest and the principal, or initial amount. The ratio of yearly interest to principal is the interest rate.

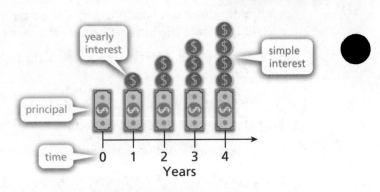

Do You Understand?

1. **? Essential Question** How does simple interest show proportional reasoning and relate to the percent equation?

2. **Reasoning** If the interest earned on an account after 2 years is $15, how much would it be after 10 years? Why?

3. **Be Precise** Angelina is deciding which bank would give her the best simple interest rate on a $300 deposit. One bank says that she will have $320 in her account if she leaves the principal for 2 years. Is this enough information for Angelina to find the interest rate? Explain.

Do You Know How?

4. Find the missing value in each row. Use the percent equation.

Principal (P)	Interest Rate (r)	Time in years (t)	Interest Earned (I)
$100	5%	3	
$500	4%		$20
	10%	7	$35
$200		2	$6

5. Annika's older cousin borrowed $800 to repair her car. She will pay off the loan after 2 years by paying back the principal plus 4.5% simple interest for each year.

   a. How much will she pay in interest? Show your work.

   b. How much will she pay back altogether?

6. J.D. opened a savings account with $425. After 2 years, the total interest he earned was $10.20. What was the annual interest rate?

Name: _____

Practice & Problem Solving

Leveled Practice In 7–8, fill in the boxes to solve.

7. Edward deposited $6,000 into a savings account 4 years ago. The simple interest rate is 3%.

How much money did Edward earn in interest?

Interest = $ [ ] • [ ] • [ ] years

Edward earned $ [ ] in interest.

8. The interest on $2,000 for 2 years is $320. What is the simple interest rate?

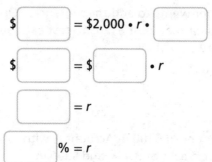

$ [ ] = $2,000 • r • [ ]

$ [ ] = $ [ ] • r

[ ] = r

[ ] % = r

9. Suppose you deposited $100 in a savings account 4 years ago with a simple interest rate of 2.2%. The interest that you earned in those 4 years is $8.80. Which of the following is true? Select all that apply.

☐ The interest rate is 0.022.

☐ The principal was $100.

☐ The interest earned is $4.

☐ The account was opened 8 years and 8 months ago.

10. A new bank customer with $3,000 wants to open a money market account. The bank is offering a simple interest rate of 1.1%.

a. How much interest will the customer earn in 20 years?

b. What will be the account balance after 20 years?

11. Boden's account has a principal of $500 and a simple interest rate of 3.3%. Complete the double number line. How much money will be in the account after 4 years, assuming Boden does not add or take out any money?

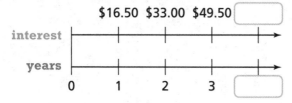

12. Critique Reasoning Monica deposits $100 into a savings account that pays a simple interest rate of 3.4%. Paul deposits $200 into a savings account that pays a simple interest rate of 2.2%. Monica says that she will earn more interest in one year because her interest rate is higher. Do you agree? Justify your response.

13. Construct Argument Tommy earned $76.00 in interest after 5 years on a principal of $400. Jane earned $82.00 in interest after 2 years on a principal of $1,000.

Which bank would you rather use, Tommy's or Jane's? Why?

14. Reasoning A bank manager wants to encourage new customers to open accounts with initial deposits of at least $3,000. He has posters made for the promotion.

EB EAST BANK

Earn

4.8%
(simple interest rate)

on

new deposits of

$3,000
or more.

   a. Under the new promotion, what is the minimum amount of interest a new account would make in one year if there were no withdrawls from the account?

   b. The manager wants to add the sentence, "Open an account with $3,000 and earn at least $120 interest each year!" to the poster. Do you agree? Explain.

---

15. Suppose you deposit $100 in Account A with a simple interest rate of 3.4%, and $300 in Account B with a simple interest rate of 1.8%. One year later, you get a bank statement that shows the interest for Account A is $3.40 and the interest for Account B is $540.00.

   a. Which account statement is incorrect?

   b. What may have been the bank's error?

16. Higher Order Thinking You have two different savings accounts. For Account A, the interest earned after 18 months is $12.00. For Account B, the interest earned after 27 months is $27.00.

   a. If the interest rate is 3.2% for Account A, how much is the principal?

   b. If the interest rate is 2.4% for Account B, how much is the principal?

   c. Which account earned you the most interest in the first year? Explain.

✔ Assessment Practice

17. A certificate of deposit with principal $150 earns 4% annual interest for 2 years.

Select all the options that would earn the same amount of interest.

☐ $300 at 2% for 2 years

☐ $150 at 6% for 18 months

☐ $400 at 3% for 1 year

☐ $100 at 1% for 8 years

☐ $50 at 48% for 6 months

18. Dakota earned $15.75 in interest in Account A and $28.00 in interest in Account B after 21 months. If the simple interest rate is for 3.0% for Account A and 4.0% for Account B, which account had the greater principal? Explain.

? Topic Essential Question

How can percents show proportional relationships between quantities and be used to solve problems?

Vocabulary Review

Complete each definition and then provide an example of each word.

| Vocabulary | markdown | markup | percent change |
| | principal | simple interest | |

Definition	Example
1. The [　　　　] is the decrease from the original price of an item to its sale price.	
2. The accuracy of a measured or estimated value compared to its actual value is described as the [　　　　].	
3. An initial amount of money that is deposited in an account is called the [　　　　].	
4. The [　　　　] describes how much a quantity has changed relative to its original amount.	

Use Vocabulary in Writing

Birute deposits $500 in a savings account with a simple interest rate of 1.3%. How could you use this information to find the interest she would earn in 4 years and determine the percent change in her savings account?

Concepts and Skills Review

LESSON 4-1 **Analyze Percents of Numbers**

Quick Review

You can use equivalent ratios to find the percent of a number. Remember that a percent is a ratio that relates a number to 100.

Example

Find 57% of 690.

$$\frac{57}{100} = \frac{x}{690}$$

$$\frac{57}{100} \cdot 690 = \frac{x}{690} \cdot 690$$

$$393.3 = x$$

Practice

1. Find 0.8% of 1,046.

2. Find 160% of 98.

3. A company charges a shipping fee that is 4.5% of the purchase price for all items it ships. What is the fee to ship an item that costs $56?

LESSON 4-2 **Connect Percent and Proportion**

Quick Review

You can use proportions to solve different types of percent problems. There are three values in a percent problem—the percent, the part, and the whole. If you know two of these values, you can set up a proportion to find the third value.

Example

What percent of 19 is 4.75?

The whole is 19 and the part is 4.75. Write a proportion, and solve for the percent, p.

$$\frac{\text{part}}{\text{whole}} = \frac{p}{100}$$

$$\frac{4.75}{19} = \frac{p}{100}$$

$$\frac{4.75}{19} \cdot 100 = \frac{p}{100} \cdot 100$$

$$25 = p$$

So, 4.75 is 25% of 19.

Practice

1. 24.94 is 29% of what number?

2. On Thursday, a restaurant serves iced tea to 35 of its 140 customers. What percent of the customers order iced tea?

3. Liam puts $40 in savings in March and 175% of this amount in savings in April. How much does Liam put in savings in April?

Represent and Use the Percent Equation

Quick Review

You can use the percent equation to solve percent problems.

$$\text{part} = \text{percent} \cdot \text{whole}$$

Substitute two of the three values to solve for the unknown value.

Example

Michael earns a 6% commission on each house he sells. If he sells a house for $180,000, how much does he earn in commission, c?

$c = 0.06 \cdot 180{,}000$

$c = 10{,}800$

Michael earns $10,800 in commission.

Practice

1. Sharon paid $78 sales tax on a new camera. If the sales tax rate is 6.5%, what was the cost of the camera?

2. There are 45 students who play a woodwind instrument in the school band. Of these, 18 play the saxophone. What percent of these students play the saxophone?

Solve Percent Change and Percent Error Problems

Quick Review

A percent change can be an increase or a decrease. You can use an equation to find a percent change.

$$\text{change} = \text{percent change} \cdot \text{original amount}$$

A percent error is always a nonnegative value. You can use an equation to find a percent error.

$$\text{difference} = \text{percent error} \cdot \text{actual}$$

Example

Juan's puppy weighed 16 pounds at the age of 2 months. The puppy weighed 60 pounds at the age of 8 months. What is the percent change in the puppy's weight?

change in pounds $= 60 - 16 = 44$

$44 = P \cdot 16$

$\dfrac{44}{16} = P$

$2.75 = P$

The puppy's weight increased by 275%.

Practice

1. In 2014, the attendance at Jefferson School's Fall Festival was 650. In 2015, the attendance was 575. What was the percent change in attendance from 2014 to 2015?

Round to the nearest whole percent.

2. Melissa estimated that she would read 250 pages last week. She read 290 pages. What is the percent error of Melissa's estimate? Round to the nearest whole percent.

LESSON 4-5 Solve Markup and Markdown Problems

Quick Review

You can use the percent equation to solve markup and markdown problems.

markup = **percent markup** • cost
markdown = **percent markdown** • selling price

Example

Bree buys a purse for $90. She sells it at her store for $135. What is the percent markup on the purse?

markup = $135 − $90 = $45

$45 = P \cdot 90$

$\dfrac{45}{90} = P$

$0.5 = P$ ◄ The decimal 0.5 is equivalent to 50%.

The percent markup on the purse is 50%.

Practice

1. Hank buys a used car for $7,200 and plans to sell it on his used car lot. What is the price of the car after a markup of 15%?

2. Nya wants to buy a sweater that had an original price of $55. The sweater is now discounted 20% and the sales tax rate is 5.5%. How much will Nya pay for the sweater?

LESSON 4-6 Solve Simple Interest Problems

Quick Review

You consider four quantities when solving problems involving simple interest.

initial amount, or principal, **p**

interest rate, **r**

time, t

amount of simple interest, I

Example

Yuni loaned $400 to her brother. He will repay the loan by paying 2.5% simple interest for 3 years. How much will he pay in interest?

$I = 400 \cdot 0.025 \cdot 3 = \$30$

He will pay $30 in interest.

Practice

1. Ethan put $700 into a Certificate of Deposit (CD) account that earns 1.8% interest each year. What will the interest of the CD account be after 6 years?

2. Kelly opened a bank account that earns 1.2% simple interest each year. After 7 years, Kelly will earn $126 in interest. How much did Kelly deposit when she opened the account?

Riddle Rearranging

Find the value of *x* in each unit rate. Then arrange the answers in order from least to greatest. The letters will spell out the answer to the riddle below.

I can...
find unit rates with ratios of fractions. © 7.RP.A.1

K
$$\frac{\frac{3}{4}\,c}{\frac{1}{3}\,h} = \frac{x\,c}{1\,h}$$

N
$$\frac{\frac{3}{5}\,mL}{\frac{2}{5}\,min} = \frac{x\,mL}{1\,min}$$

A
$$\frac{\frac{1}{4}\,mi}{\frac{5}{8}\,h} = \frac{x\,mi}{1\,h}$$

I
$$\frac{\frac{1}{4}\,ft}{\frac{3}{4}\,h} = \frac{x\,ft}{1\,h}$$

E
$$\frac{\frac{6}{5}\,m}{\frac{1}{2}\,s} = \frac{x\,m}{1\,s}$$

Y
$$\frac{\frac{5}{6}\,pt}{\frac{1}{3}\,min} = \frac{x\,pt}{1\,min}$$

S
$$\frac{\frac{1}{4}\,in.}{\frac{1}{12}\,min} = \frac{x\,in.}{1\,min}$$

O
$$\frac{\frac{5}{3}\,pt}{\frac{5}{6}\,h} = \frac{x\,pt}{1\,h}$$

P
$$\frac{\frac{3}{10}\,mm}{\frac{6}{5}\,s} = \frac{x\,mm}{1\,s}$$

What keys cannot be put in a lock?

◯ ◯ ◯ ◯ ◯   ◯ ◯ ◯ ◯

GENERATE EQUIVALENT EXPRESSIONS

How can properties of operations help to generate equivalent expressions that can be used in solving problems?

Topic Overview

Lesson Digital Resources

INTERACTIVE STUDENT EDITION
Access online or offline.

VISUAL LEARNING ANIMATION
Interact with visual learning animations.

ACTIVITY Use with *Solve & Discuss It*, *Explore It*, and *Explain It* activities, and to explore Examples.

VIDEOS Watch clips to support *3-Act Mathematical Modeling Lessons* and *STEM Projects*.

Go online

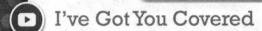

I've Got You Covered

▶ **I've Got You Covered**

Did you know that DIY stands for Do It Yourself? Do-it-yourself projects are a fun way to save money, learn new skills, and make your home unique.

From painting furniture to turning an old T-shirt into a pillow, there are plenty of projects for everyone.

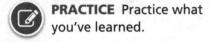 **PRACTICE** Practice what you've learned.

KEY CONCEPT Review important lesson content.

 TUTORIALS Get help from *Virtual Nerd*, right when you need it.

A-Z **GLOSSARY** Read and listen to English/Spanish definitions.

 MATH TOOLS Explore math with digital tools.

ASSESSMENT Show what you've learned.

 GAMES Play Math Games to help you learn.

ënVision® STEM Project

Did You Know?

In 2013, just over 30% of American consumers knew about activity trackers. By 2015, about **82%** recognized them.

 % of people aware of activity trackers

2013
30%

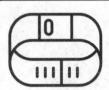 About **3.3 million** fitness bands and activity trackers were sold in the U.S. between April 2013 and March 2014.

2015
82%

The fitness tracker industry is expected to almost **triple in value** between 2014 and 2019.

$ $ $
$ $
2014 **2019**

Continued research and development leads to technological advances and breakthroughs, such as the use of biosensing apparel to track activity.

Your Task: Analyze Activity Tracker Data ▶

The ways that data are communicated and presented to the user are just as important as the types of data collected. You and your classmates will continue your exploration of activity trackers and use data to develop models based on individual fitness goals.

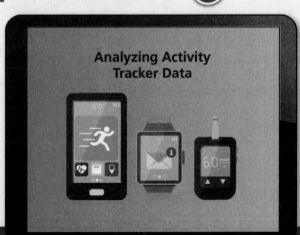

Analyzing Activity Tracker Data

Review What You Know!

Vocabulary

Choose the best term from the box to complete each definition.

evaluate
expression
factor
order of operations
substitute
term

1. When you _____ an expression, you replace each variable with a given value.

2. To evaluate $a + 3$ when $a = 7$, you can _____ 7 for a in the expression.

3. The set of rules used to determine the order in which operations are performed is called the _____.

4. Each part of an expression that is separated by a plus or minus sign is a(n) _____.

5. A(n) _____ is a mathematical phrase that can contain numbers, variables, and operation symbols.

6. When two numbers are multiplied to get a product, each number is called a(n) _____.

Order of Operations

Evaluate each expression using the order of operations.

7. $3(18 - 7) + 2$

8. $(13 + 2) \div (9 - 4)$

9. $24 \div 4 \cdot 2 - 2$

Equivalent Expressions

Evaluate each expression when $a = -4$ and $b = 3$.

10. ab

11. $2a + 3b$

12. $2(a - b)$

13. Explain the difference between evaluating $3 \cdot 7 - 4 \div 2$ and evaluating $3(7 - 4) \div 2$.

Language Development

Complete each math statement using the word bank.

addition	expand	reorder
coefficient	factors	subtraction
combine like terms	group	value
constant	multiplication	variable
division	properties of operations	

To evaluate an algebraic expression, substitute a [___] for the variable in the expression.

In the algebraic expression $3(x - 2)$, 3 and $x - 2$ are [___].

To generate equivalent expressions, you can use the [___].

In the expression $4x + 2x - 6y$, you first need to [___].

You can use the Distributive Property to [___] the algebraic expression $5(x - 7)$.

In the algebraic expression, $6x + 10$, x is the [___], 6 is the [___], and 10 is the [___].

Four words that describe operations that can be used with expressions are [___], [___], [___], and [___].

In the algebraic expression $5x + 4 + 6x - 3$, you use the Commutative Property to [___] like terms next to each other and the Associative Property to [___] like terms together.

PROJECT 5A

Which emojis would you use to tell the story of your day so far?

PROJECT: WRITE AND ILLUSTRATE A CHILDREN'S BOOK

PROJECT 5B

How many different ways can you represent a dollar?

PROJECT: GENERATE EQUIVALENCE

PROJECT 5C

If you wrote a song, what would it sound like?

PROJECT: COMPOSE A SONG

PROJECT 5D

What was your favorite structure at a playground when you were younger?

PROJECT: BUILD A MODEL PLAYGROUND

Solve & Discuss It! 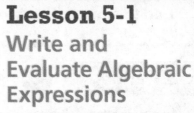 ACTIVITY

Mr. Ramirez's class was playing a game in which students
need to match sticky notes that have equivalent expressions.

How can you sort the expressions into groups?

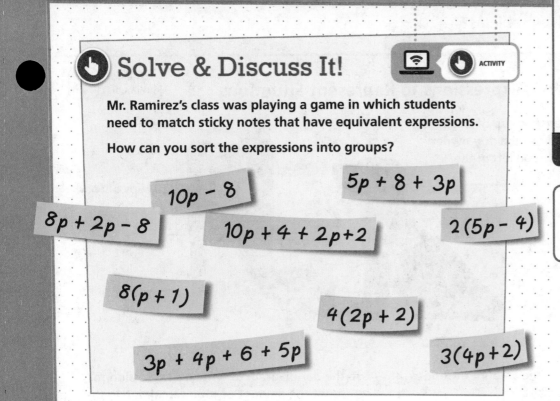

$10p - 8$

$5p + 8 + 3p$

$8p + 2p - 8$

$10p + 4 + 2p + 2$

$2(5p - 4)$

$8(p + 1)$

$4(2p + 2)$

$3p + 4p + 6 + 5p$

$3(4p + 2)$

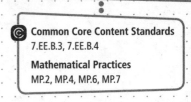

I can...
write and evaluate algebraic
expressions.

Ⓒ **Common Core Content Standards**
7.EE.B.3, 7.EE.B.4

Mathematical Practices
MP.2, MP.4, MP.6, MP.7

Focus on math practices

Reasoning Is there more than one way to group the expressions?
Give an example.

? Essential Question How can algebraic expressions be used to represent and solve problems?

 EXAMPLE 1 **Write Expressions to Represent Situations**

Scan for Multimedia

An automatic dog feeder dispenses $\frac{2}{5}$ cup of dog food each day. What expression can the dog owner use to determine the amount of food left in the feeder after d days?

Model with Math How can a bar diagram represent the situation?

20 cups of food

$\frac{2}{5}$ cup each day

Draw a bar diagram to represent the amount of food remaining in the feeder after d days.

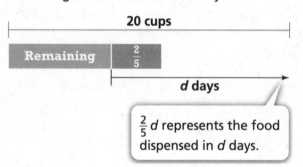

20 cups

| Remaining | $\frac{2}{5}$ |

d days

$\frac{2}{5}d$ represents the food dispensed in d days.

Use the bar diagram to write an expression to represent the amount of food remaining in the feeder after d days.

$20 - \frac{2}{5}d$

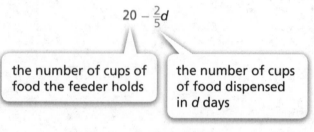

the number of cups of food the feeder holds

the number of cups of food dispensed in d days

The dog owner can use the expression $20 - \frac{2}{5}d$ to determine the amount of food left in the feeder after d days.

☑ Try It!

Misumi started with $217 in her bank account. She deposits $25.50 each week and never withdraws any money. What expression can Misumi use to determine her account balance after w weeks?

☐ + ☐ w

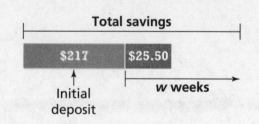

Total savings

| $217 | $25.50 |

Initial deposit

w weeks

Convince Me! How did you determine which value to use for the constant and which value to use for the coefficient?

EXAMPLE **2** **Evaluate Expressions**

The expression 9.99*d* + 12.99*c* can be used to find the total cost of *d* pounds of almonds and *c* pounds of cashews. How much does it cost to buy $1\frac{1}{2}$ pounds of almonds and $2\frac{1}{2}$ pounds of cashews?

Almonds
$9.99/lb

Cashews
$12.99/lb

Evaluate the expression for the given values.

Total cost of almonds

Total cost of cashews

$9.99d + 12.99c$

$= 9.99\left(1\frac{1}{2}\right) + 12.99\left(2\frac{1}{2}\right)$

$= 14.985 + 32.475$

$= 47.46$

It costs $47.46 to buy $1\frac{1}{2}$ pounds of almonds and $2\frac{1}{2}$ pounds of cashews.

Try It!

The cost to rent a scooter is $15.50 per hour and the cost to rent a watercraft is $22.80 per hour. Use the expression $15.5s + 22.8w$ to determine how much it would cost to rent a scooter for $3\frac{1}{2}$ hours and a watercraft for $1\frac{3}{4}$ hours.

EXAMPLE **3** **Write and Evaluate Expressions**

Malik and two friends earn *m* dollars in one week doing odd jobs. They split the earnings so that each friend gets $\frac{1}{3}$ of the total earnings. Malik uses $32.50 of his earnings on lunch each week. Last week, the three friends earned $963. How much money did Malik have left after paying for lunch?

Write an expression to represent how much Malik has left. Then evaluate the expression for the given value.

$\frac{1}{3}m - 32.5$

$= \frac{1}{3}(963) - 32.5$

$= 288.5$

Malik had $288.50 left after paying for lunch.

Try It!

Emelia earns $8.74 per hour plus a gas allowance of $3.50 per day at her job. How much does Emelia's job pay in a day when she works $5\frac{1}{2}$ hours? Write an expression and evaluate for $5\frac{1}{2}$ hours.

Algebraic expressions can be used to represent problems with unknown or variable values.

Values can be substituted for variables to evaluate the expression.

Do You Understand?

1. **? Essential Question** How are algebraic expressions used to represent and solve problems?

2. **Use Structure** How is a constant term different than a variable term for an expression that represents a real-world situation?

3. **Look for Relationships** Explain why you can have different values when evaluating an algebraic expression.

Do You Know How?

4. A tank containing 35 gallons of water is leaking at a rate of $\frac{1}{4}$ gallon per minute. Write an expression to determine the number of gallons left in the tank after m minutes.

5. Write an algebraic expression that Marshall can use to determine the total cost of buying a watermelon that weighs w pounds and some tomatoes that weigh t pounds. How much will it cost to buy a watermelon that weighs $18\frac{1}{2}$ pounds and 5 pounds of tomatoes?

6. What is the value of $\frac{3}{8}x - 4.5$ when $x = 0.4$?

7. What is the value of $8.4n - 3.2p$ when $n = 2$ and $p = 4$?

Practice & Problem Solving

Scan for
Multimedia

Leveled Practice For **8–10**, fill in the boxes to complete the problems.

8. Evaluate $10.2x + 9.4y$ when $x = 2$ and $y = 3$.

$10.2(\boxed{}) + 9.4(\boxed{})$

$= \boxed{} + 28.2$

$= \boxed{}$

9. Evaluate $\frac{1}{2}t + \frac{3}{8}$ when $t = \frac{1}{4}$.

$\frac{1}{2}(\boxed{}) + \frac{3}{8}$

$= \boxed{} + \frac{3}{8}$

$= \boxed{}$

10. Write an expression that represents the height of a tree that began at 6 feet and increases by 2 feet per year. Let y represent the number of years.

$\boxed{} + \boxed{}\,y$

For **11–14**, evaluate each expression for the given value of the variable(s).

11. $3d - 4$

$d = 1.2$

12. $0.5f - 2.3g$

$f = 12, g = 2$

13. $\frac{2}{3}p + 3$

$p = \frac{3}{5}$

14. $34 + \frac{4}{9}w$

$w = -\frac{1}{2}$

15. Model with Math What expression can be used to determine the total cost of buying g pounds of granola for $3.25 per pound and f pounds of flour for $0.74 per pound?

16. Model with Math Which expression can be used to determine the total weight of a box that by itself weighs 0.2 kilogram and contains p plaques that weigh 1.3 kilograms each?

Ⓐ $1.3p + 0.2$

Ⓑ $0.2p + 1.3$

Ⓒ $0.2 - 1.3p$

Ⓓ $1.2p$

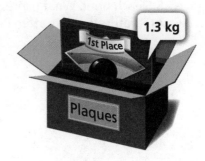

17. The expression $-120 + 13m$ represents a submarine that began at a depth of 120 feet below sea level and ascended at a rate of 13 feet per minute. What was the depth of the submarine after 6 minutes?

18. Be Precise A full grain silo empties at a constant rate. Write an expression to determine the amount of grain left after s seconds.

Capacity 3000 ft³

Rate: 3.5 ft³/s

19. Higher Order Thinking For the expression $5 - 5x$ to have a negative value, what must be true about the value of x?

☑ Assessment Practice

20. Joe bought g gallons of gasoline for $2.85 per gallon and c cans of oil for $3.15 per can.

PART A

What expression can be used to determine the total amount Joe spent on gasoline and oil?

PART B

Joe spent $15. He bought 2 cans of oil. About how many gallons of gasoline did he buy?

Ⓐ 2.5

Ⓑ 3

Ⓒ 3.5

Ⓓ 4

21. The outside temperature was 73°F at 1 P.M. and decreases at a rate of 1.5°F each hour. What expression can be used to determine the temperature h hours after 1 P.M.?

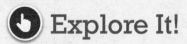 **Explore It!**

 ACTIVITY

A shipment of eggs contains some cartons with a dozen eggs and some cartons with a half-dozen eggs.

I can...
write equivalent expressions for given expressions.

© **Common Core Content Standards**
7.EE.A.1

Mathematical Practices
MP.1, MP.2, MP.3

A. How can you represent the total number of eggs in the shipment using diagrams or images? Explain your diagram.

B. How can you represent the total number of eggs in the shipment using expressions? What variables do you use? What do they represent?

Focus on math practices

Construct Arguments How do the two representations compare? How are they different?

EXAMPLE 1 **Use Properties of Operations to Write Equivalent Expressions**

Scan for Multimedia

The student council has spent $300 on the supplies needed to sponsor a dance concert fundraiser. Three council members wrote the following expressions to represent the total amount raised for *t* tickets sold. Can they all be correct? Explain.

$6t - 300$ $6(t - 50)$ $-300 + 6t$

> **Reasoning** How can you use the properties of operations to determine whether the expressions are equivalent?

STEP 1 Verify that one of the expressions represents the amount raised for *t* tickets sold.

$6t - 300$ — The cost of supplies

The amount made selling tickets

STEP 2 Use properties of operations to write equivalent expressions.

$6(t - 50)$
$= 6 \cdot t - 6 \cdot 50$ — Use the Distributive Property.
$= 6t - 300$

$-300 + 6t$
$= 6t + (-300)$ — Use the Commutative Property.
$= 6t - 300$

The council members wrote equivalent expressions. They are all correct.

 Try It!

Nancy wrote the expression $3x - 12$ to represent the relationship in a table of values. Use properties of operations to write two equivalent expressions.

$3(x - \boxed{})$

$\boxed{} + 3x$

Convince Me! What property can you use to write an equivalent expression for $-5(x - 2)$? Explain.

Write equivalent expressions by combining like terms.

a. $-5x + 2y + 3x$

$\underbrace{-5x + 3x} + 2y$ ← Use the Commutative Property.

$(-5 + 3)x + 2y$ ← Use the Distributive Property.

$-2x + 2y$

b. $\frac{1}{3}x + \left(\frac{1}{6}x + y\right)$

$\left(\frac{1}{3}x + \frac{1}{6}x\right) + y$ ← Use the Associative Property.

$\frac{3}{6}x + y$

> **Look for Relationships**
> How can you check whether the expressions are equivalent?

 Try It!

Use properties of operations to write two expressions that are equivalent to $\frac{3}{4}n + \left(8 + \frac{1}{3}z\right)$.

EXAMPLE 3 **Identify Equivalent Expressions**

Which of the expressions below are equivalent to $-\frac{2}{3}x - 2$?

$-\frac{2}{3}x + (-2)$

$= -\frac{2}{3}x - 2$ ← Subtract the additive inverse.

The expression is equivalent to $-\frac{2}{3}x - 2$.

$2 - \frac{2}{3}x$

$= -\frac{2}{3}x + 2$ ← Use the Commutative Property.

The expression is NOT equivalent to $-\frac{2}{3}x - 2$.

$-x + \left(\frac{1}{3}x + (-2)\right)$

$\left(-x + \frac{1}{3}x\right) + (-2)$ ← Use the Associative Property.

$-\frac{2}{3}x + (-2)$

The expression is equivalent to $-\frac{2}{3}x - 2$.

 Try It!

Write two expressions that are equivalent to $-\frac{5}{4}x - \frac{3}{4}$.

You can use properties of operations to write equivalent expressions.

$$-\frac{1}{2}(x + 8)$$

$$= -\frac{1}{2}x + \left(-\frac{1}{2}\right) \cdot 8$$ ◄ Use the Distributive Property.

$$= -\frac{1}{2}x + (-4)$$

$$= -4 + \left(-\frac{1}{2}x\right)$$ ◄ Use the Commutative Property.

The expressions $-\frac{1}{2}(x + 8)$, $-\frac{1}{2}x + (-4)$, and $-4 + \left(-\frac{1}{2}x\right)$ are equivalent.

Do You Understand?

1. **Essential Question** What are equivalent expressions?

2. **Make Sense and Persevere** For which operations is the Commutative Property true?

3. How can the Associative Property be applied when writing equivalent expressions with variables?

Do You Know How?

4. Write an expression equivalent to $-3 + \frac{2}{3}y - 4 - \frac{1}{3}y$.

5. Complete the tables to determine if the expressions are equivalent. If the expressions are equivalent, name the property or properties that make them equivalent.

$3(x - 5)$

x	Value of Expression
1	
2	
3	

$3x - 15$

x	Value of Expression
1	
2	
3	

6. Use the properties of operations to write an expression equivalent to $4x + \frac{1}{2} + 2x - 3$.

Name: _____

Practice & Problem Solving

Scan for Multimedia

For 7–9, write an equivalent expression.

7. $-3(7 + 5g)$

8. $(x + 7) + 3y$

9. $\frac{2}{9} - \frac{1}{5} \cdot x$

10. Which expression is equivalent to $t + 4 + 3 - 2t$?

   Ⓐ $t + 7$

   Ⓑ $-t + 7$

   Ⓒ $6t$

   Ⓓ $10t$

11. The distance in feet that Karina swims in a race is represented by $4d - 4$, where d is the distance for each lap. What is an expression equivalent to $4d - 4$?

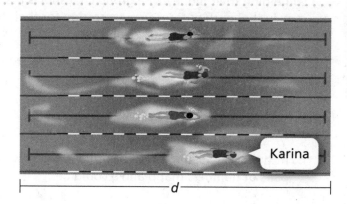

12. Use the Associative Property to write an expression equivalent to $(w + 9) + 3$.

13. Nigel is planning his training schedule for a marathon over a 4-day period. He is uncertain how many miles he will run on two days. One expression for the total miles he will run is $12 + y + 17 + z$.

Use the Commutative Property to write an equivalent expression.

Marathon Training Plan

Day	Miles to Run
1	12
2	y
3	17
4	z

14. Maria said the expression $-4n + 3 + 9n - 4$ is equivalent to $4n$. What error did Maria likely make?

15. Write an expression equivalent to $x - 3y + 4$.

16. Andre wrote the expression $-2 + 4x \div 3$ to represent the relationship shown in the table.

Write two other expressions that also represent the relationship shown in the table.

x	Value of Expression
0	−2
6	6
12	14

17. Higher Order Thinking To rent a car for a trip, four friends are combining their money. The group chat shows the amount of money that each puts in. One expression for their total amount of money is 189 plus p plus 224 plus q.

a. Use the Commutative Property to write two equivalent expressions.

Group MMS

Travel Fund?

I've got $189.

Not sure amount yet.

I've got $224.

Get back to you!

$p

$q

b. If they need $500 to rent a car, find at least two different pairs of numbers that p and q could be.

✓ **Assessment Practice**

18. Select all expressions equivalent to $\frac{3}{5}x + 3$.

☐ $\frac{2}{5}x + 3\frac{1}{5}x$

☐ $\frac{4}{5}x - \frac{1}{5}x + 3$

☐ $\frac{2}{5}x + 3\frac{3}{5}x - 1$

☐ $1 + \frac{3}{5}x + 2$

☐ $1 + \frac{x}{5} + 2$

☐ $1 + \frac{2}{5}x + 3$

Solve & Discuss It! ACTIVITY

How can the tiles below be sorted?

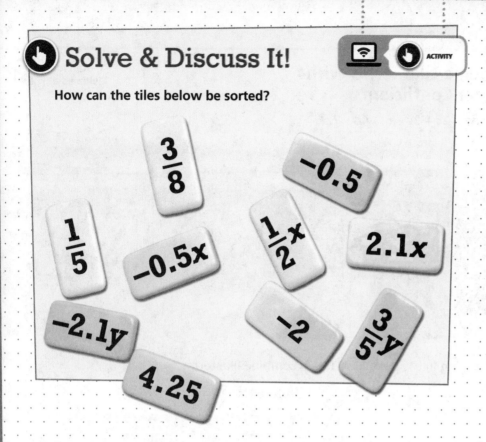

I can...
use properties of operations to simplify expressions.

© **Common Core Content Standards**
7.EE.A.1

Mathematical Practices
MP.1, MP.2, MP.3, MP.7

Focus on math practices

Reasoning Would sorting the tiles with positive coefficients together and tiles with negative coefficients together help to simplify an expression that involves all the tiles? Explain.

Essential Question How are properties of operations used to simplify expressions?

VISUAL LEARNING

ASSESS

EXAMPLE 1 Combine Like Terms with Integer Coefficients

Scan for Multimedia

A teacher used algebra tiles to model $-2c + 3c - 5 - 4c + 7$.

Simplify the expression.

STEP 1 Write the expression by grouping like terms together.

> Use the Commutative and Associative Properties to reorder and group like terms.

$-2c + 3c - 5 - 4c + 7$

$= -2c + 3c - 4c - 5 + 7$

$= -2c - 4c + 3c - 5 + 7$

$= (-2c - 4c + 3c) + (-5 + 7)$

STEP 2 Combine like terms.

$$(-2c - 4c + 3c) + (-5 + 7)$$

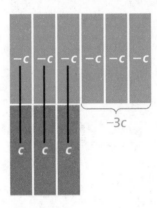

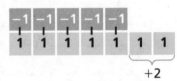

Use Structure Why can you not combine unlike terms?

The simplified expression is $-3c + 2$.

 **Try It!**

Simplify the expression $-6 - 6f + 7 - 3f - 9$.

☐ $- 3f -$ ☐ $+ 7 -$ ☐

☐ $-$ ☐

Convince Me! How do you decide in what way to reorder the terms of an expression when simplifying it?

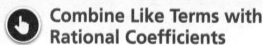 

EXAMPLE 2 — Combine Like Terms with Rational Coefficients

Simplify the expression $-3 + \frac{1}{3}x + (-4.5) - \frac{1}{5}x$.

$$-3 + \frac{1}{3}x + (-4.5) - \frac{1}{5}x$$

$$= \left(\frac{1}{3}x - \frac{1}{5}x\right) + (-3 + (-4.5))$$

> Use the Commutative and Associative Properties to reorder and group like terms.

> **Use Structure** Include the signs of terms when reordering the terms.

$$= \left(\frac{5}{15}x - \frac{3}{15}x\right) + (-3 + (-4.5))$$

$$= \frac{2}{15}x + (-7.5)$$

> Combine like terms.

The simplified expression is $\frac{2}{15}x - 7.5$.

☑ Try It!

Simplify each expression.

a. $59.95m - 30 + 7.95m + 45 + 9.49m$

b. $-0.5p + \frac{1}{2}p - 2.75 + \frac{2}{3}p$

EXAMPLE 3 Combine Like Terms with Two Variables

Simplify the expression $4a - 5b - 6 + 2b - 3a$.

$$4a - 5b - 6 + 2b - 3a$$

$$= (4a - 3a) + (-5b + 2b) - 6$$

> Use the Commutative and Associative Properties to reorder and group like terms.

$$= 1a - 3b - 6$$

The simplified expression is $a - 3b - 6$.

☑ Try It!

Simplify the expression $-3.7 + 5g + 4k + 11.1 - 10g$.

$$\left(\boxed{} - 10g\right) + 4k + \left(\boxed{} + 11.1\right)$$

$$= \boxed{} + 4k + \boxed{}$$

The simplified expression is $\boxed{}$.

When simplifying algebraic expressions, use properties of operations to combine like terms.

To simplify the expression below, group like terms.

$\frac{3}{10}y - 3.5x - \frac{3}{8} + 0.53x + 5.25 - 2.75y - 12$

$(-3.5x + 0.53x) + \left(\frac{3}{10}y - 2.75y\right) + \left(-\frac{3}{8} + 5.25 - 12\right)$

Then combine like terms.

$-2.97x - 2.45y - 7.125$

Do You Understand?

1. **? Essential Question** How are properties of operations used to simplify expressions?

2. **Make Sense and Persevere** Explain why constant terms expressed as different rational number types can be combined.

3. **Reasoning** How do you know when an expression is in its simplest form?

Do You Know How?

4. Simplify $-4b + (-9k) - 6 - 3b + 12$.

5. Simplify $-2 + 6.45z - 6 + (-3.25z)$.

6. Simplify $-9 + \left(-\frac{1}{3}y\right) + 6 - \frac{4}{3}y$.

Name: _____

Practice & Problem Solving

Scan for Multimedia

In 7–10, simplify each expression.

7. $-2.8f + 0.9f - 12 - 4$

8. $3.2 - 5.1n - 3n + 5$

9. $2n + 5.5 - 0.9n - 8 + 4.5p$

10. $12 + (-4) - \frac{2}{5}j - \frac{4}{5}j + 5$

---

11. Which expression is equivalent to $-5v + (-2) + 1 + (-2v)$?

Ⓐ $-9v$

Ⓑ $-4v$

Ⓒ $-7v - 1$

Ⓓ $-7v + 3$

12. Which expression is equivalent to $\frac{2}{3}x + (-3) + (-2) - \frac{1}{3}x$?

Ⓐ $x + 5$

Ⓑ $-\frac{1}{3}x - 5$

Ⓒ $\frac{1}{3}x - 1$

Ⓓ $\frac{1}{3}x - 5$

---

13. The dimensions of a garden are shown. Write an expression to find the perimeter.

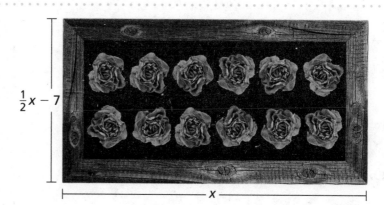

$\frac{1}{2}x - 7$

x

14. Simplify the expression $8h + (-7.3d) - 14 + 5d - 3.2h$.

15. Simply $4 - 2y + (-8y) + 6.2$.

16. Simplify $\frac{4}{9}z - \frac{3}{9}z + 5 - \frac{5}{9}z - 8$.

17. Construct Arguments Explain whether $11t - 4t$ is equivalent to $4t - 11t$. Support your answer by evaluating the expression for $t = 2$.

18. The signs show the costs of different games at a math festival. How much would it cost n people to play Decimal Decisions and Ratio Rage?

M A T H F E S T

PROBABILITY POSSIBILITIES
Cost ($) of 1 Game: $5.5n - 3$

DECIMAL DECISIONS
Cost ($) of 1 Game: $12.70 - n + 9$

RATIO RAGE!
Cost ($) of 1 Game: $\frac{n}{4}$

19. Higher Order Thinking In the expression $ax + bx$, a is a decimal and b is a fraction. How do you decide whether to write a as a fraction or b as a decimal?

✓ Assessment Practice

20. Select all expressions equivalent to $-6z + (-5.5) + 3.5z + 5y - 2.5$.

☐ $-8 + 5y + 2.5z$

☐ $-2.5z + 5y - 8$

☐ $-8 + 5y + (-2.5z)$

☐ $2.5y + (-2.5z) - 5.5$

☐ $5y - 8 - 2.5z$

Solve & Discuss It!

The school is planning to add a weight room to the gym. If the total area of the gym and weight room should stay under 5,500 square feet, what is one possible length for the new weight room? Show your work. Are there other lengths that would work? Why or why not?

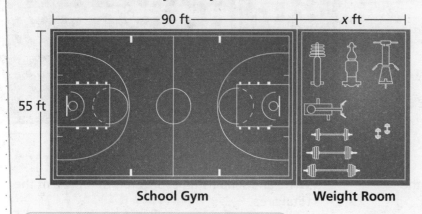

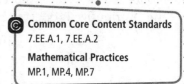

90 ft ——— x ft

55 ft

School Gym   **Weight Room**

Look for Relationships What is the relationship between the areas of the gym and weight room?

I can...
expand expressions using the Distributive Property.

Ⓒ **Common Core Content Standards**
7.EE.A.1, 7.EE.A.2

Mathematical Practices
MP.1, MP.4, MP.7

Focus on math practices

Model with Math What is an expression using x that represents the total area of the gym and the weight room?

295

? Essential Question How does the value of an expression change when it is expanded?

EXAMPLE 1 **Expand Expressions Using the Distributive Property**

Scan for Multimedia

A family farm plans to add a blueberry patch to the end of their apple orchard. What is the total area of land that will be covered by the blueberry patch and apple orchard?

Model with Math An area model can be used to represent the Distributive Property.

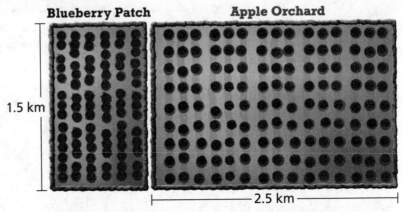

Blueberry Patch   Apple Orchard

1.5 km

2.5 km

Use a diagram to represent the areas of the blueberry patch and apple orchard.

You can add the two lengths and multiply by the width to find the total area.

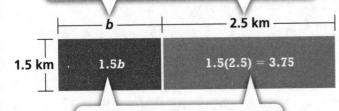

You can also add the two areas to find the total area.

Write and simplify an expression to represent the total area.

$1.5(b + 2.5)$

Use the Distributive Property to expand the expression. Multiply each term inside the parentheses by 1.5.

$= 1.5b + 1.5(2.5)$

$= 1.5b + 3.75$

The expression that represents the total land area is $1.5b + 3.75$.

☑ **Try It!**

What is the expanded form of the expression $3.6(t + 5)$?

$3.6(t + 5)$

$= \boxed{}\, t + \boxed{} \cdot 5$

$= \boxed{} + \boxed{}$

The expanded expression is $\boxed{}$.

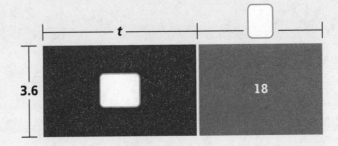

Convince Me! If you know the value of t, would the evaluated expression be different if you added the known value of t and 5 and then multiplied by 3.6? Explain.

EXAMPLE 2 Expand Expressions with a Variable ACTIVITY ASSESS

Use the Distributive Property to expand the expression $x(-2 - 0.5y)$.

$x(-2 - 0.5y)$

$= (x)(-2) + (x)(-0.5y)$ Distribute the x to both terms inside the parentheses.

$= -2x + (-0.5xy)$

$= -2x - 0.5xy$

The expanded expression is $-2x - 0.5xy$.

 Try It!

Expand the expression $t(-1.2w + 3)$.

EXAMPLE 3 **Expand More Complex Expressions**

Simplify the expression $-\frac{1}{3}(2 - 3x + 3)$.

ONE WAY Use the Distributive Property first to distribute the coefficient $-\frac{1}{3}$.

$-\frac{1}{3}(2 - 3x + 3)$

$= \left(-\frac{1}{3} \cdot 2\right) + \left(-\frac{1}{3} \cdot -3x\right) + \left(-\frac{1}{3} \cdot 3\right)$

$= -\frac{2}{3} + x - 1$

$= -\frac{5}{3} + x$

The simplified expression is $-\frac{5}{3} + x$.

ANOTHER WAY Simplify within parentheses first. Then distribute the coefficient $-\frac{1}{3}$.

$-\frac{1}{3}(2 - 3x + 3)$

$= -\frac{1}{3}(5 - 3x)$

$= \left(-\frac{1}{3} \cdot 5\right) + \left(-\frac{1}{3} \cdot -3x\right)$

$= -\frac{5}{3} + x$

The simplified expression is $-\frac{5}{3} + x$.

 Try It!

Simplify the expression $-\frac{2}{5}(10 + 15m - 20n)$.

You can expand an expression using the Distributive Property.

> Multiply, or distribute, the factor outside the parentheses with each term inside the parentheses.

$-7(3y - 1)$

$= (-7)(3y) + (-7)(-1)$

$= -21y + 7$

> The sign of each term is included in all calculations.

Do You Understand?

1. **? Essential Question** How does the value of an expression change when it is expanded?

2. **Use Structure** How does the subtraction part of the expression change when $a(b - c)$ is expanded?

3. **Make Sense and Persevere** When does expanding and simplifying $a(b + c)$ result in a positive value for ac?

Do You Know How?

4. Shoes and hats are on sale. The expression $\frac{1}{4}(s + 24.80)$ can be used to determine the discount when you buy shoes with a retail price of s dollars and a hat with a retail price of $24.80. Write another expression that can be used to determine the discount.

5. Expand $x(4 - 3.4y)$.

6. Expand $-\frac{2}{10}(1 - 2x + 2)$.

Practice & Problem Solving

Leveled Practice For 7–8, fill in the boxes to expand each expression.

7. $3(n + 7)$

$= (3)(\boxed{}) + (3)(\boxed{})$

$= \boxed{} + \boxed{}$

8. $4(x - 3)$

$= \boxed{}\,x - \boxed{}(3)$

$= \boxed{} - \boxed{}$

For **9–14**, write the expanded form of the expression.

9. $y(0.5 + 8)$

10. $4(3 + 4x - 2)$

11. $6(y + x)$

12. $-2.5(-3 + 4n + 8)$

13. $-\frac{1}{3}(y - x)$

14. $8(6x - 4)$

15. Higher Order Thinking A grocery store has a 13%-off sale on all bread. You decide to purchase 6 loaves of bread. Let b be the original price of a loaf of bread. Expand the expression $6(b - 0.13b)$. Once the expression is expanded, what do the terms represent?

16. A gardener plans to extend the length of a rectangular garden. Let x represent the garden's original length. The expression $4(x + 7)$ represents the area of the extended garden. When asked for the area of the extended portion, the gardener incorrectly said it was 11 square feet. Describe the error the gardener made.

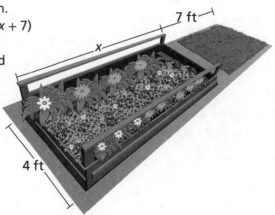

7 ft

x

4 ft

17. Find a difference equivalent to the product $11(x - y)$.

18. Use the Distributive Property to write an expression equivalent to $0.4(-5 - 7y - 13.8)$.

19. Make Sense and Persevere Use the Distributive Property to expand $7(7x - 3y) - 6$.

20. Use the Distributive Property to write an expression equivalent to $y(-3 - 8x)$.

21. An architect plans to build an extension to Meiling's rectangular deck. Let x represent the increase, in meters, of her deck's length. The expression $5(x + 8)$ represents the area of the deck, where 5 is the width, in meters, and $(x + 8)$ represents the extended length, in meters. Use the Distributive Property to write an expression that represents the total area of Meiling's new deck.

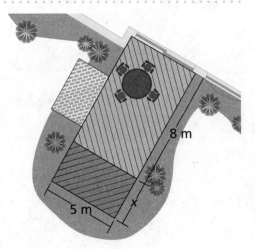

8 m

5 m   x

☑ Assessment Practice

22. Select all expressions equivalent to $-\frac{1}{2}(4 - 2 + 8x)$.

☐ $-4x - 1$

☐ $4x - 1$

☐ $3x$

☐ $-2 + 1 - 4x$

☐ $2 + 1 - 4x$

☐ $4x + 1$

23. An expression is shown.

$\frac{1}{5}(5 - 7y + 10)$

Create an equivalent expression without parentheses.

 Explain It!

ACTIVITY

Tasha is packing gift bags that include the same items. She has 72 glow sticks, 36 markers, and 24 bottles of bubbles. Tasha believes that she can pack no more than 6 bags using all of her supplies.

I can...
use common factors and the Distributive Property to factor expressions.

 Common Core Content Standards
7.EE.A.1, 7.EE.A.2
Mathematical Practices
MP.1, MP.2, MP.3, MP.8

Make Sense and Persevere
How can you use what you know about common factors to solve the problem?

A. Critique Reasoning Do you agree with Tasha? Explain.

B. If Tasha creates the greatest number of gift bags, how many of each item is in each bag? Explain how you know.

Focus on math practices

Reasoning Tasha added more markers and now has a total of 48 markers. Does this change the possible number of gift bags? Explain.

Scan for Multimedia

EXAMPLE 1 **Factor Expressions**

Kiana painted a rectangular wall blue to start an ocean mural. She used 3 cans of paint, each of which covered *x* square meters, and a different-sized can that covered 12 square meters. What are possible length and height dimensions of Kiana's mural?

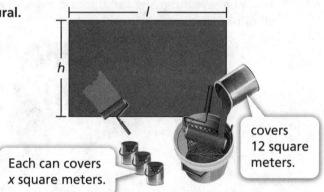

Each can covers *x* square meters.

covers 12 square meters.

> **Model with Math** The expression $3x + 12$ represents the area of the mural.

ONE WAY Use an area model to represent the area of the mural, $3x + 12$.

	x	4
3	3*x*	12

So, one possible set of dimensions of the mural could be $x + 4$ meters long and 3 meters tall.

ANOTHER WAY Use a common factor and the Distributive Property to factor the expression $3x + 12$.

$3x + 12$

$3x + (3 \cdot 4)$ ← The GCF of 3*x* and 12 is 3.

$3(x + 4)$ ← This represents the area of the mural as a product of two factors.

So, one possible set of dimensions of the mural could be 3 meters long and $x + 4$ meters tall.

Try It!

Use factoring to write an expression for the length of the pool with the given width.

$4x + 20 = \boxed{}(x + \boxed{})$

So, the length of the pool is $\boxed{}$ meters.

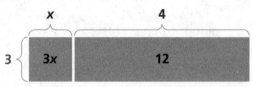

? meters

4 meters { 4*x* | 20

Convince Me! How can you use the Distributive Property to check the factored expression? Use the factored expression for Example 1 in your explanation.

EXAMPLE 2 | Factor Expressions with Negative Coefficients

Rodrigo and Jordan each factor the expression $-2x - 6$. Who factored the expression correctly?

Rodrigo uses a positive common factor, 2, to factor the expression.

2 is a common factor of $-2x$ and -6.

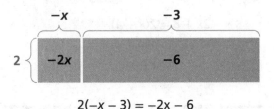

$$2(-x - 3) = -2x - 6$$

Jordan uses a negative common factor , -2, to factor the expression.

-2 is a common factor of $-2x$ and -6.

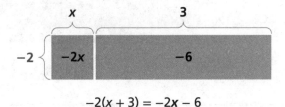

$$-2(x + 3) = -2x - 6$$

$2(-x - 3)$ and $-2(x + 3)$ are equivalent expressions. So, both Rodrigo and Jordan are correct.

 **Try It!**

Show two different ways to factor $-4x - 28$).

EXAMPLE 3 | **Factor Three-Term Expressions**

Use the GCF to factor the expression $6x - 18 - 12y$.

STEP 1 Find the GCF of $6x$, -18, and $-12y$

Factors of 6: 1, 2, 3, 6

Factors of 18: 1, 2, 3, 6, 9, 18

Factors of 12: 1, 2, 3, 4, 6, 12

The GCF is 6.

STEP 2 Use the GCF and the Distributive Property to factor the expression.

$6x - 18 - 12y$

$= (6)(x) - (6)(3) - (6)(2y)$

$= 6(x - 3 - 2y)$

The factored expression of $6x - 18 - 12y$ is $6(x - 3 - 2y)$.

Try It!

Write an equivalent expression for the expression above using a negative factor.

The greatest common factor (GCF) can be used to factor expressions.

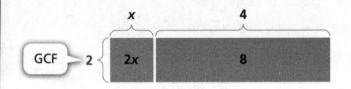

The Distributive Property can be applied to factor an expression. Factoring an expression creates an equivalent expression.

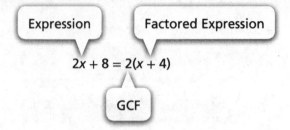

Do You Understand?

1. ? **Essential Question** How does the Distributive Property relate to factoring expressions?

2. Susan incorrectly factored the expression below.

$$12a - 15b + 6$$
$$3(4a + 5b + 3)$$

a. Explain any errors Susan may have made when factoring.

b. Factor the expression correctly.

Do You Know How?

3. Sahil is putting together supply kits and has 36 packs of x pencils, 12 packs of y crayons, and 24 erasers.

a. Write an expression to show the total number of items.

b. Use factoring to show many kits Sahil can make while putting every type of item in each kit.

c. Use the factored expression to find the number of each item in each kit.

4. Show two different ways to factor $-12x + 24 - 18y$.

5. How can you use the Distributive Property to factor the expression $6x + 15$?

Name: _____

Practice & Problem Solving

Leveled Practice In 6–9, factor the expression.

6. $16a + 10$.

The GCF of $16a$ and 10 is 2.

$2 \times \boxed{} = 16a \qquad 2 \times \boxed{} = 10$

The factored expression is $\boxed{}$.

7. $-9y - 3$.

The positive GCF of $-9y$ and -3 is 3.

$3 \times \boxed{} = -9y \qquad 3 \times \boxed{} = -3$

The factored expression is $\boxed{}$.

8. $14x + 49$

9. $12y - 16$

---

10. This model shows the area of a garden. Write two expressions that represent the area.

---

11. Use the GCF to write the factored form of the expression $18x + 24y$.

---

12. Find the dimensions of the sports field at the right if the width is at least 60 yards.

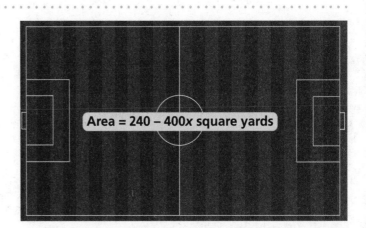

Area = $240 - 400x$ square yards

---

13. Your friend incorrectly factors the expression $15x - 20xy$ as $5x(\,3 - 4xy)$.

a. Factor the expression correctly.

b. What error did your friend likely make?

14. You are given the expression $12x + 18y + 26$.

a. Make Sense and Persevere What is the first step in factoring the expression?

b. Factor the expression.

15. A hotel manager is adding a tile border around the hotel's rectangular pool. Let x represent the width of the pool, in feet. The length is 3 more than 2 times the width, as shown. Write two expressions that give the perimeter of the pool.

16. Higher Order Thinking Use the expressions below.

$14m + mn$ $\qquad$ $2y + 2x + 4$

$-\frac{3}{4}m + 8m + m$ $\qquad$ $4 - 3p$

$5.75t + 7.75t - t$ $\qquad$ $8xy - 6xy$

a. Circle the expressions that have like terms.

b. Explain why the other expressions do not have like terms.

17. Construct Arguments Ryan says the expression $3 + 5y$ cannot be factored using a GCF. Is he correct? Explain why or why not.

18. Select all the expressions equivalent to $12 + 30y$.

☐ $3(4 + 10y)$

☐ $4(3 + 10y)$

☐ $6(2 + 5y)$

☐ $2(6 + 30y)$

☐ $6(3 + 10y)$

19. Write an expression that is the product of two factors and is equivalent to $-2x - 10$.

1. **Vocabulary** If you write an expression to represent the following situation, how can you determine which is the constant and which is the coefficient of the variable? *Lesson 5-1*

   The zoo charges the Garcia family an admission fee of $5.25 per person and a one-time fee of $3.50 to rent a wagon for their young children.

2. An online photo service charges $20 to make a photo book with 16 pages. Each extra page costs $1.75. The cost to ship the completed photo book is $5. Write an expression to determine the total cost in dollars to make and ship a photo book with *x* extra pages. *Lesson 5-1*

3. Write an expression equivalent to $2a + \left(\frac{3}{4}a + \frac{1}{5}b\right)$ by combining like terms. *Lesson 5-3*

4. Which expression is equivalent to $3.2y - \frac{1}{3} + (-7y) + \frac{2}{3}$? *Lesson 5-2*

   Ⓐ $-10.2y + \frac{1}{3}$ Ⓑ $-3.8y + \frac{1}{3}$ Ⓒ $-3\frac{7}{15}y$ Ⓓ $-3y$

5. Ray wants to buy a hat that costs $10 and some shirts that cost $12 each. The sales tax rate is 6.5%. Write an expression to determine the amount of sales tax that Ray will pay on his entire purchase. Expand to simplify the expression. *Lesson 5-4*

6. Factor the expression $28r + 42s - 35$. *Lesson 5-5*

7. Describe two ways the Distributive Property can be used to write equivalent expressions. *Lessons 5-4 and 5-5*

How well did you do on the mid-topic checkpoint? Fill in the stars.

Alison is a buyer for a chain of 6 flower shops. This means that she buys flowers in bulk from a supplier and then distributes them to the 6 flower shops in the chain.

PART A

This week Alison bought 108 bunches of carnations and 96 bunches of roses from the supplier. Let c represent the number of carnations in each bunch, and let r represent the number of roses in each bunch. Write an expression to show the total number of carnations and roses that Alison bought.

PART B

Alison wants to distribute the carnations and roses equally among the 6 flower shops. Factor the expression from Part A using 6 as the common factor. How does the factored expression help Alison determine how many carnations and how many roses each flower shop should get?

PART C

There are 24 carnations in each bunch and 12 roses in each bunch. Use your answer to Part B to determine the total number of carnations and the total number of roses Alison will distribute to each flower shop this week.

PART D

Jake manages one of the flower shops. He wants to use the carnations and roses to make bouquets. He wants each bouquet to have the same combination of carnations and roses, with no flowers left over. Determine a way that Jake can divide the flowers to make the bouquets. How many bouquets will there be?

3-ACT MATH ⊙ ⊙ ⊙

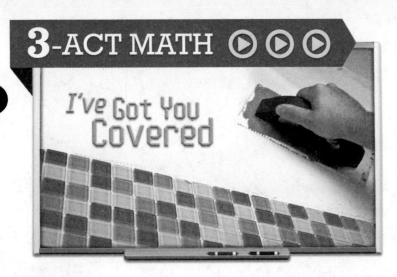

© **Common Core Content Standards**
7.EE.A.1, 7.EE.A.2

Mathematical Practices
MP.4, MP.1, MP.2, MP.3, MP.5, MP.7, MP.8

ACT 1

1. After watching the video, what is the first question that comes to mind?

2. Write the Main Question you will answer.

3. Construct Arguments Predict an answer to this Main Question. Explain your prediction.

4. On the number line below, write a number that is too small to be the answer. Write a number that is too large.

Too small   Too large

5. Plot your prediction on the same number line.

6. What information in this situation would be helpful to know? How would you use that information?

7. Use Appropriate Tools What tools can you use to solve the problem? Explain how you would use them strategically.

8. Model with Math Represent the situation using mathematics. Use your representation to answer the Main Question.

9. What is your answer to the Main Question? Is it higher or lower than your prediction? Explain why.

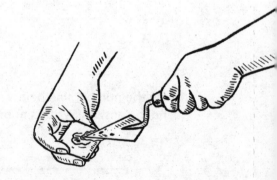

10. Write the answer you saw in the video.

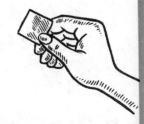

11. Reasoning Does your answer match the answer in the video? If not, what are some reasons that would explain the difference?

12. Make Sense and Persevere Would you change your model now that you know the answer? Explain.

Reflect

13. Model with Math Explain how you used a mathematical model to represent the situation. How did the model help you answer the Main Question?

14. Generalize What pattern did you notice in your calculations? How did that pattern help you solve the problem?

SEQUEL

15. Reasoning A classmate says that another object needs 512 tiles. What do you know about the dimensions of the object?

 Solve & Discuss It!

 ACTIVITY

The Smith family took a 2-day road trip. On the second day, they drove $\frac{3}{4}$ the distance they traveled on the first day. What is a possible distance they could have traveled over the 2 days? Is there more than one possible distance? Justify your response.

I can...
add expressions that represent real-world problems.

© **Common Core Content Standards**
7.EE.A.1, 7.EE.A.2

Mathematical Practices
MP.1, MP.2, MP.4, MP.6, MP.7

Make Sense and Persevere
How are the quantities in the problem related?

Focus on math practices
Use Structure How can two different expressions be used to represent the total distance?

? **Essential Question** How can properties of operations be used to add expressions?

  VISUAL LEARNING ASSESS

 EXAMPLE 1 **Add Expressions by Using Properties**

Scan for Multimedia

Delilah signs up for a health club and a rock-climbing gym. What expression represents her total fitness cost after m months?

Model with Math Each bill can be represented with an expression.

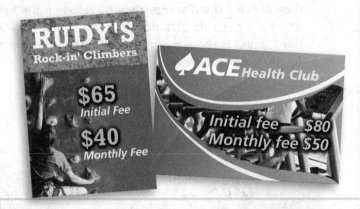

Use bar diagrams to represent the situation and write an expression for the cost of each club.

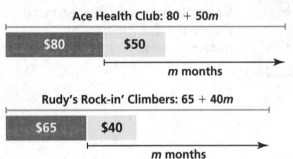

Ace Health Club: 80 + 50m

| $80 | $50 |

m months

Rudy's Rock-in' Climbers: 65 + 40m

| $65 | $40 |

m months

Add the expressions to find the combined cost.

$(80 + 50m) + (65 + 40m)$

$= (80 + 65) + (50m + 40m)$

Use the Commutative and Associative Properties.

$= 145 + 90m$

The expression $145 + 90m$ can be used to determine the total cost for the health club and rock-climbing gym after m months.

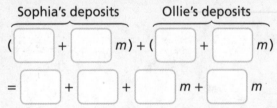 **Try It!**

Sophia and Ollie each deposit $120 to open a joint account. They each make monthly deposits as shown. What expression represents the amount in the account after m months?

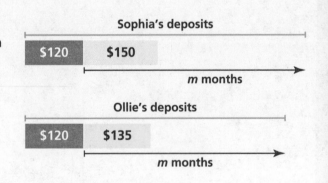

Sophia's deposits

| $120 | $150 |

m months

Ollie's deposits

| $120 | $135 |

m months

Sophia's deposits   Ollie's deposits

$(\boxed{} + \boxed{}\,m) + (\boxed{} + \boxed{}\,m)$

$= \boxed{} + \boxed{} + \boxed{}\,m + \boxed{}\,m$

The amount of money in the joint account after m months

is $\boxed{} + \boxed{}$.

Convince Me! Explain why the initial deposits and monthly deposits are not combined into one term?

EXAMPLE **2** **Add Expressions with More Than One Variable**

Cindy spent $125 on ingredients for muffins and $92.40 on ingredients for bagels. Write an expression to represent Cindy's profit for *m* muffins and *b* bagels.

muffin income	cost of ingredients		bagel income	cost of ingredients

$$2.40m - 125 \qquad\qquad 1.80b - 92.40$$

$(2.40m - 125) + (1.80b - 92.40)$

$= 2.40m + 1.80b + (-125 - 92.40)$ — Use the Commutative and Associative Properties.

$= 2.40m + 1.80b - 217.4$

The expression $2.40m + 1.80b - 217.4$ represents the profit from selling the muffins and bagels.

EXAMPLE **3** **Add More Complex Expressions**

Add the expressions.

$$\left(\tfrac{1}{2}x - 3 - 2y\right) + \left(\tfrac{1}{4}x - 2y + 5\right)$$

$$= \left(\tfrac{1}{2}x + \tfrac{1}{4}x\right) + (-2y + (-2y)) + (-3 + 5)$$ — Use the Commutative and Associative Properties to reorder and group like terms.

$$= \quad \tfrac{3}{4}x \quad + \quad (-4y) \quad + \quad 2$$

$$= \tfrac{3}{4}x - 4y + 2$$

✅ Try It!

Find each sum.

a. $(9.74c - 250.50) + (-5.48p + 185.70)$

b. $\left(\tfrac{2}{11}x - 3 - 5y\right) + \left(-\tfrac{3}{11}x + 5y + 5.5\right)$

c. $(-14.2b - 97.35) + (6.76d - 118.7 - 3.4d)$

d. $\left(\tfrac{3}{8} - \tfrac{1}{6}m + 5t\right) + \left(\tfrac{7}{10}m + 9t + \tfrac{1}{4}\right)$

Adding expressions may require combining like terms.

Terms with the same variables are added together and constants are added together.

When adding terms with the same variables, the rules for adding rational numbers apply to their coefficients.

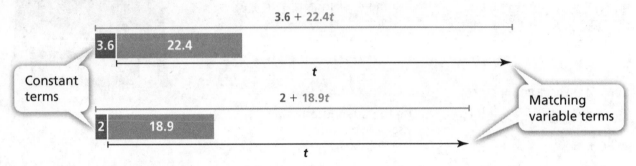

$(3.6 + 22.4t) + (2 + 18.9t) = 5.6 + 41.3t$

Do You Understand?

1. **? Essential Question** How can properties of operations be used to add expressions?

2. **Reasoning** Explain whether the coefficients of two terms with different variables can be added to make one new term.

3. **Be Precise** Which properties of operations could be used to show that $(-5p + 9) + (-2 + p)$ is equivalent to $(-5p) + p + 9 - 2$?

Do You Know How?

4. Dillon says that $4b$ and $-2b$ are not like terms because $4b$ is positive and $-2b$ is negative. Is he correct? Explain.

5. Joel spent $28 for an Internet data service and pays $14.50 per month. He spent $24.50 to join an online movie streaming site and pays $13.25 per month. Write an expression to represent Joel's total cost for both memberships after m months.

6. Add $\frac{1}{3}n + \frac{2}{3}$ and $-\frac{1}{6}n + \frac{1}{6}m$.

7. Find the sum.

$(-3.5t - 4s + 4.5) + (-7.1 - 0.3s + 4.1t)$

Name: _____

Practice & Problem Solving

Leveled Practice For 8–9, fill in the boxes to add the expressions.

8. $(2a + 8) + (4a + 5)$

$= \left(2a + \boxed{}\right) + \left(8 + \boxed{}\right)$

$= \boxed{} + 13$

9. $\left(\frac{2}{7}x - 7\right) + \left(\frac{1}{7}x + 8\right)$

$= \left(\boxed{} + \boxed{}\right) + \left(-7 + \boxed{}\right)$

$= \boxed{}x + \boxed{}$

---

10. Find the sum.

$(8b + 7) + (6x - 4) + (5c + 8)$

11. Combine like terms.

$(-3y - 5) + (5m + 7y) + (6 + 9m)$

---

12. Felipe is going to plant b sunflower seeds in one garden and $5b + 10$ sunflower seeds in another. How many seeds is Felipe going to plant altogether?

---

13. An art class is making a mural for the school that has a triangle drawn in the middle. The length of the bottom of the triangle is x. Another side is 1 more than three times the length of the bottom of the triangle. The last side is 2 more than the bottom of the triangle. Write and simplify an expression for the perimeter of the triangle.

---

14. On a math test, Sarah has to identify all the coefficients and constants of the expression $4 + n + 7m$. Sarah identifies the only coefficient as 7 and the only constant as 4.

a. Identify all the coefficients of the expression.

b. Identify all the constants of the expression.

c. What error did Sarah likely make?

15. The width of a rectangle is $5x - 2.5$ feet and the length is $2.5x + 8$ feet. Find the perimeter of the rectangle.

16. Nina has x coins. Clayton has 5 fewer coins than six times the number of coins Nina has. Write an expression for the total number of coins Nina and Clayton have altogether. Then simplify the expression.

17. Higher Order Thinking Use the expression $(8x + 2) + (-9x + 7)$.

  a. Find the sum.

  b. Reasoning Explain how you know when to combine terms with variables.

18. Gabe went to the Florida Mall. He bought k model planes and spent \$24 on books. Then he spent another \$25 at another store.

  a. Write an expression that represents the amount Gabe spent at the mall.

  b. How much did Gabe spend in all if he bought 3 model planes?

Each model plane costs \$14.99.

☑ Assessment Practice

19. A middle school with x students conducted a survey to determine students' Tuesday afternoon activities.

  PART A Write an expression for each activity.

| 25 more than one-tenth of the students dance. | 20 fewer than three-tenths of the students play soccer. | 21 more than one-tenth of the students play baseball. |

  PART B Write a simplified expression to represent the number of students who either dance or play baseball on Tuesday afternoons.

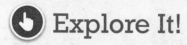 Explore It!

 ACTIVITY

The East Side Bulldogs and the West Side Bears are playing a football game. A fan is keeping score using T for a touchdown plus extra point, worth 7 points total, and F for a field goal, worth 3 points.

East Side Bulldogs	West Side Bears
1st quarter — TT F	FFF
2nd quarter — TT F	T FF
3rd quarter — T FF	TTT
4th quarter — TT FF	T

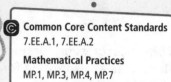

I can...
subtract expressions using properties of operations.

© **Common Core Content Standards**
7.EE.A.1, 7.EE.A.2

Mathematical Practices
MP.1, MP.3, MP.4, MP.7

A. How can you represent the score of each team using expressions?

B. How can you represent the difference of the teams' scores using an expression?

C. How can you determine how many more points the winning team had than the losing team?

Focus on math practices

Look for Relationships How can looking at the coefficients help you determine which team scored the greater number of points?

EXAMPLE 1 👁 **Subtract Expressions by Using Properties**

Scan for Multimedia

Lita's family wants to put a tiled border around their swimming pool. What expression represents the total area of the border?

Make Sense and Persevere
How can you use subtraction to find the area of the tiled border?

2 ft   (2x + 14) ft   2 ft

14 ft

2 ft

Write an expression for the area of the pool only. Then write an expression for the area of the pool plus the tiled border.

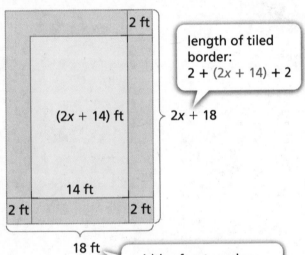

2 ft

length of tiled border:
2 + (2x + 14) + 2

(2x + 14) ft } 2x + 18

14 ft

2 ft   2 ft

18 ft

width of outer edge of walkway: 2 + 14 + 2

Area of pool:
width • length
$14 \times (2x + 14)$ ft^2

Area of pool and tiled border:
$18 \times (2x + 18)$ ft^2

Use properties of operations to subtract the expressions.

(area of pool + tiles) − (area of pool)

$= 18(2x + 18) - 14(2x + 14)$

$= 36x + 324 - 28x - 196$

$= 36x - 28x + 324 - 196$

$= 8x + 128$

First, use the Distributive Property.

Then, use the Commutative Property.

The area of the tiled border is $8x + 128$ ft^2.

☑ Try It!

A frame holds a picture that is 15 inches long and x inches wide. The frame border is 3 inches wide around the picture. What expression represents the area of the frame border?

Area of frame border = Area of entire frame − Area of photo = ⬚ − ⬚

The area of the frame is ⬚ in^2.

Convince Me! Why can you choose to add or subtract when subtracting an expression?

EXAMPLE 2 Subtract Expressions with Rational Coefficients

Jada is comparing membership costs for two gyms. What is the difference in membership costs after m months if she joins Be Strong instead of Zippy Health Club?

Write an expression for each membership cost for m months and subtract them.

(Be Strong) − (Zippy's Health Club)

$(24.99m - 10) - (19.95m + 49.95)$

$= 24.99m - 10 + (-1)(19.95m + 49.95)$

$= 24.99m - 10 + (-1)(19.95m) + (-1)(49.95)$ ◁ Use the Distributive Property.

$= 24.99m - 10 - 19.95m - 49.95$

$= (24.99m - 19.95m) - 10 - 49.95$ ◁ Use the Commutative and Associative Properties to reorder and group like terms.

$= 5.04m - 59.95$

> **Use Structure** How did the signs of the terms in the second expression change after distributing −1?

Jada will pay $5.04 more each month at Be Strong, but will start with an initial savings of $59.95.

Try It!

Subtract $(0.95x - 0.04) - (0.99x - 0.13)$.

EXAMPLE 3   Subtract More Complex Expressions

Subtract the expressions.

$\left(5j - 2q + \frac{2}{5}\right) - \left(4 - 3j - \frac{1}{2}q\right)$

$= \left(5j - 2q + \frac{2}{5}\right) + \left(-4 + 3j + \frac{1}{2}q\right)$ ◁ Distribute the minus sign, or −1, to all terms in the second expression.

$= 5j - 2q + \frac{2}{5} - 4 + 3j + \frac{1}{2}q$

$= 5j + 3j - 2q + \frac{1}{2}q + \frac{2}{5} - 4$

$= 8j - 1\frac{1}{2}q - 3\frac{3}{5}$

The simplified expression is $8j - 1\frac{1}{2}q - 3\frac{3}{5}$.

Try It!

Subtract $(17 + 4.5m + 8k) - (7.5m - 9 + 4k)$.

To subtract expressions, you can use properties of operations.

> Write the subtraction as addition and use the Distributive Property to multiply −1 to the terms in the expression being subtracted.

$$5 - (-2x - 7)$$
$$= 5 + (-1)(-2x - 7)$$
$$= 5 + (-1)(-2)x + (-1)(-7)$$
$$= 5 + 2x + 7$$

$$5 - (-2x - 7)$$

$$= 5 + 2x + 7$$

> You can use the Distributive Property to distribute the minus sign to the second expression, which changes the signs of the terms.

Do You Understand?

1. **Essential Question** How can properties of operations be used to subtract expressions?

2. **Use Structure** How is subtracting −4x from 9x similar to subtracting −4 from 9?

3. Is adding the quantity −12 + 8r to an expression the same as subtracting −8r + 12 from the same expression? Explain your reasoning.

Do You Know How?

4. Subtract.

   a. $(21x) - (-16 + 7x)$

   b. $(-13n) - (17 - 5n)$

   c. $(4y - 7) - (y - 7)$

   d. $(-w + 0.4) - (-w - 0.4)$

5. Jude has 5 pairs of sunglasses that cost the same in his online shopping cart, but then decides to get only 2. Each pair of sunglasses is the same price. Let p represent the cost of each pair. Write an expression for the original cost, the updated cost, and the difference in cost.

6. Subtract and simplify.

$$\frac{1}{6}m - \left(-\frac{5}{8}m + \frac{1}{3}\right)$$

Name: _____

Practice & Problem Solving

Leveled Practice In 7–9, fill in the missing signs or numbers.

7. Rewrite the expression $14m - (5 + 8m)$ without parentheses.

$14m \bigcirc 5 \bigcirc 8m$

8. Rewrite the expression $13d - (-9d - 4)$ without parentheses.

$13d \bigcirc 9d \bigcirc 4$

9. Write an equivalent expression to $8k - (5 + 2k)$ without parentheses. Then simplify.

$8k - (5 + 2k) = 8k \bigcirc 5 \bigcirc 2k$

$= 8k \bigcirc 2k \bigcirc 5$

$= \boxed{} k \bigcirc 5$

10. A company has two manufacturing plants with daily production levels of $5x + 11$ items and $2x - 3$ items, respectively, where x represents a minimum quantity. The first plant produces how many more items daily than the second plant?

11. Two communications companies offer calling plans. With Company X, it costs 35¢ to connect and then 5¢ for each minute. With Company Y, it costs 15¢ to connect and then 4¢ for each minute.

Write and simplify an expression that represents how much more Company X charges than Company Y, in cents, for n minutes.

12. Make Sense and Persevere
The base and height of a triangle are each extended 2 cm. What is the area of the shaded region? How do you know?

2 cm

x cm

8 cm   2 cm

13. Two friends shop for fresh fruit. Jackson buys a watermelon for $7.65 and 5 pounds of cherries. Tim buys a pineapple for $2.45 and 4 pounds of cherries. Use the variable p to represent the price, in dollars, per pound of cherries. Write and simplify an expression to represent how much more Jackson spent.

14. Yu's family wants to rent a car to go on vacation. EnvoCar charges $50.50 and 8¢ per mile. Freedomride charges $70.50 and 12¢ per mile. How much more does Freedomride charge for driving d miles than EnvoCar?

15. A rectangular garden has a walkway around it. Find the area of the walkway.

21 ft
15 ft
6.5x + 5 ft
8x + 6.5 ft

16. **Critique Reasoning** Tim incorrectly rewrote the expression $\frac{1}{2}p - \left(\frac{1}{4}p + 4\right)$ as $\frac{1}{2}p + \frac{1}{4}p - 4$. Rewrite the expression without parentheses. What was Tim's error?

17. **Higher Order Thinking** Find the difference.

$$\left(7x - 6\frac{2}{3}\right) - \left(-3x + 4\frac{3}{4}\right)$$

18. Each month, a shopkeeper spends $5x + 11$ dollars on rent and electricity. If he spends $2x - 3$ dollars on rent, how much does he spend on electricity?

19. Use the expression $\frac{1}{4}p - \left(1 - \frac{1}{3}p\right)$.

   a. Rewrite the expression without parentheses. Simplify. Show your work.

   b. Use a different method to write the expression without parentheses. Do not simplify.

☑ **Assessment Practice**

20. An expression is shown.

   $(0.25n - 0.3) - (0.8n - 0.25)$

   Create an equivalent expression without parentheses.

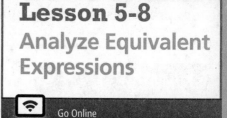
Solve & Discuss It!

ACTIVITY

How many toothpicks make a triangle? Two triangles? Write an expression that represents the number of toothpicks needed to make *x* triangles that appear side-by-side in a single row, as shown. Explain your reasoning.

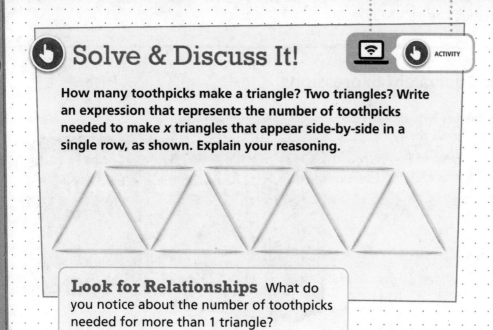

Look for Relationships What do you notice about the number of toothpicks needed for more than 1 triangle?

I can...
use an equivalent expression to find new information.

Common Core Content Standards
7.EE.A.2

Mathematical Practices
MP.2, MP.7

Focus on math practices

Reasoning Can there be more than one expression that represents the total number of toothpicks needed to make *x* triangles in the arrangement shown? Explain.

Essential Question How can writing equivalent expressions show how quantities are related?

VISUAL LEARNING

ASSESS

EXAMPLE 1 Write Equivalent Expressions

Scan for Multimedia

A new box of pasta claims that it contains 25% more than the usual box. What expression shows the amount of pasta, *p*, in the new box?

Use Structure What expressions can you write to represent a percent greater than the original amount?

25% MORE!

Penne Pasta

Penne Pasta

Draw a bar diagram to represent the problem situation. Then write an expression to represent the amount of pasta in the new box.

$p + 0.25p$

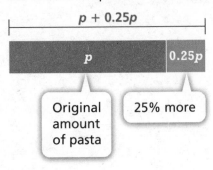

Original amount of pasta

25% more

$p + 0.25p$

Combine like terms to write an equivalent expression.

The coefficient of *p* is 1.

$(1)p + 0.25p$

$= 1.25p$

25% more than 100% is the same as 125%.

Try It!

Joe is buying gift cards that are on sale for 15% off. He uses $c - 0.15c$ to determine the sale price of gift cards. What is an equivalent expression that Joe could also use to determine the sale price of a gift card?

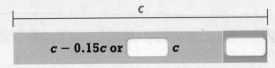

c

$c - 0.15c$ or [   ] *c* [   ]

Convince Me! How do you know if an expression is describing a percent increase or a percent decrease?

EXAMPLE 2 **Analyze Equivalent Expressions**

  ACTIVITY ASSESS

Some middle school students will use 1-foot tiles to create a frame around a large square mural painting with side lengths *s* feet. Three students each wrote an expression to determine the number of tiles needed. Are these expressions equivalent? Explain.

$4(s + 1)$

$s + 1$

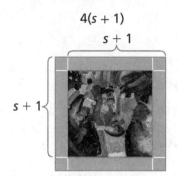

$s + 1$

$s + s + s + s + 4$

s

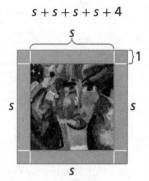

s s

s

$2s + 2(s + 2)$

$s + 2$

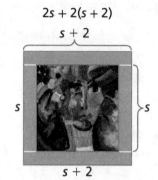

s }s

$s + 2$

> **Look for Relationships**
> What does each expression tell you about the relationship among quantities and variables?

Each section requires $s + 1$ tiles and there are 4 sections.

Each side requires *s* tiles and there are 4 sides, so $s + s + s + s$, plus 4 corner tiles.

The top and bottom of the frame require $s + 2$ tiles and the two sides require *s* tiles.

The three expressions are equivalent because they each represent the number of tiles needed for the frame around the painting.

EXAMPLE 3 **Interpret Equivalent Expressions**

A table with a rectangular top has been extended with a table leaf as shown.

Multiply 3.5(6.5 + x) to write an equivalent expression for the total area of the extended table. What does each term of the equivalent expression tell you about the table?

$3.5(6.5 + x)$

$= (3.5 \cdot 6.5) + (3.5 \cdot x)$

$= 22.75 + 3.5x$

Area, in ft², of table leaf

Area, in ft², of original table

|— 6.5 feet —|— x feet —|

3.5 feet

Table top   Leaf

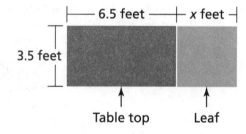

Try It!

The total area, in square feet, of a rectangular stage that has been widened by *x* feet is represented by $1,900 + 76x$. Use the Distributive Property to factor the expression. What does each factor in the equivalent expression tell you about the stage?

original stage

x { extension

Rewriting expressions can clarify relationships among quantities or variables.

When you *rewrite* an expression, you are writing an *equivalent* expression.

$4x + 12$ is equivalent to $4(x + 3)$ is equivalent to $x + x + x + x + 3 + 3 + 3 + 3$

Do You Understand?

1. **? Essential Question** How can writing equivalent expressions show how quantities are related?

2. **Use Structure** The total area, in square feet, of a rectangular mural that has been extended by x feet is represented by $5.5(7.5 + x)$. Expand the expression using the Distributive Property. What do each of the terms in the equivalent expression tell you about the mural?

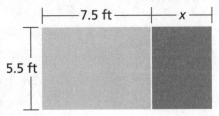

5.5 ft
7.5 ft
x

3. The expression $(2x + 6) + x$ represents the perimeter of an isosceles triangle. If x represents the length of one side of the triangle, explain how you can use the Distributive Property to find the length of each of the two equivalent sides?

Do You Know How?

4. Rewrite the expression $12x + 8$ to find an equivalent expression. Show three possible expressions. What do the rewritten expressions tell you about the relationships among the quantities?

5. A rope is used to make a fence in the shape of an equilateral triangle around a newly planted tree. The length of the rope is represented with the expression $9x + 15$

   a. Rewrite the expression to represent the three side lengths of the rope fence.

   b. What is the length of one side?

6. The expression $(x - 0.35x)$ represents 35% off the cost of an item x. How is this equivalent to multiplying x by 0.65?

Name: _____

Practice & Problem Solving

7. Reasoning Eric is planning an event at a hotel. Let g stand for the number of Eric's guests. The two expressions represent the difference between the cost of the rooms. Expression 1: $(326 + 37g) - (287 + 23g)$. Expression 2: $39 + 14g$. What can you tell about Expression 2 and Expression 1?

Hotel
Function Rooms

Ocean
Booking Fee $326
Price per Guest $37

Harbor
Booking Fee $287
Price per Guest $23

---

8. A student received a coupon for 17% off the total purchase price at a clothing store. Let b be the original price of the purchase. Use the expression $b - 0.17b$ for the new price of the purchase. Write an equivalent expression by combining like terms.

9. Kirana buys boxes of crackers that each have the same cost, c. She represents the cost of 3 boxes of cheese crackers, 2 boxes of poppy seed crackers, and 2 boxes of plain crackers using the expression $3c + 2c + 2c$. What equivalent expression can represent the cost?

---

10. A student received a coupon for 14% off the total purchase price at a clothing store. Let c be the original price of the purchase. The expression $c - 0.14c$ represents the new price of the purchase. Write an equivalent expression to show another way to represent the new price.

---

11. A farmer recently sold a large plot of land. The sale decreased his total acreage by 8%. Let v be the original acreage.

a. Find two equivalent expressions that will give the new acreage.

b. Use the expressions to describe two ways to find the new acreage.

12. An art teacher enlarged the area of a copy of a painting by 49%. Let d represent the area of the original painting. The expression $d + 0.49d$ is one way to represent the area of the new painting. Write two additional expressions that will give the area of the new painting.

13. Use Structure The area of a rectangular playground has been extended on one side. The total area of the playground, in square meters, can be written as $352 + 22x$.

Rewrite the expression to give a possible set of dimensions for the playground.

14. The manager of a store increases the price of the bathing suits by 7%. Let t be the original price of a bathing suit. The new price is $t + 0.07t$.

a. Find an expression equivalent to $t + 0.07t$.

b. If the original price of a bathing suit was $19.99, estimate the new price by first rounding the original price to the nearest dollar.

15. Higher Order Thinking A customer at a clothing store is buying a pair of pants and a shirt. The customer can choose between a sale that offers a discount on pants, or a coupon for a discount on the entire purchase. Let n represent the original price of the pants and s represent the price of the shirt.

a. Write two expressions that represent the "15% off sale on all pants" option.

b. Write two expressions that represent the "10% off her entire purchase" option.

c. If the original cost of the pants is $25 and the shirt is $10, which option should the customer choose? Explain.

15% OFF SALE on all pants

SAVE 10% OFF Entire Purchase
Cannot be combined with any other offers.
TROPICAL CLOTHES SHOP
Serving greater Orlando for over 40 years

✓ Assessment Practice

16. At a college, the cost of tuition increased by 10%. Let b represent the former cost of tuition. Use the expression $b + 0.10b$ for the new cost of tuition.

PART A

Write an equivalent expression for the new cost of tuition.

PART B

What does your equivalent expression tell you about how to find the new cost of tuition?

? Topic Essential Question

How can properties of operations help to generate equivalent expressions that can be used in solving problems?

Vocabulary Review

Complete each definition and then provide an example of each vocabulary word.

Vocabulary   coefficient   constant   variable   factor   expression

Definition	Example
1. A term that contains only a number is a [____].	
2. The number part of a term that contains a variable is a [____].	
3. A [____] is a letter that represents an unknown value.	

Use Vocabulary in Writing

Membership in a digital library has a $5 startup fee and then costs $9.95 per month. Membership in a video streaming service costs $7.99 per month with no startup fee. Use vocabulary words to explain how this information could be used to write an expression for the total cost of both memberships after m months.

Concepts and Skills Review

LESSON 5-1 › Write and Evaluate Algebraic Expressions

Quick Review

You can use an algebraic expression to represent and solve a problem with unknown values. The expression can consist of coefficients, constants, and variables. You can substitute values for variables to evaluate expressions.

Example

A farm charges $1.75 for each pound of strawberries picked and $2 for a basket to hold the strawberries. What is the total cost to pick 5 pounds of strawberries?

Write an expression to represent the total cost in dollars to pick p pounds of strawberries.

$1.75p + 2$

Substitute 5 for p.

$1.75(5) + 2 = 8.75 + 2 = 10.75$

It costs $10.75 to pick 5 pounds of strawberries.

Practice

1. Haddie makes and sells knit scarves. Next week she will pay a $25 fee for the use of a booth at a craft fair. She will charge $12 for each scarf she sells at the fair. Write an expression to determine Haddie's profit for selling s scarves after paying the fee for the use of the booth.

2. The cost to buy p pounds of potatoes at $0.32 per pound and n pounds of onions at $0.48 per pound can be determined by using the expression $0.32p + 0.48n$. How much will it cost to buy 4.5 pounds of potatoes and 2.5 pounds of onions?

LESSONS 5-2 AND 5-3 › Generate Equivalent Expressions and Simplify Expressions

Quick Review

You can use properties of operations and combine like terms to simplify expressions. Like terms are terms that have the same variable part.

Example

Simplify the expression below.

$-7 + \frac{1}{3}n - \frac{4}{3} + 2n$

Use the Commutative Property to put like terms together,

$\frac{1}{3}n + 2n - 7 - \frac{4}{3}$

Combine like terms.

$2\frac{1}{3}n - 8\frac{1}{3}$

Practice

Simplify each expression below.

1. $\frac{5}{8}m + 9 - \frac{3}{8}m - 15$

2. $-8w + (-4z) + 2 + 6w + 9z - 7$

3. $-6 + (-2d) + (-4d) + 3d$

Quick Review

The Distributive Property allows you to multiply each term inside parentheses by a factor that is outside the parentheses. This means that you can use the Distributive Property to expand expressions.

Example

Expand the expression $\frac{1}{4}(h + 7)$.

$\left(\frac{1}{4} \times h\right) + \left(\frac{1}{4} \times 7\right) = \frac{1}{4}h + 1.75$

Practice

1. Expand the expression $3.5(-3n + 4)$.

2. Simplify the expression $-\frac{3}{5}\left(-8 + \frac{5}{9}x - 3\right)$.

Quick Review

When you factor an expression, you write it as a product of two expressions. The new expression is equivalent to the original expression. The greatest common factor (GCF) and the Distributive Property are tools that you use when you need to factor an expression.

Example

Factor the expression $12x - 9y + 15$.

The GCF of $12x$, 15, and $-9y$ is 3.

Rewrite each term using 3 as a factor.

$12x = 3 \cdot 4x$

$-9y = 3 \cdot (-3y)$

$15 = 3 \cdot 5$

Use the Distributive Property to factor the expression.

$3(4x - 3y + 5)$

Practice

Factor each expression.

1. $63a - 42b$

2. $81y + 54$

3. Which show a way to factor the expression $32t - 48$? Select all that apply.

☐ $2(16t - 24)$

☐ $4(12t - 48)$

☐ $6(26t - 42)$

☐ $8(4t - 6)$

☐ $16(2t - 3)$

Quick Review

Adding and subtracting expressions may require combining like terms. This means that you must use the Commutative and Associative Properties to reorder and group terms as needed.

Example

Kerry has n markers. Rachel has 1 marker fewer than twice the number of markers Kerry has. Write and simplify an expression for the total number of markers they have.

Number of markers Kerry has: n

Number of markers Rachel has: $2n - 1$

Total number of markers:

$n + (2n - 1)$

$(n + 2n) - 1$

$3n - 1$

Practice

Add the expressions.

1. $(5.2c - 7.35) + (-3.9c + 2.65)$

2. $(6x - 2y - 5) - (-5 + 9y - 8x)$

3. Last week Jean ran 2 fewer than $4m$ miles. This week she ran 0.5 miles more than last week. Write and simplify an expression for the total number of miles Jean ran in the two weeks.

Quick Review

Equivalent expressions can help to show new information about a problem. Sometimes the equivalent expression will be an expanded expression. In other cases, it will be a factored expression.

Example

The perimeter of a square is represented with the expression $84 + 44s$. What is the length of one side of the square?

A square has 4 sides, so factor 4 out of each term in the expression for the perimeter.

$84 + 44s = 4 \cdot 21 + 4 \cdot 11s = 4(21 + 11s)$

The factor within the parentheses represents the length of one side of the square.

The length of one side is $21 + 11s$.

Practice

1. Hal earns n dollars per hour. Next month he will receive a 2% raise in pay per hour. The expression $n + 0.02n$ is one way to represent Hal's pay per hour after the raise. Write an equivalent simplified expression that will represent his pay per hour after the raise.

2. The area of a garden plot can be represented by the expression $84z - 54$. The garden will be divided into six sections for planting six different vegetables. The sections will be equal in area. Write an expression that represents the area of each section.

Hidden Clue

For each ordered pair, solve the percent problems to find the coordinates. Then locate and label the corresponding point on the graph. Draw line segments to connect the points in alphabetical order. Use the completed picture to help you answer the riddle below.

I can...
represent and solve percent problems.

© 7.RP.A.2c

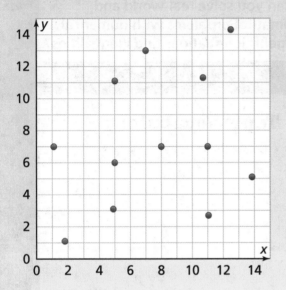

What occurs once in every minute, twice in every moment, yet never in a thousand years?

A (x is 85% of 13, 60% of 4.5 is y) ____ , ____

B (x is 110% of 10, y% of 50 is 3.5) ____ , ____

C (x% of 31 is 3.317, 4.407 is 39% of y) ____ , ____

D (1.36 is 17% of x, 1.05 is y% of 15) ____ , ____

E (x% of 60 is 3.006, 10% of 111 is y) ____ , ____

F (x is 16% of 31.25, y is 24% of 25) ____ , ____

G (78% of x is 3.822, y% of 8 is 0.248) ____ , ____

SOLVE PROBLEMS USING EQUATIONS AND INEQUALITIES

? Topic Essential Question

How can you solve real-world and mathematical problems with numerical and algebraic equations and inequalities?

Topic Overview

Topic Vocabulary

• isolate the variable

Lesson Digital Resources

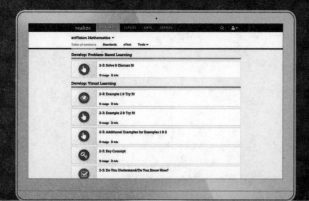

 INTERACTIVE STUDENT EDITION
Access online or offline.

 VISUAL LEARNING ANIMATION
Interact with visual learning animations.

 ACTIVITY Use with *Solve & Discuss It, Explore It,* and *Explain It* activities, and to explore Examples.

 VIDEOS Watch clips to support *3-Act Mathematical Modeling Lessons* and *STEM Projects*.

Go online

Digital Downloads

Experts estimate that almost a billion dollars' worth of gift cards go unused every year! However, gift cards may still be your preference. They prevent waste, and you can choose the exact items you want. Plus, if you know you won't use the gift card, it's easy to regift it to someone who can use it.

There are a number of clever ways to get the most out of your gift card. Think about this during the 3-Act Mathematical Modeling lesson.

PRACTICE Practice what you've learned.

TUTORIALS Get help from *Virtual Nerd*, right when you need it.

MATH TOOLS Explore math with digital tools.

GAMES Play Math Games to help you learn.

KEY CONCEPT Review important lesson content.

GLOSSARY Read and listen to English/Spanish definitions.

ASSESSMENT Show what you've learned.

:enVision® STEM Project

Did You Know?

Total world population in 2015
7.4 billion

According to the World Health Organization, 2.6 billion people have gained access to safe drinking water since 1990.

A 2015 WHO report states that 663 million people do not have access to clean, safe water. 8 out of 10 of these people live in rural areas.

80% of all illness and death in developing countries is a result of water-related disease.

Water filtration systems purify water by removing contaminates. In developing countries, water filters need to be affordable and easy to use.

Three common water filters used in developing countries are:

Ceramic Water Filters

Sand Filters

Hollow Fiber Microfiltration System

Your Task:
Water is Life!

You have water to drink, to use to brush your teeth, and to bathe. You and your classmates will research the need for safe, clean water in developing countries. Based on your research, you will determine the type, size, and cost of a water filtration system needed to provide clean, safe water to a community. You will also develop a plan to raise money to purchase the needed filtration system.

Review What You Know!

Vocabulary

Choose the best term from the box to complete each definition.

> inverse relationship
> like terms
> inequality
> properties of equality

1. A statement that contains the symbols <, >, ≤, or ≥ is called a(n)

   _____.

2. Properties that state that performing the same operation on both sides of

   an equation will keep the equation true are called _____.

3. Addition and subtraction have a(n) _____ because they can "undo" each other.

4. Terms that have the same variable are called _____.

Properties of Equality

Use properties to solve each equation for *x*.

5. $x + 9.8 = 14.2$

6. $14x = 91$

7. $\frac{1}{3}x = 24$

Like Terms

Combine like terms in each expression.

8. $\frac{1}{4}k + \frac{1}{4}m - \frac{2}{3}k + \frac{5}{9}m$

9. $-4b + 2w + (-4b) + 8w$

10. $6 - 5z + 8 - 4z + 1$

Inequalities

11. Write an inequality that represents the situation: *A large box of golf balls has more than 12 balls.* Describe how your inequality represents the situation.

Language Development

Fill in the Venn diagram to compare and contrast equations and inequalities.

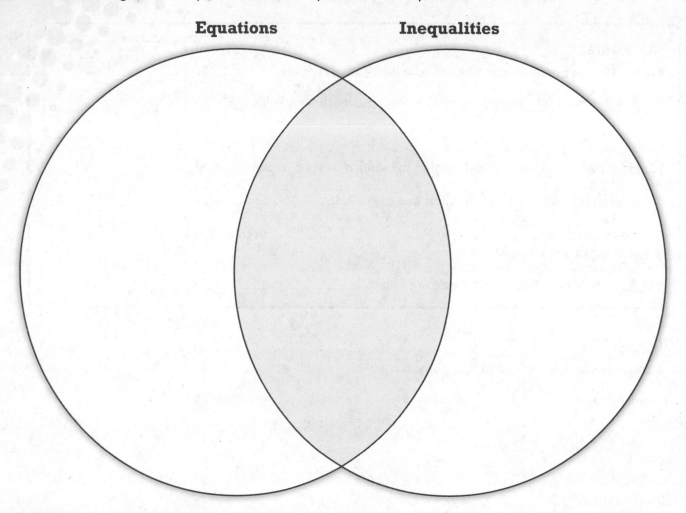

Equations   **Inequalities**

In the box below, draw pictures to represent the terms and phrases in the overlap section of your diagram.

PROJECT 6A

How many different ways could you sort a basket of vegetables?

PROJECT: COMPARING WITH A VENN DIAGRAM

PROJECT 6B

Which character would you be from your favorite play? Why?

PROJECT: WRITE A PLAY

PROJECT
6C

If you could live in another country, where would you live, and why?

PROJECT: EXCHANGE SOUVENIRS

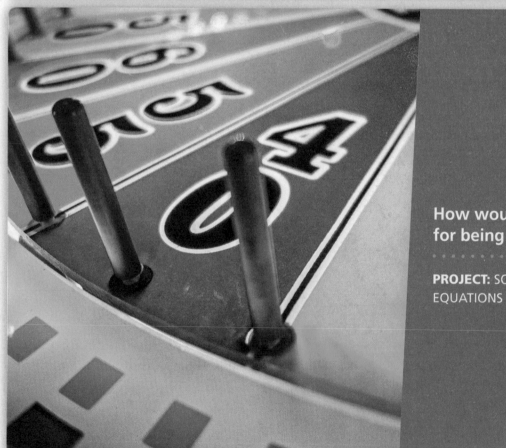

PROJECT
6D

How would you prepare for being on a game show?

PROJECT: SOLVE RANDOMIZED EQUATIONS AND INEQUALITIES

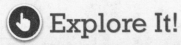 **Explore It!**

 ACTIVITY

Marley collects golf balls. His neighbor Tucker collects 3 more than twice as many golf balls as Marley.

I can...
represent a problem with a two-step equation.

© **Common Core Content Standards**
7.EE.B.4

Mathematical Practices
MP.2, MP.4, MP.7

A. How can you use a table to represent the number of golf balls in Marley's collection, m, and the number of golf balls in Tucker's collection?

B. How can you use an algebraic expression to represent the number of golf balls in Tucker's collection?

Focus on math practices

Look for Relationships How do the terms of the expression you wrote in Part B relate to the values in the table?

343

? **Essential Question** How does an equation show the relationship between variables and other quantities in a situation?

EXAMPLE 1 👁 **Write a Two-Step Equation to Represent a Situation**

Scan for Multimedia 🅱

What equation can be used to represent the numbers of golf balls in Marley's and Tucker's collections?

159 golf balls

Model with Math
How can an equation represent a given situation?

Tucker has 3 more than twice Marley's golf ball collection.

Marley's Collection   Tucker's Collection

Use a bar diagram to represent the situation.

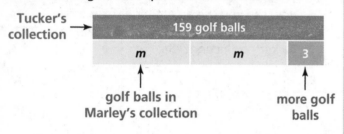

Tucker's collection

159 golf balls		
m	m	3

golf balls in Marley's collection

more golf balls

Use the bar diagram to write an equation.

Tucker's collection	=	twice Marley's collection	+	more golf balls
159	=	2m	+	3

The equation $159 = 2m + 3$ can be used to represent Marley's and Tucker's golf ball collections.

☑ **Try It!**

Cole buys a new laptop for $335. He makes a down payment of $50 and pays the rest in 6 equal monthly payments, *p*. What equation represents the relationship between the cost of the laptop and Cole's payments?

Cost of laptop →
Down payment →

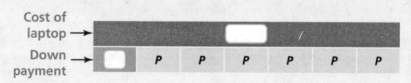

	P	P	P	P	P	P

cost = [　　　　] + [　　　　] × monthly payment

[　] = [　] + [　] × [　]

[　] = [　　　]

Convince Me! Why are both multiplication and addition used in the equation that represents Cole's monthly payments?

EXAMPLE **2** Write More Two-Step Equations

  ACTIVITY ASSESS

A baseball weighs 25.75 ounces less than a bat. Write an equation that represents the relationship between the weights of a baseball and a bat in terms of the weight of the box, w.

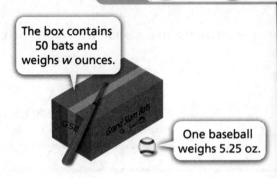

The box contains 50 bats and weighs w ounces.

One baseball weighs 5.25 oz.

$$\text{weight of one baseball} = \text{weight of one bat} - \text{difference in weight}$$

$$5.25 = \frac{\text{weight of box}}{\text{number of bats in box}} - 25.75$$

$$5.25 = \frac{w}{50} - 25.75$$

The equation $5.25 = \frac{w}{50} - 25.75$ can be used to represent the relationship between the weights of a baseball and a bat.

Try It!

Marcia and Tamara are running a race. Marcia has run 4 kilometers. Tamara has completed $\frac{3}{4}$ of the race and is 2.5 kilometers ahead of Marcia. Write an equation that represents the relationship between the distances each girl has run. Let k represent the total length of the race in kilometers.

EXAMPLE **3** Interpret Quantities and Operations in Equations

Claire bought 8 tickets for a total cost of $104. She had used a coupon code to get $3 off each ticket. Let x be the original cost of each ticket. Which of the following equations correctly represents the situation?

$3(x - 8) = 104$ ◁ Total cost

$8x - 3 = 104$ ◁ Total cost

$8(x - 3) = 104$ ◁ Total cost

$3 discount times the difference of 8 tickets and the cost per ticket

8 tickets times the cost per ticket minus a total discount of $3

8 tickets times the difference of the cost per ticket and $3.

The equation $8(x - 3) = 104$ represents this situation.

Try It!

At the mall, Claire buys a hat that is 60% off and socks that are reduced to $5.49. She spends a total of $9.49. Let x represent the cost of the hat. Which of the following equations correctly represents Claire's shopping trip?

$0.4x + 5.49 = 5.09$ $0.4x + 5.49 = 9.49$ $0.6x + 9.49 = 5.49$

You can write an equation with more than one operation to represent a situation.

$$3(x + 5) = 24 \qquad\qquad \frac{x}{4} - 15 = 18$$

> This two-step equation uses multiplication and addition.

> This two-step equation uses division and subtraction.

Do You Understand?

1. **? Essential Question** How does an equation show the relationship between variables and other quantities in a situation?

2. **Use Structure** Do the equations $\frac{1}{5}x + 2 = 6$ and $\frac{1}{5}(x + 2) = 6$ represent the same situation? Explain.

3. How do you decide which operations to use when writing an equation?

Do You Know How?

4. Rita started the day with r apps. Then she deleted 5 apps and still had twice as many apps as Cora has. Write an equation that represents the number of apps each girl has.

5. Write a problem that could be represented by the equation $5n - 6 = 19$.

6. Kayleigh babysat for 11 hours this week. That was 5 fewer than $\frac{2}{3}$ as many hours as she babysat last week, h. Write an equation to represent the number of hours she babysat each week.

Name: _____

Practice & Problem Solving

7. A farmer ships oranges in wooden crates. Suppose each orange weighs the same amount. The total weight of a crate filled with *g* oranges is 24.5 pounds. Write an equation that represents the relationship between the weight of the crate and the number of oranges it contains.

$$24.5 = \boxed{} + \boxed{} \times \boxed{}$$

empty crate: 15 lb

0.38 lb

---

8. Jordan wrote the following description: Three fewer than one fourth of *x* is 12. Write an equation to represent the description.

9. At a graduation dinner, an equal number of guests were seated at each of 3 large tables, and 7 late-arriving guests were seated at a smaller table. There were 37 guests in all. If *n* represents the number of people seated at each of the large tables, what equation represents the situation?

---

10. Last night, 4 friends went out to dinner at a restaurant. They split the bill evenly. Each friend paid $12.75 for his or her meal and each left the same amount for a tip, *t*. The total dinner bill including the tip was $61. What equation could you use to describe the situation?

11. Mia buys $4\frac{1}{5}$ pounds of plums. The total cost after using a coupon for 55¢ off her entire purchase was $3.23. If *c* represents the cost of the plums in dollars per pound, what equation could represent the situation?

For 12 and 13, use the equation shown at the right.

12. Describe a situation that the equation could represent.

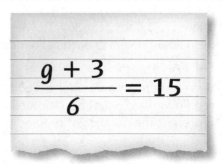

$$\frac{g + 3}{6} = 15$$

13. Reasoning Would the situation you wrote for Problem 12 work if the denominator in the equation were doubled? Explain why or why not.

14. You want to buy a pet iguana. You already have $12 and plan to save $9 per week.

Iguana $48

   a. **Model with Math** If *w* represents the number of weeks until you have enough money to buy the iguana, what equation represents your plan to afford the iguana?

   b. Explain how you could set up an equation to find the amount of money you should save each week to buy the iguana in 6 weeks.

15. In a certain country, the life expectancy of a woman born in 1995 was 80.2 years. Between 1995 and 2005, the life expectancy increased 0.4 year every 5 years.

   a. If *L* represents the life expectancy of a woman born in 2005, what equation could you use to represent the situation?

   b. **Reasoning** Could two different equations be used to find the value of *L*? Explain.

16. **Higher Order Thinking** Use the equation $5x - 13 = 12$.

   a. Write a description that represents the equation.

   b. Of the numbers 1, 2, 3, 4, and 5, which are solutions to the equation?

☑ Assessment Practice

17. A garden contains 135 flowers, each of which is either red or yellow. There are 3 beds of yellow flowers and 3 beds of red flowers. There are 30 yellow flowers in each yellow flower bed.

   PART A

   If *r* represents the number of red flowers in each red flower bed, what equation could you use to represent the number of red and yellow flowers?

   PART B

   Write another real-world situation that your equation from Part A could represent.

Solve & Discuss It!  ACTIVITY

Elizabeth wrote the following clues. What is the relationship between the shapes?

Use Structure How can you use properties of equality to reason about these equations?

I can...
solve a problem with a two-step equation.

© **Common Core Content Standards**
7.EE.B.3, 7.EE.B.4a

Mathematical Practices
MP.1, MP.7

Focus on math practices

Look for Relationships Complete the equation with only triangles using the relationships from the clues shown above.

EXAMPLE 1 — Solve Two-Step Equations Using Models

Scan for Multimedia

Nala and two friends spent $21 on movie tickets and a box of popcorn. How could they figure out how much each movie ticket costs?

> **Use Structure** Two-step equations can be solved in two steps by using two different properties of equality.

Use a bar diagram and an equation to represent the situation.

total spent →

$21			
m	m	m	$6

↑ cost of one movie ticket   ↑ cost of popcorn

Total spent $= 3 \cdot$ Cost of one movie ticket $+$ Cost of popcorn

$21 = 3 \cdot m + 6$

Use the Subtraction Property of Equality to isolate the term containing the variable.

$15			$6
m	m	m	$6

$21 = 3m + 6$

$21 - 6 = 3m + 6 - 6$

$15 = 3m$

Use the Division Property of Equality to **isolate the variable**, or get the variable by itself on one side of the equation.

$5	$5	$5	$6
m	m	m	$6

$15 = 3m$

$\dfrac{15}{3} = \dfrac{3m}{3}$

$5 = m$

So, each movie ticket costs $5.

✓ Try It!

Andrew rents bowling shoes for $4. He bowls 2 games. Andrew spent a total of $22. How much was the cost of each game, b?

Complete the bar diagrams, and then solve the problem.

total spent →

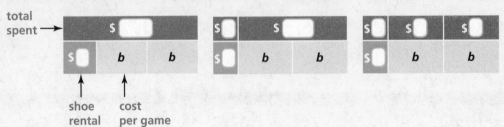

↑ shoe rental   ↑ cost per game

Each game cost ☐ .

Convince Me! What were the two steps you used to solve this equation?

EXAMPLE 2 Solve Two-Step Equations Algebraically

Jon has a $21.61 balance on a gift card that can be used to purchase online music. He bought some songs that each cost $1.29. Now he has $10 left. How many songs did Jon purchase?

Write and solve a two-step equation.

Let d represent the number of songs Jon purchased.

Balance on gift card	−	Cost of one song	•	Number of songs	=	$10 balance
21.61	−	1.29	•	d	=	10

$$21.61 - 1.29d = 10$$

> Use inverse operations and the Subtraction Property of Equality to isolate the term with the variable.

$$21.61 - 1.29d - 21.61 = 10 - 21.61$$

$$-1.29d = -11.61$$

> Use the inverse operations and the Division Property of Equality to isolate the variable.

$$\frac{-1.29d}{-1.29} = \frac{-11.61}{-1.29}$$

$$d = 9$$

Jon purchased 9 songs.

EXAMPLE 3 Compare Algebraic and Arithmetic Solutions

The number of trumpet players is 2 more than $\frac{1}{4}$ of the entire band. How many students are in the band?

An algebraic and an arithmetic solution are shown to find b, the total number of students in the band.

Algebraic Solution

$$\frac{1}{4}b + 2 = 18$$

$$\frac{1}{4}b + 2 - 2 = 18 - 2$$

> Subtract 2.

$$\frac{1}{4}b = 16$$

$$\frac{4}{1} \cdot \frac{1}{4}b = \frac{4}{1} \cdot 16$$

> Multiply by 4.

$$b = 64$$

Arithmetic Solution

$$4 \cdot (18 - 2)$$

$$4 \cdot (16)$$

$$64$$

So, there are 64 students in the band.

> 18 students play the trumpet in the band.

 Try It!

Kirsty ran 24 laps in a charity run and then walked 0.2 kilometer to the presentation table. The total distance Kirsty traveled was 29.6 kilometers. What was the distance of each lap? Explain how you solved the problem.

The properties of equality can be applied the same way when solving two-step equations as when solving one-step equations.

The inverse relationship between operations determines the property of equality needed to "undo" the operations in the equation.

$$5x + 27 = 122$$
$$5x + 27 - 27 = 122 - 27$$
$$\frac{5x}{5} = \frac{95}{5}$$
$$x = 19$$

Do You Understand?

1. **? Essential Question** How is solving a two-step equation similar to solving a one-step equation?

2. **Use Structure** Preston uses the bar diagram below to represent $4x - 3 = 13$. How would you use the bar diagram to solve for x?

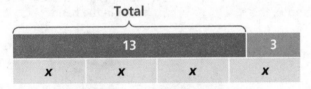

Total

13			3
x	x	x	x

3. Clara has solved the problem $6p - 12 = 72$ and says that $p = 14$. How can you check to see if Clara is correct?

Do You Know How?

4. Clyde is baking, and the recipe requires $1\frac{1}{3}$ cups of flour. Clyde has 2 cups of flour, but he is doubling the recipe to make twice as much. How much more flour does Clyde need?

a. Write an equation to represent the problem. Let c represent the amount of flour Clyde needs.

b. Solve the equation.

5. Four times a number, n, added to 3 is 47.

a. Write an equation that you can use to find the number.

b. What is the number represented by n?

Practice & Problem Solving

6. Use the bar diagram to help you solve the equation $4x - 12 = 16$.

Total

16	12
x	x	x	x

7. Complete the steps to solve the equation.

$\frac{1}{5}t + 2 - \boxed{} = 17 - \boxed{}$

$\frac{1}{5}t = \boxed{}$

$\boxed{} \cdot \frac{1}{5}t = \boxed{}$

$t = \boxed{}$

8. Use the bar diagram to write an equation. Then solve for *x*.

Total

7	5
x	x	x

9. While shopping for clothes, Tracy spent $38 less than 3 times what Daniel spent. Write and solve an equation to find how much Daniel spent. Let *x* represent how much Daniel spent.

Tracy spent
$10.

10. Solve the equation $0.5p - 3.45 = -1.2$.

11. Solve the equation $\frac{n}{10} + 7 = 10$.

12. A group of 4 friends went to the movies. In addition to their tickets, they bought a large bag of popcorn to share for $6.25. The total was $44.25.

   a. Write and solve an equation to find the cost of one movie ticket, m.

   b. Draw a model to represent the equation.

13. Oliver incorrectly solved the equation $2x + 4 = 10$. He says the solution is $x = 7$.

   a. What is the correct solution?

   b. What mistake might Oliver have made?

14. Use the equation $4.9x - 1.9 = 27.5$.

   a. Make Sense and Persevere What two properties of equality do you need to use to solve the equation?

   b. The solution is $x = \boxed{}$.

15. Higher Order Thinking
At a party, the number of people who ate meatballs was 11 fewer than $\frac{1}{3}$ of the total number of people. Five people ate meatballs.

   a. Write and solve an equation to find the number of people at the party. Let x represent the number of people at the party.

   b. Write a one-step equation that has the same solution.

✓ Assessment Practice

16. In a week, Tracy earns $12.45 less than twice the amount Kayla earns. Tracy earns $102.45. How much does Kayla earn?

17. Solve the equation $2x + 4\frac{1}{5} = 9$. Explain the steps and properties you used.

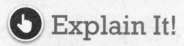 **Explain It!**

 ACTIVITY

Six friends go jet skiing. The total cost for the adventure is $683.88, including a $12 fee per person to rent flotation vests. Marcella says they can use the equation $6r + 12 = 683.88$ to find the jet ski rental cost, r, per person. Julia says they need to use the equation $6(r + 12) = 683.88$.

I can...
use the Distributive Property to solve equations.

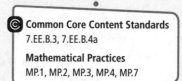
Common Core Content Standards
7.EE.B.3, 7.EE.B.4a

Mathematical Practices
MP.1, MP.2, MP.3, MP.4, MP.7

A. Construct Arguments Whose equation accurately represents the situation? Construct an argument to support your response.

B. What error in thinking might explain the inaccurate equation?

Focus on math practices

Use Structure How can you use the correct equation to determine the jet ski rental cost per person?

VISUAL LEARNING

ASSESS

EXAMPLE 1 Solve Equations Using the Distributive Property

Scan for Multimedia

Each of the graphic novels in Chen's collection increased in value by $3.50 in the last few years. If each graphic novel has the same value, what was the original value of one graphic novel?

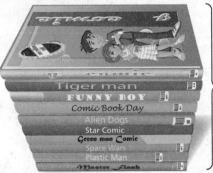

10 graphic novels

Current total value: $75

> **Model with Math** How can you write an equation in the form $p(x + q) = r$ to relate the quantities in the problem?

Use an area model to represent the situation and write an equation.

> Let g represent the original value of a graphic novel.

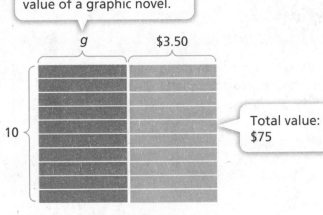

g $3.50

10

Total value: $75

$10(g + 3.50) = 75$

Solve for g to find the original cost of each graphic novel.

$$10(g + 3.50) = 75$$

$$(10 \cdot g) + (10 \cdot 3.50) = 75$$

> Use the Distributive Property.

$$10g + 35 = 75$$

$$10g + 35 - 35 = 75 - 35$$

$$\frac{10g}{10} = \frac{40}{10}$$

$$g = 4$$

> Use mental math to check that the solution is reasonable.
> Think: 10(4 + 3.50) is 10(7.5), or 75.

The original value of one graphic novel was $4.00.

✓ **Try It!**

A collector has a box of 32 figurines. The value of each figurine increased by $2.32 over the past year. The box of figurines is now worth $114.24. What was the original cost, x, of one figurine?

The original cost of one figurine was ⬚ .

Convince Me! Can the equation $32x + 2.32 = 114.24$ be used to find the original cost of each figurine in the problem above? Explain.

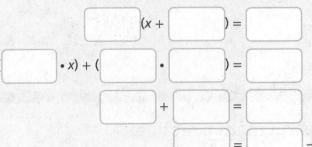

$$\boxed{}(x + \boxed{}) = \boxed{}$$

$$(\boxed{} \cdot x) + (\boxed{} \cdot \boxed{}) = \boxed{}$$

$$\boxed{} + \boxed{} = \boxed{}$$

$$\boxed{} = \boxed{} - \boxed{}$$

$$x = \boxed{} \div \boxed{}$$

$$x = \boxed{}$$

EXAMPLE 2

Solve Equations by Distributing a Negative Number

Solve the equation $-5(s + 30) = -17$.

$$-5(s + 30) = -17$$

$$-5s + (-5)(30) = -17$$ ◁ Use the Distributive Property to distribute the negative number.

$$-5s - 150 = -17$$ ◁ Remember the rules for multiplying negative integers.

$$-5s - 150 + 150 = -17 + 150$$

$$-5s = 133$$

$$\frac{-5s}{-5} = \frac{133}{-5}$$

$$s = -26\frac{3}{5}$$

EXAMPLE 3

Solve Equations by Distributing a Rational Number

The cheerleading squad received $\frac{1}{4}$ of the total sales of foam fingers and pom-poms at a pep rally. The squad received a total of $136.75. What was the value of the pom-poms sales, p?

$258 in sales of foam fingers

Write and solve an equation.

$$\frac{1}{4} \text{ of } \left(\begin{matrix} \text{pom-pom} \\ \text{sales} \end{matrix} + \begin{matrix} \text{foam finger} \\ \text{sales} \end{matrix} \right) = \begin{matrix} \text{total amount} \\ \text{squad received} \end{matrix}$$

$$\frac{1}{4}(p + 258) = 136.75$$

$$\frac{1}{4}p + \frac{1}{4}(258) = 136.75$$ ◁ Use the Distributive Property.

$$\frac{1}{4}p + 64.5 = 136.75$$

$$\frac{1}{4}p + 64.5 - 64.5 = 136.75 - 64.5$$

$$\frac{1}{4}p = 72.25$$

$$\left(\frac{4}{1}\right)\frac{1}{4}p = 72.25\left(\frac{4}{1}\right)$$

$$p = 289$$

The total received from pom-pom sales was $289.

☑ Try It!

Use the Distributive Property to solve each equation.

a. $-\frac{1}{2}(b - 6) = 5$

b. $0.4(x - 0.45) = 9.2$

c. $-4(p - 212) = 44$

When solving equations written in the form $p(x + q) = r$, you can use the Distributive Property to multiply the two terms in the parentheses by the term outside the parentheses.

$$6(x + 8.5) = 123$$
$$6x + 51 = 123$$
$$6x = 72$$
$$x = 12$$

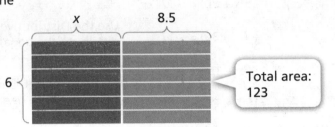

Total area: 123

Do You Understand?

1. **? Essential Question** How does the Distributive Property help you solve equations?

2. **Make Sense and Persevere** How are the terms in parentheses affected when multiplied by a negative coefficient when the Distributive Property is applied?

3. **Reasoning** How can an area model help you set up an equation for a problem situation?

Do You Know How?

4. A family of 7 bought tickets to the circus. Each family member also bought a souvenir that cost $6. The total amount they spent was $147. How much did one ticket cost?

5. David reads the problem:

    Ally bought a T-shirt and a pair of shorts on sale, which reduced prices by $\frac{1}{4}$. The total savings on the two garments was $10.25. Find the original price for the pair of shorts.

    David says that the original price of the shorts was $41. Does his answer seem reasonable? Defend your answer by writing and solving an equation that represents the situation.

6. Which of the following shows the correct use of the Distributive Property when solving $\frac{1}{3}(33 - x) = 135.2$?

    Ⓐ $(33 - x) = 1 \_- 3 \cdot 135.2$

    Ⓑ $\frac{1}{3} \cdot 33 - \frac{1}{3}x = \frac{1}{3} \cdot 135.2$

    Ⓒ $\frac{1}{3} \cdot 33 + \frac{1}{3}x = 135.2$

    Ⓓ $\frac{1}{3} \cdot 33 - \frac{1}{3}x = 135.2$

Practice & Problem Solving

Leveled Practice For 7–10, use the Distributive Property to solve the equations.

7. $-2(x + 5) = 4$

$$\left(\boxed{} \cdot x\right) + \left(\boxed{} \cdot 5\right) = 4$$

$$\boxed{} + \boxed{} = 4$$

$$\boxed{} = 4 + \boxed{}$$

$$x = \dfrac{14}{\boxed{}}$$

$$x = \boxed{}$$

8. $3.2 = \frac{4}{5}(b - 5)$

$$3.2 = \left(\frac{4}{5} \cdot \boxed{}\right) + \left(\frac{4}{5} \cdot \boxed{}\right)$$

$$3.2 = \boxed{} - 4$$

$$3.2 + \boxed{} = \boxed{}$$

$$\frac{5}{4} \cdot \boxed{} = \boxed{}$$

$$9 = b$$

9. $\frac{1}{8}(p + 24) = 9$

$$\left(\boxed{}\right) + \left(\boxed{}\right) = \boxed{}$$

$$p = \boxed{}$$

10. $\frac{2}{3}(6a + 9) = 20.4$

$$\left(\boxed{}\right) + \left(\boxed{}\right) = \boxed{}$$

$$a = \boxed{}$$

11. Use the equation at the right.

a. Make Sense and Persevere If you apply the Distributive Property first to solve the equation, what operation will you need to use last?

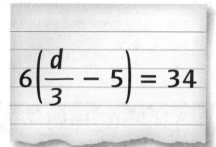

$$6\left(\frac{d}{3} - 5\right) = 34$$

b. If instead you divide first to solve the equation, what operation would you need to use last?

12. A family buys 4 airline tickets online. The family buys travel insurance that costs $19 per ticket. The total cost is $752. Let x represent the price of one ticket.

a. Write an equation to represent this situation.

b. What is the price of one ticket?

13. A local charity receives $\frac{1}{3}$ of funds raised during a craft fair and a bake sale. The total amount given to charity was $137.45. How much did the bake sale raise?

Craft Fair	Bake Sale
Funds raised.	Funds raised.
$252.60	$?

14. The solution shown for the equation is incorrect.

   a. What is the correct solution?

   b. What was the likely error?

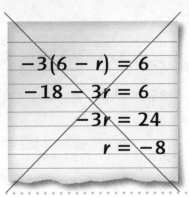

$$-3(6 - r) = 6$$
$$-18 - 3r = 6$$
$$-3r = 24$$
$$r = -8$$

15. Vita wants to center a towel bar on her door that is $27\frac{1}{2}$ inches wide. She determines that the distance from each end of the towel bar to the end of the door is 9 inches. Write and solve an equation to find the length of the towel bar.

16. Higher Order Thinking A cell phone plan is shown at the right. The rates, which include an unlimited data plan, are the same each month for 7 months. The total cost for all 7 months is $180.39. Let m represent the average number of minutes that exceeds 700 minutes each month.

   a. Write an equation to represent the given situation.

   b. Solve the equation to determine how many additional minutes, on average, you use each month.

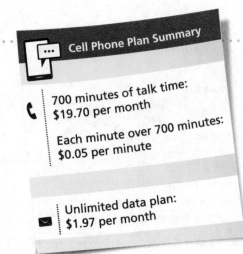

Cell Phone Plan Summary

700 minutes of talk time:
$19.70 per month

Each minute over 700 minutes:
$0.05 per minute

Unlimited data plan:
$1.97 per month

✓ Assessment Practice

17. Fidel earns a fixed amount, m, for each television he sells, and an additional $15 if the buyer gets an extended warranty. Fidel sells 12 televisions with extended warranties, earning $900. Write an equation to represent the situation. Then solve the equation to find the amount earned for each television sold.

1. Vocabulary Explain how to *isolate the variable* in the equation $-\frac{2}{3}n + 7 = 15$. *Lesson 6-2*

2. Jake paid $13.50 for admission to the county fair and bought 9 tickets to play games. If he spent a total of $36, what is the cost, c, of one ticket? Write and solve an equation. *Lessons 6-1 and 6-2*

3. Select all the equations that are equivalent to $\frac{1}{2}(4 + 8x) = 17$. *Lesson 6-3*

☐ $2 + 4x = 8.5$ ☐ $4x = 15$ ☐ $4 + 8x = 8.5$

☐ $4 + 8x = 34$ ☐ $2 = 17 - 8x$

4. Clara has 9 pounds of apples. She needs $1\frac{1}{4}$ pounds to make one apple pie. If she sets aside 1.5 pounds of apples to make applesauce, how many pies, p, can she make? Write and solve an equation. *Lessons 6-1 and 6-2*

5. Solve the equation $-4(1.75 + x) = 18$. Show your work. *Lesson 6-3*

6. Four friends attend a school play and pay $6.75 per ticket. Each also buys a Healthy Snack Bag sold by the Theater Club. If the friends spent a total of $37.00, how much did each Healthy Snack Bag cost, b? Write and solve an equation. *Lessons 6-1, 6-2, 6-3*

How well did you do on the mid-topic checkpoint? Fill in the stars.

MID-TOPIC
PERFORMANCE TASK

Marven and three friends are renting a car for a trip. Rental prices are shown in the table.

Item	Price
Small car rental fee – seats 4 passengers	$39/day
Full-size car rental fee – seats 4 passengers	$49/day
Insurance	$21/day

PART A

Marven has a coupon that discounts the rental of a full-size car by $25. They decide to buy insurance for each day. If the cost is $465, how many days, d, will they rent the car? Write and solve an equation.

PART B

If they still use the coupon, how many days could they rent the small car with insurance if they have $465 to spend?

PART C

They rent a car with insurance for 5 days but lost their coupon. If Marven and the three friends spend $75 each, which car did they rent? Write and solve an equation to justify your answer.

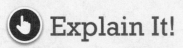 # Explain It!

 ACTIVITY

Selena and Martin are waiting at the bus stop. The number lines show the possible wait times in minutes, *t*, for Selena and Martin.

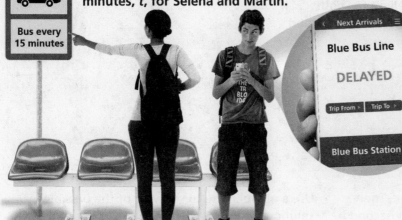

Bus every 15 minutes

I can...
solve inequalities using addition or subtraction.

Common Core Content Standards
7.EE.B.4b

Mathematical Practices
MP.2, MP.4

Selena's Possible Wait Time

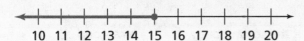

Martin's Possible Wait Time

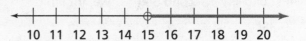

A. Construct Arguments Who anticipates a longer wait? Justify your response with a mathematical explanation.

B. If Selena and Martin both wait 10 minutes for the bus, whose possible wait time was closer to his or her actual wait time? Explain.

Focus on math practices

Be Precise If Selena and Martin both wait exactly 15 minutes for the bus, whose possible wait time was closer to his or her actual wait time? Explain.

VISUAL LEARNING ASSESS

EXAMPLE 1 Solve Inequalities That Involve Addition

Scan for Multimedia

On the airline that Raul is using, the weight limit for both suitcases combined is 50 pounds. How much can Raul's second bag weigh without going over the limit?

Reasoning Is there more than one possible weight for Raul's second bag?

38 lbs

Write an inequality to represent the situation. Then solve the inequality to find the weight of the second bag, p.

Weight of first bag	+	Weight of second bag	≤	Baggage weight limit
38	+	p	≤	50

Solve the inequality as you would an equation.

$$38 + p \leq 50$$
$$38 + p - 38 \leq 50 - 38$$
$$p \leq 12$$

> Use the inverse relationship between addition and subtraction to isolate the variable.

> The *Subtraction Property of Inequality* is like the Subtraction Property of Equality: subtracting the same number from both sides maintains the inequality.

Use a number line to show all of the possible solutions to $p \leq 12$

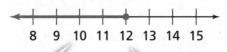

> If the second bag weighs 10 pounds, the total weight is 38 + 10 = 48, which is ≤ 50.

> The second bag can weigh at most 12 pounds.

Raul's second bag must weigh 12 pounds or less to avoid going over the weight limit for both suitcases combined.

✓ Try It!

Kyoko has completed 26 hours of community service. Her goal is to complete at least 90 hours this semester. Write and solve an inequality to show how many more hours, h, Kyoko needs to complete to meet her goal. Use the number line to graph the solutions.

Convince Me! Is there more than one solution to the problem about Kyoko? Explain. Give one value that is a solution and one value that is not a solution.

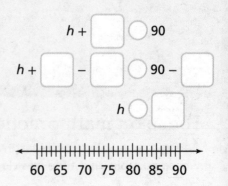

$h + \boxed{} \bigcirc 90$

$h + \boxed{} - \boxed{} \bigcirc 90 - \boxed{}$

$h \bigcirc \boxed{}$

60 65 70 75 80 85 90

EXAMPLE 2 | Solve Inequalities That Involve Subtraction

The weather forecast predicted that the evening temperature could get as low as −12.5°F. Between afternoon and evening, the temperature dropped by 7.5°F, which was consistent with the forecast. What could the afternoon temperature, t, have been?

MONDAY EVENING

Low of −12.5°F

Tue	Wed	Thu	Fri	Sat
−12°	−14°	−15°	−11°	−10°

Write an inequality to represent the situation. Then solve as you would an equation.

$$t - 7.5 \geq -12.5$$
$$t - 7.5 + 7.5 \geq -12.5 + 7.5$$
$$t \geq -5$$

> The *Addition Property of Inequality* is like the Addition Property of Equality: adding the same number to both sides maintains the inequality.

A number line showing a closed dot at −5 with shading to the right, labeled from −6 to −2.

The afternoon temperature could have been −5°F or warmer.

> **Look for Relationships** How is the Addition Property of Inequality similar to the Subtraction Property of Inequality?

☑ Try It!

The speed limit on a road drops down to 15 miles per hour around a curve. Mr. Gerard slows down by 10 miles per hour as he drives around the curve. He never drives above the speed limit. At what speed was Mr. Gerard driving before the curve? Graph the solution.

EXAMPLE 3 | Solve More Inequalities

Solve the inequality $x - \frac{1}{2} < -\frac{2}{3}$. Then graph the solution.

$$x - \frac{1}{2} < -\frac{2}{3}$$
$$x - \frac{1}{2} + \frac{1}{2} < -\frac{2}{3} + \frac{1}{2}$$
$$x < -\frac{1}{6}$$

> Remember to isolate the variable.

A number line showing an open circle at $-\frac{1}{6}$ with shading to the left, labeled −1, $-\frac{2}{3}$, $-\frac{1}{3}$, 0, $\frac{1}{3}$.

☑ Try It!

Solve the inequality $n - 1\frac{3}{4} \leq -\frac{5}{8}$. Then graph the solution.

Solving inequalities with addition and subtraction is the same as solving equations with addition and subtraction. Use the inverse relationship between addition and subtraction to isolate the variable.

$x + 15.76 > 26.05$

$x + 15.76 - 15.76 > 26.05 - 15.76$

$x > 10.29$

> Remember: The Addition and Subtraction Properties of Inequality are like the Addition and Subtraction Properties of Equality.

$-6\frac{4}{5} + y \le 3\frac{1}{10}$

$-6\frac{4}{5} + y + 6\frac{4}{5} \le 3\frac{1}{10} + 6\frac{4}{5}$

$y \le 9\frac{9}{10}$

Do You Understand?

1. **? Essential Question** How is solving inequalities with addition and subtraction similar to and different from solving equations with addition and subtraction?

2. **Be Precise** How do the solutions of the two inequalities differ? Are any of the solutions the same? Explain.

   a. $x + 5 < 8$ and $x + 5 > 8$

   b. $x + 5 \le 8$ and $x + 5 \ge 8$

3. **Reasoning** Write two different inequalities in which one of the solutions is the same as the solution to $x - 23 = 191$.

Do You Know How?

4. Solve each inequality. Then graph the solution.

   a. $x + 5 > 3$

   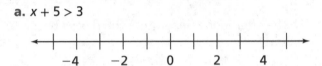

   b. $x + 5 \le 3$

   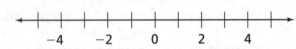

   c. $x - \frac{3}{2} < -3$

   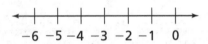

5. Elanor is driving below the speed limit on a highway.

   a. Write the inequality to show how much faster Elanor can drive without going over the speed limit.

   b. Solve the inequality you wrote. By how much can Elanor increase her speed?

Name: _____

Practice & Problem Solving

Leveled Practice In 6 and 7, fill in the boxes to solve each inequality. Then graph the solutions.

6. $x + 5 < 7$

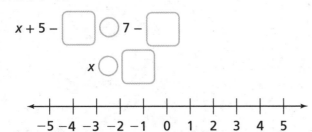

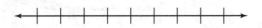

$$-5 \; -4 \; -3 \; -2 \; -1 \quad 0 \quad 1 \quad 2 \quad 3 \quad 4 \quad 5$$

7. $x - 4 \geq 12$

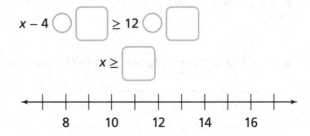

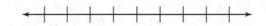

$$8 \qquad 10 \qquad 12 \qquad 14 \qquad 16$$

8. Solve $x + 10 \geq 14$. Then graph the solution.

9. Solve $x - 20 \leq -11$. Then graph the solution.

10. The maximum number of students in a classroom is 26. If there are 16 students signed up for the art class, how many more students can join the class without exceeding the maximum?

11. Higher Order Thinking The inequality $x + c > -2.55$ has the solution $x > 4.85$ What is the value of c? How do you know?

12. Rina is climbing a mountain. She has not yet reached base camp. Write an inequality to show the remaining distance, d, in feet she must climb to reach the peak.

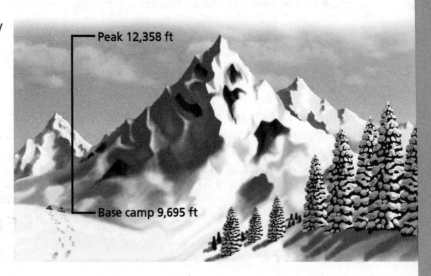

Peak 12,358 ft

Base camp 9,695 ft

13. On a math test, students must solve the inequality $x - 5 < 11$ and then graph the solution. Mason said the solution is $x < 6$ and graphed the solution as shown below.

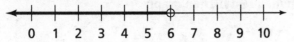

a. What error did Mason make?

b. Show the correct solution on the number line.

14. Model with Math Dani's neighbors paid her to take care of their bird during their vacation. Dani spent $4 of her earnings on an afternoon snack and $16 on a new book. Afterward, she had at least $8 left. Write an inequality to represent how much Dani's neighbors paid her.

15. Reasoning The temperature in a greenhouse should be 67°F or higher. One morning, the heater stopped working. The temperature dropped 4 degrees before someone fixed the heater. The temperature was still at least 67°F when the heater started working again. How can you best describe the temperature in the greenhouse before the heater stopped working?

Keep at least
67°F
or higher

16. Ramiro has $21. He wants to buy a skateboard that costs $47. How much more money does he need to have at least $47? Write an inequality that represents the situation. Solve the inequality and graph your solution.

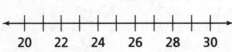

17. Kendra has $7.35 in her purse. She needs at least $2.87 more to buy a special bead. What is the total amount, x, she needs for the bead? Which inequalities can be used to represent the situation? Select all that apply.

☐ $x + 7.35 \leq 2.87$

☐ $x - 7.35 \leq 2.87$

☐ $x + 7.35 \geq 2.87$

☐ $x - 7.35 \geq 2.87$

☐ $x \geq 10.22$

☐ $x \leq 2.87$

☐ $x \leq 10.22$

☐ $x \leq 4.48$

Solve & Discuss It!

 ACTIVITY

Alex and Hope were trying to solve $-6x > 24$.

Whose inequality shows the solution? Show your work.

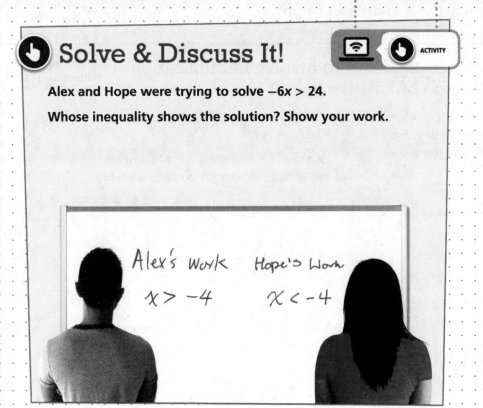

Alex's Work
$x > -4$

Hope's Work
$x < -4$

I can...
solve inequalities using multiplication or division.

© **Common Core Content Standards**
7.EE.B.4b

Mathematical Practices
MP.2, MP.3, MP.6, MP.7

Construct Arguments Why does more than one value of x make the inequality true?

Focus on math practices

Be Precise What do you notice about the inequality symbols used in the original inequality and in the correct solution?

369

? Essential Question How is solving inequalities with multiplication and division similar to and different from solving equations with multiplication and division?

 VISUAL LEARNING ASSESS

EXAMPLE 1 **Solve Inequalities That Involve Multiplication or Division of Positive Values**

Scan for Multimedia

Gina's pet pot-bellied pig is on a diet. He can have no more than 18 ounces of pig food per day. How many scoops of pig food can Gina feed the pig without going over 18 ounces?

Look for Relationships How can the Multiplication Property of Equality help you solve this problem?

STEP 1 Write an inequality to represent the situation.

Ounces per scoop $\cdot$ Number of scoops $\leq$ Maximum daily ounces

$$4 \cdot s \leq 18$$

The total can be equal to but not more than 18.

STEP 2 Solve the inequality as you would an equation. Then graph the solution.

$$4s \leq 18$$
$$\frac{4s}{4} \leq \frac{18}{4}$$
$$s \leq 4.5$$

Use the inverse relationship between multiplication and division and the *Division Property of Inequality* to isolate the variable.

Gina can feed her pig up to $4\frac{1}{2}$ scoops of food.

 Try It!

Solve the inequality $\frac{d}{7} > 15$. Then graph the solution.

$$\frac{d}{7} > 15$$

$$\boxed{} \cdot \frac{d}{7} \bigcirc 15 \cdot \boxed{}$$

$$d \bigcirc \boxed{}$$

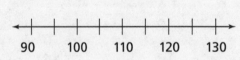

Convince Me! Frances solved the inequality $5g \geq 35$. She says that 7 is a solution to the inequality. Is Frances correct? Explain.

EXAMPLE 2 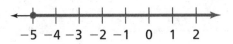 **Solve Inequalities Using Division by a Negative Value**

Solve the inequality $-3.4m \leq 17$. Then graph the solution.

$$-3.4m \leq 17$$

$$\frac{-3.4m}{-3.4} \geq \frac{17}{-3.4}$$

> Use the inverse relationship between multiplication and division and the *Division Property of Inequality* to isolate the variable.

$$m \geq -5$$

> Dividing by a negative value reverses the inequality symbol.

```
←——•——+——+——+——+——+——+——→
  -5 -4 -3 -2 -1  0  1  2
```

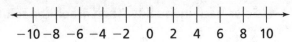 **Try It!**

Solve each inequality. Then graph the solution.

a. $149.76 > -19.2x$

```
←—+——+——+——+——+——+——+——+——+——→
 -10 -8 -6 -4 -2  0  2  4  6  8  10
```

b. $-3.25y < -61.75$

```
←—+——+——+——+——+——+——+——+——+——→
   8  10 12 14 16 18 20 22 24 26
```

EXAMPLE 3 **Solve Inequalities Using Multiplication by a Negative Value**

Solve the inequality $\frac{r}{-2.25} \geq 7$. Then graph the solution.

$$\frac{r}{-2.25} \geq 7$$

$$-2.25 \cdot \frac{r}{-2.25} \leq 7 \cdot -2.25$$

> Use the inverse relationship between multiplication and division and the *Multiplication Property of Inequality* to isolate the variable.

$$r \leq -15.75$$

> Multiplying by a negative value reverses the inequality symbol.

```
←—+——+——+——+——+——•——+——+——+——+——→
    -17        -16        -15
```

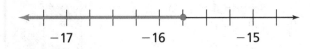 **Try It!**

Solve each inequality. Then graph the solution.

a. $\frac{k}{-0.5} < 12$

```
←——+——+——+——+——+——+——+——+——+——→
```

b. $-\frac{5}{4}h \geq 25$

```
←——+——+——+——+——+——+——+——+——+——→
```

Solving inequalities with multiplication and division is the same as solving equations with multiplication and division when the values are positive. Use the inverse relationship between multiplication and division to isolate the variable.

$2.5x \geq 15$

$\dfrac{2.5x}{2.5} \geq \dfrac{15}{2.5}$ ◁ Use inverse relationships and properties of inequality to isolate the variable.

$x \geq 6$

When multiplying or dividing by negative values, the inequality symbol is reversed.

$-2.5x \geq 15$

$\dfrac{-2.5x}{-2.5} \leq \dfrac{15}{-2.5}$ ◁ Multiplying or dividing by a negative value reverses the inequality.

$x \leq -6$

Do You Understand?

1. **? Essential Question** How is solving inequalities with multiplication and division similar to and different from solving equations with multiplication and division?

2. **Construct Arguments** Why is $-x < 3$ equivalent to $x > -3$? Provide a convincing argument.

3. If a, b, and c are rational numbers and $a > b$, is $ac > bc$ always true? Justify your answer.

Do You Know How?

4. Solve each inequality. Then graph the solution.

   a. $4x > 12$

   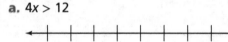

   b. $\dfrac{x}{4} \leq -12$

   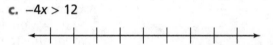

   c. $-4x > 12$

5. Vanna is saving for a trip. The hotel room will be $298.17 for 3 nights, and there will be additional fees. What is her daily cost?

   $298.17 for 3 nights

   a. Write an inequality for the situation.

   b. Solve the inequality. Then provide a statement that represents the solution of the problem.

Name: _____

Practice & Problem Solving

Leveled Practice In 6–9, fill in the boxes to solve the inequality. Then graph the solution.

6.

$$8m \leq 56$$

$$\frac{8m}{\boxed{}} \leq \frac{56}{\boxed{}}$$

$$x \leq \boxed{}$$

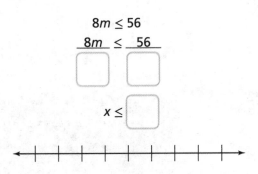

7.

$$-\frac{4}{3}x < -8$$

$$\boxed{} \cdot -\frac{4}{3}x \bigcirc -8 \cdot \boxed{}$$

$$x \bigcirc \boxed{}$$

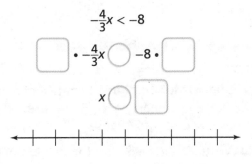

8.

$$-7x > 56$$

$$\frac{7x}{\boxed{}} \bigcirc \frac{56}{\boxed{}}$$

$$x \bigcirc \boxed{}$$

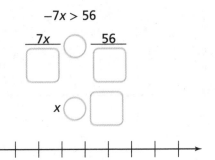

9.

$$\frac{m}{-5} \geq 2$$

$$\boxed{} \cdot \frac{m}{-5} \bigcirc 2 \cdot \boxed{}$$

$$m \bigcirc \boxed{}$$

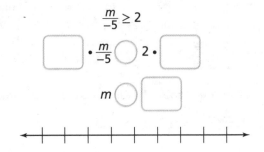

10. Kyra and five friends shared a bag of fruit snacks. Each person got no more than 3 fruit snacks. The inequality $x \div 6 \leq 3$ represents this situation. Solve the inequality to find the possible numbers of fruit snacks that were in the bag.

11. Over the next 17 months, Eli needs to read more than 102 e-books. The inequality $17x > 102$ represents the number of e-books he needs to read per month. Solve the inequality to find the number of e-books Eli needs to read per month.

12. Brittney can spend no more than $15 for new fish in her aquarium.

  a. Let f be the number of fish she can buy. What inequality represents the problem?

  b. How many fish can Brittney buy?

$3.00 each

13. Isaac has a bag of n peanuts. He shares the peanuts with 5 of his friends. Each person gets at least 18 peanuts. The inequality $18 \leq n \div 6$ represents this situation. Graph the solution of this inequality.

14. a. Solve the inequality $-3x < 12$.

   b. Reasoning Describe how you know the direction of the inequality sign without solving the inequality.

15. Higher Order Thinking Renata and her family go through an average of more than 15 cans of sparkling water each day. They buy cases of 24 cans at $3.50 a case.

   a. Write an inequality for the number of cases they go through in 30 days.

   b. Solve the inequality in part **a.** If they buy only full cases, how much do they spend on sparkling water in 30 days?

Sparkling water $3.50 PER CASE

16. Solve the inequality. Graph the solution on the number line.

$$-6.25x > -38\frac{3}{4}$$

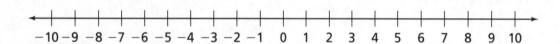

-10 -9 -8 -7 -6 -5 -4 -3 -2 -1 0 1 2 3 4 5 6 7 8 9 10

✅ Assessment Practice

17. Cynthia plans to build a tree house that is $\frac{1}{3}$ the size of Andrew's tree house. Cynthia plans to make the area of her tree house at least 13 square feet.

PART A

Write and solve an inequality to find the area of Andrew's tree house. Let x be the area of Andrew's tree house.

PART B

Describe how you know which tree house is larger without solving the inequality.

3-Act Mathematical Modeling:
Digital Downloads

  Go Online

ⓒ **Common Core Content Standards**
7.EE.B.3, 7.EE.B.4

Mathematical Practices
MP.4, MP.1, MP.2, MP.3, MP.5, MP.7, MP.8

ACT 1

1. After watching the video, what is the first question that comes to mind?

2. Write the Main Question you will answer.

3. **Construct Arguments** Make a prediction to answer this Main Question. Explain your prediction.

4. On the number line below, write a number that is too small to be the answer. Write a number that is too large.

Too small   Too large

←————————————————————————————→

5. Plot your prediction on the same number line.

6. What information in this situation would be helpful to know? How would you use that information?

7. Use Appropriate Tools What tools can you use to solve the problem? Explain how you would use them strategically.

8. Model with Math Represent the situation using mathematics. Use your representation to answer the Main Question.

9. What is your answer to the Main Question? Is it higher or lower than your initial prediction? Explain why.

10. Write the answer you saw in the video.

11. Reasoning Does your answer match the answer in the video? If not, what are some reasons that would explain the difference?

12. Make Sense and Persevere Would you change your model now that you know the answer? Explain.

Reflect

13. Model with Math Explain how you used a mathematical model to represent the situation. How did the model help you answer the Main Question?

14. Reasoning If all single tracks were on sale for 10% off, how would your model change? How would the answer to the Main Question change?

15. Make Sense and Persevere Suppose you have a $50 gift card to the same site. You want to buy an album with 16 tracks for $12.99 and then use the rest of the gift card for single tracks. How many songs can you buy with the gift card?

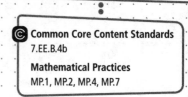

I can...
write and solve two-step inequalities.

Common Core Content Standards
7.EE.B.4b

Mathematical Practices
MP.1, MP.2, MP.4, MP.7

👆 Solve & Discuss It!

Rico and Halima are shopping for craft sticks, glue, and electrical tape for a science project. Together, they have $30 to spend on supplies. How should they spend their $30 if they need at least 1,000 craft sticks?

Focus on math practices

Make Sense and Persevere At the store, Rico and Halima find boxes of 500 craft sticks for $7.50. Which boxes of craft sticks should they buy?

? **Essential Question** How is solving a two-step inequality similar to and different from solving a two-step equation?

EXAMPLE 1 **Solve Two-Step Inequalities**

Hamish has $25.97 in his pocket to spend at the craft store. He wants to buy a paint canvas and some paint pens. How many paint pens, *p*, can Hamish buy?

> **Use Structure** How are inverse relationships and properties used to solve equations and inequalities?

Canvas $14.00

Paint Pens $3.15ea.

Write an inequality to represent the situation.

Cost of the canvas	+	Cost of one pen	·	Number of pens	≤	Money available
14	+	3.15	·	*p*	≤	25.97

> The total cost can be equal to but not more than $25.97.

Solve the inequality as you would an equation. Then graph the solution.

$$14 - 14 + 3.15p \leq 25.97 - 14$$

> Use the Subtraction Property of Inequality.

$$\frac{3.15p}{3.15} \leq \frac{11.97}{3.15}$$

> Use the Division Property of Inequality.

$$p \leq 3.80$$

> Only whole numbers are solutions.

```
←--+--+--+--+--+--+--+--→
   0  1  2  3  4  5  6
```

Hamish can purchase only a whole number of paint pens. So, Hamish can buy 3 or fewer paint pens.

☑ Try It!

Erin has $52 to spend at the florist. She wants to buy a vase for $11.75 and several roses for $3.50 each. What are the possible numbers of roses Erin can buy?

$$\boxed{} + \boxed{} \; r \bigcirc 52$$

$$r \bigcirc \boxed{}$$

Erin can buy up to $\boxed{}$ roses

Convince Me! What properties did you use to solve the inequality?

EXAMPLE **2** Solve More Two-Step Inequalities

 ACTIVITY ASSESS

Members of the science club are selling coupon booklets for $17.95 as a fundraiser. They hope to exceed the amount of money they raised last year. How many more coupon booklets, b, must the club members sell to achieve their goal?

Write an inequality to represent the situation. Then solve.

SCIENCE CLUB FUNDRAISER

← Last year's total
$658.35

← Here's where we are
$498.75

Current funds raised	+	Cost of one booklet	•	Number of booklets	>	Last year's total funds raised
498.75	+	17.95	•	b	>	658.35

> The amount raised this year should exceed last year's amount.

$$498.75 + 17.95b > 658.35$$

$$498.15 + 17.95b - 498.75 > 658.35 - 498.75$$

$$17.95b > 159.6$$

$$\frac{17.95b}{17.95} > \frac{159.6}{17.95}$$

$$b > 8.89$$

> **Make Sense and Persevere** What values for b make sense in the context of the problem?

The members of the science club must sell at least 9 booklets to exceed last year's total fundraising amount.

 Try It!

The Jazz Band needs to raise at least $600 to travel to an upcoming competition. The members of the band have already raised $350. If they sell calendars for $8 each, how many calendars would they need to sell to exceed their goal?

EXAMPLE **3** Solve Inequalities with Negative Values

Solve the inequality $-10 - \frac{9}{2}x < 80$.

$$-10 + 10 - \frac{9}{2}x < 80 + 10$$

$$-\frac{2}{9} \cdot -\frac{9}{2}x > -\frac{2}{9} \cdot 90$$

$$x > -20$$

> Remember: When you multiply or divide by a negative value, the inequality symbol is reversed.

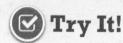 **Try It!**

Solve the inequality $5 - \frac{1}{2}x > 30$.

Like two-step equations, solving two-step inequalities involves carrying out two different operations—addition or subtraction, and multiplication or division. Unlike two-step equations, which have a single solution, two-step inequalities have multiple solutions.

Do You Understand?

1. **❓ Essential Question** How is solving a two-step inequality similar to and different from solving a two-step equation?

2. **Reasoning** What is the difference between the number of solutions for a two-step equation and for a two-step inequality?

3. Why are inverse relationships between operations used to solve two-step inequalities?

Do You Know How?

4. Joe ran 3 miles yesterday and wants to run at least 12 miles this week. Write an inequality that can be used to determine the additional number of days Joe must run this week if each run is 3 miles. Then solve the inequality.

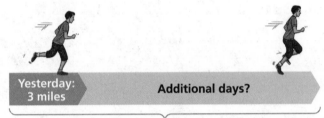

Joe's goal this week: Run at least 12 miles

5. Solve $4 + 6.5x < 36.5$.

6. Tomas has $1,000 to spend on a vacation. His plane ticket costs $348.25. If he stays 5.5 days at his destination, how much can he spend each day? Write an inequality and then solve.

7. Solve $12 - \frac{3}{5}x > 39$.

Practice & Problem Solving

Leveled Practice For **8** and **9**, fill in the boxes to write and solve each inequality.

8. Eight less than the product of a number n and $\frac{1}{5}$ is no more than 95.

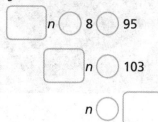

9. Seven more than the quotient of a number b and 45 is greater than 5.

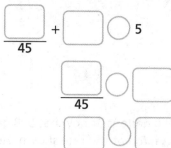

---

10. Solve the inequalities and compare.

  a. Solve $2x + 6 < 10$.

  b. Solve $-2x + 22 < 18$.

  c. Which is the correct comparison of solutions for $2x + 6 < 10$ and $-2x + 22 < 18$?

    Ⓐ The inequalities have some common solutions.

    Ⓑ The inequalities have one common solution.

    Ⓒ The inequalities have no common solutions.

    Ⓓ The inequalities have the same solutions.

---

11. Make Sense and Persevere Talia has a daily budget of $94 for a car rental. Write and solve an inequality to find the greatest distance Talia can drive each day while staying within her budget.

Car Rental
$30 per day
plus $0.20 per mile

---

12. Model with Math A manager needs to rope off a rectangular section for a private party. The length of the section must be 7.6 meters. The manager can use no more than 28 meters of rope. What inequality could you use to find the possible width, w, of the roped-off section?

13. **Higher Order Thinking** Andrea went to the store to buy a sweater that was on sale for 40% off the original price. It was then put on clearance at an additional 25% off the sale price. She also used a coupon that saved her an additional $5. Andrea did not spend more than $7.60 for the sweater. What are the possible values for the original price of the sweater?

14. A pool can hold 850 gallons. It now has 598 gallons of water and is being filled at the rate shown. How many more minutes, *m*, can water continue to flow into the pool before it overflows? Write and solve an inequality.

filling rate of 15.75 gallons per minute

☑ Assessment Practice

15. Use the rectangle diagram at the right.

    PART A

    Write and solve an inequality to find the values of *x* for which the perimeter of the rectangle is less than 120.

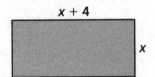

    x + 4

    x

    PART B

    Based on your answer to Part A, are there any values that can be eliminated from the solution set? Explain.

16. Kari is building a rectangular garden bed. The length is 6 feet. She has 20 feet of boards to make the sides. Write and solve an inequality to find the possible width of her garden bed.

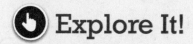 **Explore It!**

Charlene has 2 flash drives of the same size that she uses to store pictures and videos. Each drive is holding the same number of GB of data, *d*. She wants to move everything to a memory card that can hold up to 8 GB.

I can...
solve inequalities that require multiple steps.

© **Common Core Content Standards**
7.EE.B.4b

Mathematical Practices
MP.2, MP.3, MP.4, MP.7

A. Charlene is going to delete 1 GB of data from each flash drive. How can the total amount of data left on the two flash drives be represented as an expression?

B. How can the expression you wrote be used to write an inequality that shows the maximum amount of data each flash drive can have on it in order to have all the data transfer to the 8 GB memory card?

Focus on math practices

Reasoning If each flash drive has 5 GB of memory, can all of the data be transferred to the memory card? Explain.

385

? Essential Question How is solving a multi-step inequality similar to and different from solving a multi-step equation

EXAMPLE 1 **Write and Solve Multi-Step Inequalities**

Scan for
Multimedia

Gabriela likes to make people guess her age. She gives them this clue:

Add 13 to the product of 3 and the sum of my age and 2, and you get a number greater than my height in inches.

What are possible ages for Gabriela? Graph the solution.

← 55 inches

STEP 1 Write an inequality to represent Gabriela's age, x.

Multiply by 3	The sum of Gabriela's age and 2	Add 13	>	Gabriela's height
3 •	$(x + 2)$ +	13	>	55

STEP 2 Solve the inequality. Then graph the solution.

$3(x + 2) + 13 > 55$

$3x + 6 + 13 > 55$ ◁ Use the Distributive Property.

$3x + 19 > 55$

$3x + 19 - 19 > 55 - 19$ ◁ Use the Subtraction and Division Properties of Inequality to isolate the variable.

$\dfrac{3x}{3} > \dfrac{36}{3}$

$x > 12$

11 12 13 14 15 16

Gabriela is more than 12 years old.

☑ Try It!

Twice the difference of Felipe's age, f, and 4 is at least 2.
What are possible values for Felipe's age? Graph the solution.

Write the inequality. ☐ (☐) ◯ ☐

Use the Distributive Property to rewrite the inequality as $2f - \boxed{} \geq 2$.

Solve the inequality.   Graph the solution.

$2f \geq \boxed{}$

3 4 5 6 7 8

$f \geq \boxed{}$

Convince Me! Describe the similarity between the process of solving an inequality with two steps and solving an inequality with more than two steps.

EXAMPLE 2 **Solve More Multi-Step Inequalities**

  ACTIVITY ASSESS

Solve the inequality $-3(x + 4) + 3 \geq 9$. Then graph the solution.

$$-3(x + 4) + 3 \geq 9$$

> Remember to use the Distributive Property.

$$-3x - 12 + 3 \geq 9$$

$$-3x - 9 \geq 9$$

$$-3x \geq 18$$

$$\frac{-3x}{-3} \leq \frac{18}{-3}$$

> Remember: When multiplying or dividing by a negative value, the inequality symbol is reversed.

$$x \leq -6$$

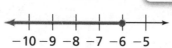

EXAMPLE 3 **Solve Multi-Step Inequalities by Combining Like Terms**

Solve the inequality $2(3.5t - 2) + 6t \geq -2$. Then graph the solution.

$$2(3.5t - 2) + 6t \geq -2$$

> Distribute and then combine like terms.

$$7t - 4 + 6t \geq -2$$

$$13t - 4 \geq -2$$

$$13t - 4 + 4 \geq -2 + 4$$

$$13t \geq 2$$

> Use the Division Property of Inequality.

$$t \geq \frac{2}{13}$$

 Try It!

Solve the inequality $-1-6(6 + 2x) < 11$. Then graph the solution.

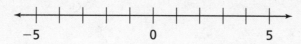

Solve the inequality $3(4 - 6) + 2 \geq 2(-t + 3) + 4$. Then graph the solution.

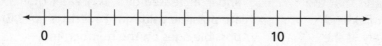

Solving multi-step inequalities is similar to solving multi-step equations. You may need to use the Distributive Property, combine like terms, and use inverse relationships and properties to solve them.

$4(y - 4) + 8 \leq 20$

$4y - 16 + 8 \leq 20$

$4y - 8 \leq 20$

$4y - 8 + 8 \leq 20 + 8$

$4y \leq 28$

$\dfrac{4y}{4} \leq \dfrac{28}{4}$

$y \leq 7$

0   10

Do You Understand?

1. ❓ Essential Question How is solving a multi-step inequality similar to and different from solving a multi-step equation?

2. Be Precise Explain how you would combine like terms and use properties of operations to solve the inequality $5(2t + 3) - 3t < 16$.

3. Critique Reasoning Gloria's solution to a multi-step inequality is $r > 7$. She states that the graph will have an open dot at 7 and extend with an arrow to the right indefinitely. Is she correct? Explain.

Do You Know How?

4. Solve the inequality $2(n + 3) - 4 < 6$. Then graph the solution.

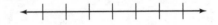

5. Solve the inequality $-2(x + 3) + 2 \geq 6$. Then graph the solution.

6. Three times the difference of Federico's age and 4, increased by 7, is greater than 37. What are possible values of Federico's age? Graph his possible ages on the number line.

Name: _____

Practice & Problem Solving

7. Use the inequality $18 < -3(4x - 2)$.

  a. Solve the inequality for x.

  b. Which graph shows the solution to the inequality?

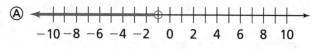

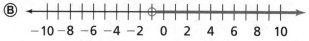

  Ⓒ
$$\underset{\substack{-10\ -8\ -6\ -4\ -2\quad 0\quad 2\quad 4\quad 6\quad 8\quad 10}}{\longleftarrow\!+\!+\!+\!+\!+\!+\!+\!\bullet\!+\!+\!+\!+\!+\!+\!+\!+\!\longrightarrow}$$

  Ⓓ
$$\underset{\substack{-10\ -8\ -6\ -4\ -2\quad 0\quad 2\quad 4\quad 6\quad 8\quad 10}}{\longleftarrow\!+\!+\!+\!+\!+\!\bullet\!+\!+\!+\!+\!+\!+\!+\!+\!+\!+\!\longrightarrow}$$

8. Michelle says that the solution to the inequality $2(4y - 3) > -22$ is $y > -3.5$. Her work is shown.

$$2(4y - 3) > -22$$
$$8y > -28$$
$$y > -3.5$$

  a. What was Michelle's mistake?

  b. What is the solution to the inequality?

9. Model with Math The length of a picture frame is 7 inches more than the width. For what values of x is the perimeter of the picture frame greater than 154 inches?

10. Critique Reasoning Sierra says that she can simplify the left side of the inequality $2(-3 + 5) + 2 \geq -4(x - 2) - 3$ by combining the terms within the parentheses, but that she can't do the same on the right side. Is Sierra correct? Explain.

11. a. Solve the inequality $30 \geq 6\left(\frac{2}{3}z + \frac{1}{3}\right)$.

  b. Solve the inequality $15.6 < 2.7(z - 1) - 0.6$.

  c. Are there any values of z that solve both inequalities? Use a number line to support your answer.

12. Mr. Lin baked banana bread for a bake sale to raise money for the math team. He said that he added a spoonful of walnuts for each of the students in his three classes, and that he added more than 250 walnuts. He used the inequality $16w + 24w + 10w > 250$ to represent the situation, where w represents the number of walnuts in each spoonful. How many walnuts could be in each spoonful?

13. Use both the Addition and Multiplication Properties of Inequality to solve the inequality. Graph the solutions on a number line.

$2(3y - 5) < -16$

14. Higher Order Thinking Solve each of the given inequalities for z. Which of the inequalities has 5 as a solution?

Inequality 1	Inequality 2
$4(2.8z + 1.75) > -26.6$	$2(1.9z + 1.5) \leq 18.2$

☑ Assessment Practice

15. The school band needs $500 to buy new hats. They already have $200. They are selling bumper stickers for $1.50 each. How many bumper stickers do they need to sell to have at least $500? Write and solve an inequality that represents the situation.

? Topic Essential Question

How can you solve real-world and mathematical problems with numerical and algebraic equations and inequalities?

Vocabulary Review

Complete each definition and then provide an example of each vocabulary word used.

Vocabulary
isolate the variable   equation
Distributive Property   inequality

Definition	Example
1. You [ ] when you divide both sides of the equation $3n = 12$ by 3.	
2. A statement that contains $>$, $<$, $\geq$, $\leq$, or $\neq$ to compare two expressions is a(n) [ ].	
3. You can use the [ ] to remove parentheses in the process of solving the equation $-10(x + 5) = 40$.	

Use Vocabulary in Writing

Write an equation or inequality to represent the following situation: *17 is at least 5 more than 3 times x*. Explain how you wrote your equation or inequality. Use vocabulary from Topic 5 in your explanation.

Concepts and Skills Review

Write Two-Step Equations | Solve Two-Step Equations

Quick Review

Equations can be used to represent situations. Two-step equations have two different operations. The properties of equality can be applied the same way when solving two-step equations as when solving one-step equations.

Example

There are red and yellow flowers in a city park. The number of yellow flowers is 3 more than $\frac{1}{3}$ of the number of red flowers. There are 21 yellow flowers. Write an equation to find the number of red flowers. Let r represent the number of red flowers. Then solve for r.

$$\frac{1}{3}r + 3 = 21$$

$$\frac{1}{3}r + 3 - 3 = 21 - 3$$

$$\frac{1}{3}r = 18$$

$$(3)\frac{1}{3}r = 18(3)$$

$$r = 54$$

The garden has 54 red flowers.

Practice

1. The total number of students in the seventh grade is 9 more than 4 times as many students as are in the art class. There are 101 students in the seventh grade. Write and solve an equation to find the number of students in the art class. Let x represent the number of students in the art class.

2. List the steps to solve the following equation: $5x - 6 = 44$. Then solve for x.

3. Solve for the given variable.

   a. $4y + 3 = 19$ b. $\frac{1}{2}n - 3 = 5$

Solve Equations Using the Distributive Property

Quick Review

Use the Distributive Property to solve problems of the form $p(x + q) = r$.

Example

Solve the equation $2(4.3 + n) = 17.63$.

$$8.6 + 2n = 17.63$$

$$2n = 9.03$$

$$n = 4.515$$

Practice

1. There are 450 seats in the lower level of a concert hall with b balcony seats in the upper level. So far, 170 tickets have been sold, which is $\frac{1}{5}$ of the total number of seats in the concert hall. How many tickets sold are balcony seats?

2. Solve the equation $-4(8 + y) = 90$.

LESSON 6-4 · Solve Inequalities Using Addition or Subtraction

Quick Review

When you add or subtract the same number on both sides of an inequality, the relationship between the sides stays the same. Solutions to inequalities can be graphed on number lines.

Example

Solve $x + 13 \geq 43$. Then graph the solution.

$x + 13 - 13 \geq 43 - 13$

$\qquad x \geq 30$

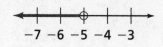

Practice

1. Carson's wheelbarrow can hold 345 pounds. If he has 121 pounds of rock in the wheelbarrow, what number of pounds, p, can he put in the wheelbarrow without going over the weight limit?

2. Solve $x - 19 < 81$. Then graph the solution.

LESSON 6-5 · Solve Inequalities Using Multiplication or Division

Quick Review

When you multiply or divide both sides of an inequality by the same positive number, the inequality remains true. When you multiply or divide both sides of an inequality by the same negative number, you need to reverse the inequality symbol, but the inequality remains true.

Example

Solve $-15n > 75$. Then graph the solution.

$-15n > 75$

$\dfrac{-15n}{-15} < \dfrac{75}{-15}$

$\qquad n < -5$

Practice

1. Travis has 3 months to save money for a trip. An airplane ticket costs more than $300. If he saves the same amount of money, a, each month, how much does he need to save each month to pay for the ticket?

2. Solve $-\frac{1}{8}y \leq 34$. Then graph the solution.

Quick Review

Inverse relationships and properties can be used to isolate the variable and solve two-step inequalities in the form $px + q < r$ or $px + q > r$ in the same way that they are used to solve two-step equations.

Example

Write and solve the inequality.

9 less than the product of 6 and x is greater than 54.

$$6x - 9 > 54$$
$$6x - 9 + 9 > 54 + 9$$
$$6x > 63$$
$$\frac{6x}{6} > \frac{63}{6}$$
$$x > 10\frac{1}{2}$$

Practice

1. The school band gets $5 for each T-shirt they sell at a fundraiser. They have a goal of raising $150. If $45 has been raised so far, how many more T-shirts do they have to sell to reach or exceed the goal?

2. Solve the inequality $-8 - \frac{1}{3}n \leq -25$.

Quick Review

Solving a multi-step inequality is similar to solving a multi-step equation. All of the rules and properties for solving one- and two-step inequalities apply to solving multi-step inequalities.

Example

Solve the inequality $7(x + 8) - 4 < 143$. Then graph the solution.

$$7(x + 8) - 4 < 143$$
$$7x + 56 - 4 < 143$$
$$7x + 52 < 143$$
$$7x < 91$$
$$x < 13$$

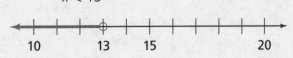

Practice

1. Solve $1.9(2.3n + 6) + 10.45 > 43.7$. Then graph the solution.

2. Solve $4(-2n + 2.5) - 8 \leq 50$. Then graph the solution.

Crisscrossed

Solve each problem. Write your answers in the cross-number puzzle below. Each digit, decimal point, dollar sign, and percent symbol of your answer goes in its own box. Round money amounts to the nearest cent as needed.

I can...
use the percent equation to solve problems. © 7.RP.A.3

ACROSS

A Antonia buys 0.75 yard of fabric at $12.00 per yard. If she pays 5% sales tax, what is the total cost of the fabric?

B Five friends plan to split a restaurant bill evenly. The total cost of the meal is $89.75, and they want to leave a 20% tip. What amount should each friend pay?

E Kaylie buys a sweater on sale for $40.11. If the discount is 20% off and she pays $1.91 in sales tax, what is the original price of the sweater?

F Randy buys a pair of shoes that were originally priced at $147. He receives a 35% discount and pays 8.5% sales tax. How much does Randy pay?

G A basketball player makes 8 of 22 shots in Game 1, 6 of 15 shots in Game 2, and 10 of 23 shots in Game 3. What percent of the shots did the player make in the three games?

DOWN

A Jack buys a tablet that costs $99 and a memory card that costs $15. He has a coupon for a 15% discount. What is the amount of the discount on the two items?

B Tara buys two pairs of socks for $4.99 each and three T-shirts for $11.45 each. If she pays 6% sales tax, what is the total amount of her purchase?

C Sunil receives a 20% discount on a concert ticket that costs $75. If Sunil pays $3.30 in sales tax on the discounted ticket, what is the sales tax rate?

D Dylan works for 4 hours and is paid $17.50 per hour. He must pay 15% in income taxes. What amount does he earn after taxes?

E Miles earns a 6% commission on each vehicle he sells. Today he sold a truck for $18,500 and a car for $9,600. What is the total amount of his commission for these vehicles?

GLOSSARY

ENGLISH	SPANISH

A

action In a probability situation, an action is a process with an uncertain result.

acción En una situación de probabilidad, una acción es el proceso con un resultado incierto.

additive inverses Two numbers that have a sum of 0.

inversos de suma Dos números cuya suma es 0.

Example 7 and −7 are additive inverses.

adjacent angles Two angles are adjacent angles if they share a vertex and a side, but have no interior points in common.

ángulos adyacentes Dos ángulos son adyacentes si tienen un vértice y un lado en común, pero no comparten puntos internos.

Example ∠ABD and ∠DBC are adjacent angles.

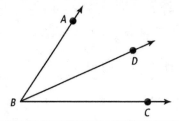

alternate interior angles Alternate interior angles lie within a pair of lines and on opposite sides of a transversal.

ángulos alternos internos Los ángulos alternos internos están ubicados dentro de un par de rectas y a lados opuestos de una secante.

Example ∠1 and ∠4 are alternate interior angles. ∠2 and ∠3 are also alternate interior angles.

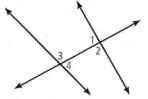

angle of rotation The angle of rotation is the number of degrees a figure is rotated.

ángulo de rotación El ángulo de rotación es el número de grados que se rota una figura.

Example The angle of rotation is 180°.

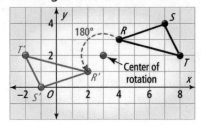

balance The balance in an account is the principal amount plus the interest earned.

saldo El saldo de una cuenta es el capital más el interés ganado.

Example You deposit $100 in an account and earn $5 in interest. The balance is $105.

biased sample In a biased sample, the number of subjects in the sample with the trait that you are studying is not proportional to the number of members in the population with that trait. A biased sample does not accurately represent the population.

muestra sesgada En una muestra sesgada, el número de sujetos de la muestra que tiene la característica que se está estudiando no es proporcional al número de miembros de la población que tienen esa característica. Una muestra sesgada no representa con exactitud la población.

Example The population:

12 females   4 males
75% female   25% male

A biased sample:

4 females   4 males
50% female   50% male

Does *not* accurately represent the population.

center of rotation The center of rotation is a fixed point about which a figure is rotated.

centro de rotación El centro de rotación es el punto fijo alrededor del cual se rota una figura.

Example *O* is the center of rotation.

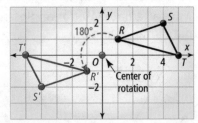

circumference of a circle The circumference of a circle is the distance around the circle. The formula for the circumference of a circle is $C = \pi d$, where C represents the circumference and d represents the diameter of the circle.

circunferencia de un círculo La circunferencia de un círculo es la distancia alrededor del círculo. La fórmula de la circunferencia de un círculo es $C = \pi d$, donde C representa la circunferencia y d representa el diámetro del círculo.

Example

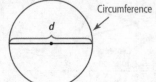

Circumference

d

ENGLISH	SPANISH

comparative inference A comparative inference is an inference made by interpreting and comparing two sets of data.

inferencia comparativa Una inferencia comparativa es una inferencia que se hace al interpretar y comparar dos conjuntos de datos.

Example Inference: Based on Sample *A*, 65% of Population *A* loves to sing.

Inference: Based on Sample *B*, 30% of Population *B* loves to sing.

Comparative Inference: Based on Sample *A* and Sample *B*, a greater percent of Population *A* loves to sing than Population *B*.

complementary angles Two angles are complementary angles if the sum of their measures is 90°. Complementary angles that are adjacent form a right angle.

ángulos complementarios Dos ángulos son complementarios si la suma de sus medidas es 90°. Los ángulos complementarios que son adyacentes forman un ángulo recto.

Example

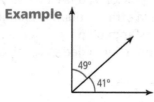 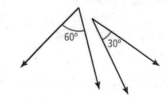

complex fraction A complex fraction is a fraction $\frac{A}{B}$ where *A* and/or *B* are fractions and *B* is not zero.

fracción compleja Una fracción compleja es una fracción $\frac{A}{B}$ donde *A* y/o *B* son fracciones y *B* es distinto de cero.

Example $\frac{\frac{1}{2}}{\frac{3}{4}}$

composite figure A composite figure is the combination of two or more figures into one object.

figura compuesta Una figura compuesta es la combinación de dos o más figuras en un objeto.

compound event A compound event is an event associated with a multi-step action. A compound event is composed of events that are the outcomes of the steps of the action.

evento compuesto Un evento compuesto es un evento que se relaciona con una acción de varios pasos. Un evento compuesto se compone de eventos que son los resultados de los pasos de una acción.

Example Action: Toss a coin. Roll a number cube.

Compound event: tails, 3

cone A cone is a three-dimensional figure with one circular base and one vertex.

cono Un cono es una figura tridimensional con una base circular y un vértice.

Example

ENGLISH

SPANISH

congruent figures Two two-dimensional figures are congruent ($\cong$) if the second can be obtained from the first by a sequence of rotations, reflections, and translations.

figuras congruentes Dos figuras bidimensionales son congruentes $\cong$ si la segunda puede obtenerse a partir de la primera mediante una secuencia de rotaciones, reflexiones y traslaciones.

Example $\triangle SRQ \cong \triangle ABC$

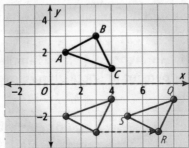

---

constant of proportionality In a proportional relationship, one quantity y is a constant multiple of the other quantity x. The constant multiple is called the constant of proportionality. The constant of proportionality is equal to the ratio $\frac{y}{x}$.

constante de proporcionalidad En una relación proporcional, una cantidad y es un múltiplo constante de la otra cantidad x. El múltiplo constante se llama constante de proporcionalidad. La constante de proporcionalidad es igual a la razón $\frac{y}{x}$.

Example In the equation $y = 4x$, the constant of proportionality is 4.

Converse of the Pythagorean Theorem If the sum of the squares of the lengths of two sides of a triangle equals the square of the length of the third side, then the triangle is a right triangle. If $a^2 + b^2 = c^2$, then the triangle is a right triangle.

expresión recíproca del Teorema de Pitágoras Si la suma del cuadrado de la longitud de dos lados de un triángulo es igual al cuadrado de la longitud del tercer lado, entonces el triángulo es un triángulo rectángulo. Si $a^2 + b^2 = c^2$, entonces el triángulo es un triángulo rectángulo.

Example Since $3^2 + 4^2 = 25$, or 5^2, the triangle is a right triangle.

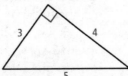

---

corresponding angles Corresponding angles lie on the same side of a transversal and in corresponding positions.

ángulos correspondientes Los ángulos correspondientes se ubican al mismo lado de una secante y en posiciones correspondientes.

Example $\angle 1$ and $\angle 3$ are corresponding angles. $\angle 2$ and $\angle 4$ are also corresponding angles.

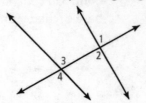

ENGLISH	SPANISH

cross section A cross section is the intersection of a three-dimensional figure and a plane.

corte transversal Un corte transversal es la intersección de una figura tridimensional y un plano.

Example

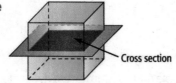

Cross section

---

cube root The cube root of a number, n, is a number whose cube equals n.

raíz cúbica La raíz cúbica de un número, n, es un número que elevado al cubo es igual a n.

Example The cube root of 27 is 3 because $3 \cdot 3 \cdot 3 = 27$. The cube root of -27 is -3 because $(-3) \cdot (-3) \cdot (-3) = -27$.

---

cylinder A cylinder is a three-dimensional figure with two parallel circular bases that are the same size.

cilindro Un cilindro es una figura tridimensional con dos bases circulares paralelas que tienen el mismo tamaño.

Example

D

dilation A dilation is a transformation that moves each point along the ray through the point, starting from a fixed center, and multiplies distances from the center by a common scale factor. If a vertex of a figure is the center of dilation, then the vertex and its image after the dilation are the same point.

dilatación Una dilatación es una transformación que mueve cada punto a lo largo de la semirrecta a través del punto, a partir de un centro fijo, y multiplica las distancias desde el centro por un factor de escala común. Si un vértice de una figura es el centro de dilatación, entonces el vértice y su imagen después de la dilatación son el mismo punto.

Example $\triangle A'B'C'$ is the image of $\triangle ABC$ after a dilation with center A and scale factor 2.

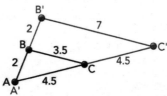

enlargement An enlargement is a dilation with a scale factor greater than 1. After an enlargement, the image is bigger than the original figure.

aumento Un aumento es una dilatación con un factor de escala mayor que 1. Después de un aumento, la imagen es más grande que la figura original.

Example The dilation is an enlargement with scale factor 2.

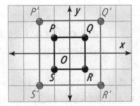

event An event is a single outcome or group of outcomes from a sample space.

evento Un evento es un resultado simple o un grupo de resultados de un espacio muestral.

Example Sample space for rolling a number cube:

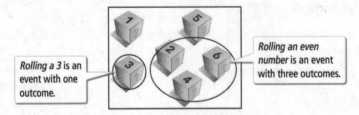

Rolling a 3 is an event with one outcome.

Rolling an even number is an event with three outcomes.

experimental probability You find the experimental probability of an event by repeating an experiment many times and using this ratio:

$$P(\text{event}) = \frac{\text{number of times event occurs}}{\text{total number of trials}}$$

probabilidad experimental Para hallar la probabilidad experimental de un evento, debes repetir un experimento muchas veces y usar esta razón: $P(\text{evento}) = \frac{\text{número de veces que sucede el evento}}{\text{número total de pruebas}}$

Example Suppose a basketball player makes 19 baskets in 28 attempts. The experimental probability that the basketball player makes a basket is $\frac{19}{28} \approx 68\%$.

exterior angle of a triangle An exterior angle of a triangle is an angle formed by a side and an extension of an adjacent side.

ángulo externo de un triángulo Un ángulo externo de un triángulo es un ángulo formado por un lado y una extensión de un lado adyacente.

Example $\angle 1$ is an exterior angle of $\triangle ABC$.

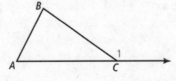

ENGLISH

SPANISH

hypotenuse In a right triangle, the longest side, which is opposite the right angle, is the hypotenuse.

hipotenusa En un triángulo rectángulo, el lado más largo, que es opuesto al ángulo recto, es la hipotenusa.

Example

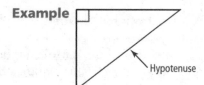

Hypotenuse

I

independent events Two events are independent events if the occurrence of one event does not affect the probability of the other event.

eventos independientes Dos eventos son eventos independientes cuando el resultado de un evento no altera la probabilidad del otro.

Example Action: Pick a marble out of a bag, and then replace it. Then pick a second marble from the same bag. The events are independent because the probability of picking the second marble is not affected by the choice of the first marble.

image An image is the result of a transformation of a point, line, or figure.

imagen Una imagen es el resultado de una transformación de un punto, una recta o una figura.

Example

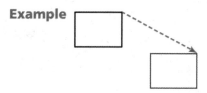

The blue figure is the image of the black figure.

inference An inference is a judgment made by interpreting data.

inferencia Una inferencia es una opinión que se forma al interpretar datos.

Example If 25% of a representative sample has Characteristic X, then a valid inference is that 25% of the population has Characteristic X.

interest rate Interest is calculated based on a percent of the principal. That percent is called the interest rate (*r*).

tasa de interés El interés se calcula con base en un porcentaje del capital. Ese porcentaje se llama tasa de interés, (*r*).

invalid inference An invalid inference is false about the population, or does not follow from the available data. A biased sample can lead to invalid inferences.

inferencia inválida Una inferencia inválida es una inferencia falsa acerca de una población, o no se deduce a partir de los datos disponibles. Una muestra sesgada puede llevar a inferencias inválidas.

irrational number An irrational number is a number that cannot be written in the form $\frac{a}{b}$, where a and b are integers and $b \neq 0$. In decimal form, an irrational number cannot be written as a terminating or repeating decimal.

número irracional Un número irracional es un número que no se puede escribir en la forma $\frac{a}{b}$ donde a y b, son enteros y $b \neq 0$. Los números racionales en forma decimal no son finitos y no son periódicos.

Example The numbers π and $\sqrt{2}$ are irrational numbers.

isolate a variable When solving equations, to isolate a variable means to get a variable with a coefficient of 1 alone on one side of an equation. Use the properties of equality and inverse operations to isolate a variable.

aislar una variable Cuando resuelves ecuaciones, aislar una variable significa poner una variable con un coeficiente de 1 sola a un lado de la ecuación. Usa las propiedades de igualdad y las operaciones inversas para aislar una variable.

Example To isolate x in $2x = 8$, divide both sides of the equation by 2.

 L

leg of a right triangle In a right triangle, the two shortest sides are legs.

cateto de un triángulo rectángulo En un triángulo rectángulo, los dos lados más cortos son los catetos.

Example
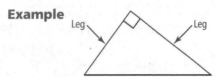

line of reflection A line of reflection is a line across which a figure is reflected.

eje de reflexión Un eje de reflexión es una línea a través de la cual se refleja una figura.

Example
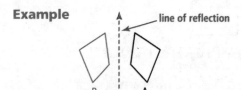
Figure B is a reflection of Figure A.

 M

markdown Markdown is the amount of decrease from the selling price to the sale price. The markdown as a percent decrease of the original selling price is called the percent markdown.

rebaja La rebaja es la cantidad de disminución de un precio de venta a un precio rebajado. La rebaja como una disminución porcentual del precio de venta original se llama porcentaje de rebaja.

Example A shirt that was originally $28 is on sale for $21. The markdown is $28 - 21 = 7$. The percent markdown is $\frac{7}{28} = \frac{1}{4} = 0.25$, or 25%.

ENGLISH	SPANISH

markup Markup is the amount of increase from the cost to the selling price. The markup as a percent increase of the original cost is called the percent markup.

margen de ganancia El margen de ganancia es la cantidad de aumento del costo al precio de venta. El margen de ganancia como un aumento porcentual del costo original se llama porcentaje del margen de ganancia.

Example The original cost of a shirt is $16, and a store is selling it for $28. The markup is 28 − 16 = 12. The percent markup is $\frac{12}{16} = \frac{3}{4} = 0.75$, or 75%.

Negative Exponent Property For every nonzero number a and integer n, $a^{-n} = \frac{1}{a^n}$.

Propiedad del exponente negativo Para todo número distinto de cero a y entero n, $a^{-n} = \frac{1}{a^n}$.

Example $8^{-5} = \frac{1}{8^5}$

outcome An outcome is a possible result of an action.

resultado Un resultado es un desenlace posible de una acción.

Example One outcome of rolling a number cube is getting a 3.

percent equation The percent equation describes the relationship between a part and a whole. You can use the percent equation to solve percent problems. part = percent • whole

ecuación de porcentaje La ecuación de porcentaje describe la relación entre una parte y un todo. Puedes usar la ecuación de porcentaje para resolver problemas de porcentaje. parte = por ciento • todo

percent error Percent error describes the accuracy of a measured or estimated value compared to an actual or accepted value.

error porcentual El error porcentual describe la exactitud de un valor medido o estimado en comparación con un valor real o aceptado.

Example A person guesses that there are 36 passengers on a bus. The actual number of passengers is 45.

$$\text{percent error} = \frac{|\text{ measured or estimated value} - \text{actual value }|}{\text{actual value}}$$

$$= \frac{|\ 36 - 45\ |}{45}$$

$$= \frac{|-9|}{45}$$

$$= 0.20, \text{ or } 20\%$$

So the guess "36 passengers" is off by 20%.

ENGLISH	SPANISH

percent of change Percent of change is the percent something increases or decreases from its original measure or amount. You can find the percent of change by using the equation:

$$\text{percent of change} = \frac{\text{amount of change}}{\text{original quantity}}$$

porcentaje de cambio El porcentaje de cambio es el porcentaje en que algo aumenta o disminuye en relación a la medida o cantidad original. Puedes hallar el porcentaje de cambio con la siguiente ecuación:

$$\text{porcentaje de cambio} = \frac{\text{cantidad de cambio}}{\text{cantidad original}}$$

Example The number of employees changed from 14 to 21.

amount of change $= 21 - 14 = 7$

percent change $= \frac{7}{14} = \frac{1}{2} = 0.5$, or 50%

perfect cube A perfect cube is the cube of an integer.

cubo perfecto Un cubo perfecto es el cubo de un entero.

Example Since $64 = 4^3$, 64 is a perfect cube.

perfect square A perfect square is the square of an integer.

cuadrado perfecto Un cuadrado perfecto es el cuadrado de un entero.

Example Since $25 = 5^2$, 25 is a perfect square.

population A population is the complete set of items being studied.

población Una población es todo el conjunto de elementos que se estudian.

Power of Powers Property To find the power of a power, keep the base and multiply the exponents.

Propiedad de la potencia de una potencia Para hallar la potencia de una potencia, se deja la misma base y se multiplican los exponentes.

Power of Products Property To multiply two powers with the same exponent and different bases, multiply the bases and keep the exponent.

Propiedad de la potencia de productos Para multiplicar dos potencias que tienen el mismo exponente y bases diferentes, se multiplican las bases y se deja el mismo exponente.

Product of Powers Property To multiply two powers with the same base, keep the common base and add the exponents.

Propiedad del producto de potencias Para multiplicar dos potencias con la misma base, se deja la misma base y se suman los exponentes.

principal The original amount of money deposited or borrowed in an account.

capital La cantidad original de dinero que se deposita o se pide prestada en una cuenta.

Example You open a savings account with $500. The principal is $500.

ENGLISH	SPANISH

probability model A probability model consists of an action, its sample space, and a list of events with their probabilities. The events and probabilities in the list have these characteristics: each outcome in the sample space is in exactly one event, and the sum of all of the probabilities must be 1.

modelo de probabilidad Un modelo de probabilidad consiste en una acción, su espacio muestral y una lista de eventos con sus probabilidades. Los eventos y las probabilidades de la lista tienen estas características: cada resultado del espacio muestral está exactamente en un evento, y la suma de todas las probabilidades debe ser 1.

Example Action: Spin the spinner once
Sample space: red, blue, green
Probabilities: $P(\text{red}) = \frac{1}{3}$, $P(\text{blue}) = \frac{1}{3}$, $P(\text{green}) = \frac{1}{3}$

probability of an event The probability of an event is a number from 0 to 1 that measures the likelihood that the event will occur. The closer the probability is to 0, the less likely it is that the event will happen. The closer the probability is to 1, the more likely it is that the event will happen. You can express probability as a fraction, decimal, or percent.

probabilidad de un evento La probabilidad de un evento es un número de 0 a 1 que mide la probabilidad de que suceda el evento. Cuanto más se acerca la probabilidad a 0, menos probable es que suceda el evento. Cuanto más se acerca la probabilidad a 1, más probable es que suceda el evento. Puedes expresar la probabilidad como una fracción, un decimal o un porcentaje.

Example

	Impossible	Unlikely	As Likely as Not	Likely	Certain
Probability (fraction):	0	$\frac{1}{4}$	$\frac{1}{2}$	$\frac{3}{4}$	1
Probability (decimal):	0	0.25	0.50	0.75	1
Probability (percent):	0%	25%	50%	75%	100%

proof A proof is a logical, deductive argument in which every statement of fact is supported by a reason.

comprobación Una comprobación es un argumento lógico y deductivo en el que cada enunciado de un hecho está apoyado por una razón.

proportion A proportion is an equation stating that two ratios are equal.

proporción Una proporción es una ecuación que establece que dos razones son iguales.

Example $\frac{2}{3} = \frac{6}{9}$ and $\frac{9}{12} = \frac{x}{4}$

ENGLISH

proportional relationship Two quantities x and y have a proportional relationship if y is always a constant multiple of x. A relationship is proportional if it can be described by equivalent ratios.

Example The equation $y = 4x$ shows a proportional relationship between x and y.

Pythagorean Theorem In any right triangle, the sum of the squares of the lengths of the legs equals the square of the length of the hypotenuse. If a triangle is a right triangle, then $a^2 + b^2 = c^2$, where a and b represent the lengths of the legs, and c represents the length of the hypotenuse.

Example $6^2 + 8^2 = 10^2$

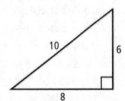

Q

Quotient of Powers Property To divide two powers with the same base, keep the common base and subtract the exponents.

R

random sample In a random sample, each member in the population has an equal chance of being selected.

reduction A reduction is a dilation with a scale factor less than 1. After a reduction, the image is smaller than the original figure.

Example The dilation is a reduction with scale factor $\frac{1}{2}$.

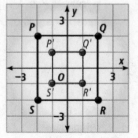

SPANISH

relación de proporción Dos cantidades x y y tienen una relación de proporción si y es siempre un múltiplo constante de x. Una relación es de proporción si se puede describir con razones equivalentes.

Teorema de Pitágoras En cualquier triángulo rectángulo, la suma del cuadrado de la longitud de los catetos es igual al cuadrado de la longitud de la hipotenusa. Si un triángulo es un triángulo rectángulo, entonces $a^2 + b^2 = c^2$, donde a y b representan la longitud de los catetos, y c representa la longitud de la hipotenusa.

Propiedad del cociente de potencias Para dividir dos potencias con la misma base, se deja la misma base y se restan los exponentes.

muestra aleatoria En una muestra aleatoria, cada miembro en la población tiene una oportunidad igual de ser seleccionado.

reducción Una reducción es una dilatación con un factor de escala menor que 1. Después de una reducción, la imagen es más pequeña que la figura original.

ENGLISH

SPANISH

reflection A reflection, or flip, is a transformation that flips a figure across a line of reflection.

reflexión Una reflexión, o inversión, es una transformación que invierte una figura a través de un eje de reflexión.

Example

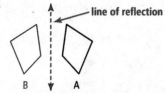

line of reflection

B   A

Figure B is a reflection of Figure A.

---

relative frequency relative frequency of an

$$\text{event} = \frac{\text{number of times event occurs}}{\text{total number of trials}}$$

frecuencia relativa frecuencia relativa de un

$$\text{evento} = \frac{\text{número de veces que sucede el evento}}{\text{número total de pruebas}}$$

Example For 40 trials, the relative frequency of 2 is $\frac{12}{40}$, or 30%.

Outcome	1	2	3	4
Frequency	10	12	4	14

---

remote interior angles Remote interior angles are the two nonadjacent interior angles corresponding to each exterior angle of a triangle.

ángulos internos no adyacentes Los ángulos internos no adyacentes son los dos ángulos internos de un triángulo que se corresponden con el ángulo externo que está más alejado de ellos.

Example ∠1 and ∠2 are remote interior angles of ∠3.

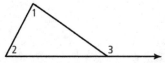

---

representative sample A representative sample is a sample of a population in which the number of subjects in the sample with the trait that you are studying is proportional to the number of members in the population with that trait. A representative sample accurately represents the population and does not have bias.

muestra representativa Una muestra representativa es una muestra de una población en la que el número de sujetos de la muestra que tiene la característica que se estudia es proporcional al número de miembros de la población que tienen esa característica. Una muestra representativa representa la población con exactitud y no está sesgada.

Example The population:

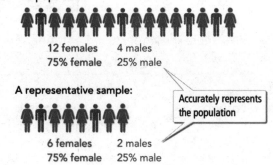

12 females   4 males
75% female 25% male

A representative sample:

Accurately represents the population

6 females   2 males
75% female 25% male

ENGLISH

SPANISH

rotation A rotation is a rigid motion that turns a figure around a fixed point, called the center of rotation.

rotación Una rotación es un movimiento rígido que hace girar una figura alrededor de un punto fijo, llamado centro de rotación.

Example A rotation about the origin maps triangle *RST* to triangle *R'S'T'*.

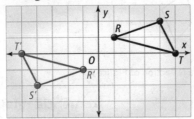

S

same-side interior angles Same-side interior angles are in the interior of two lines on the same side of a transversal.

ángulos internos del mismo lado Los ángulos internos del mismo lado se ubican dentro de dos rectas que están del mismo lado de una secante.

---

sample of a population A sample of a population is part of the population. A sample is useful when you want to find out about a population but you do not have the resources to study every member of the population.

muestra de una población Una muestra de una población es una parte de la población. Una muestra es útil cuando quieres saber algo acerca de una población, pero no tienes los recursos para estudiar a cada miembro de esa población.

Example

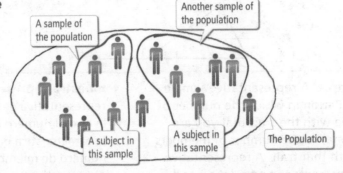

---

sample space The sample space for an action is the set of all possible outcomes of that action.

espacio muestral El espacio muestral de una acción es el conjunto de todos los resultados posibles de esa acción.

Example The sample space for rolling a standard number cube is
1, 2, 3, 4, 5, 6.

---

scale drawing A scale drawing is an enlarged or reduced drawing of an object that is proportional to the actual object.

dibujo a escala Un dibujo a escala es un dibujo ampliado o reducido de un objeto que es proporcional al objeto real.

Example Maps and blueprints are examples of scale drawings.

ENGLISH	SPANISH

scale factor The scale factor is the ratio of a length in the image to the corresponding length in the original figure.

factor de escala El factor de escala es la razón de una longitud de la imagen a la longitud correspondiente en la figura original.

Example $\triangle A'B'C'$ is a dilation of $\triangle ABC$ with center A. The scale factor is 4.

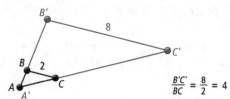

$$\frac{B'C'}{BC} = \frac{8}{2} = 4$$

scientific notation A number in scientific notation is written as the product of two factors, one greater than or equal to 1 and less than 10, and the other a power of 10.

notación científica Un número en notación científica está escrito como el producto de dos factores, uno mayor que o igual a 1 y menor que 10, y el otro una potencia de 10.

Example 37,000,000 is $3.7 \cdot 10^7$ in scientific notation.

similar figures A two-dimensional figure is similar (~) to another two-dimensional figure if you can map one figure to the other by a sequence of rotations, reflections, translations, and dilations.

figuras semejantes Una figura bidimensional es semejante (~) a otra figura bidimensional si puedes hacer corresponder una figura con otra mediante una secuencia de rotaciones, reflexiones, traslaciones y dilataciones.

Example Rectangle $ABCD \sim$ Rectangle $EFGH$

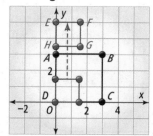

simple interest Simple interest is interest paid only on an original deposit.

interés simple El interés simple es el interés que se paga sobre un depósito original solamente.

simulation A simulation is a model of a real-world situation that is used to find probabilities.

simulación Una simulación es un modelo de una situación de la vida diaria que se usa para hallar probabilidades.

slope of a line

$$\text{slope} = \frac{\text{change in } y\text{-coordinates}}{\text{change in } x\text{-coordinates}} = \frac{\text{rise}}{\text{run}}$$

pendiente de una recta

$$\text{pendiente} = \frac{\text{cambio en las coordenadas } y}{\text{cambio en las coordenadas } x}$$

$$= \frac{\text{distancia vertical}}{\text{distancia horizontal}}$$

Example The slope of the line is $\frac{2}{4} = \frac{1}{2}$.

ENGLISH	SPANISH

slope-intercept form An equation written in the form $y = mx + b$ is in slope-intercept form. The graph is a line with slope m and y-intercept b.

forma pendiente-intercepto Una ecuación escrita en la forma $y = mx + b$ está en forma de pendiente-intercepto. La gráfica es una línea recta con pendiente m e intercepto en y b.

Example The equation $y = 2x + 1$ is written in slope-intercept form with slope 2 and y-intercept 1.

sphere A sphere is the set of all points in space that are the same distance from a center point.

esfera Una esfera es el conjunto de todos los puntos en el espacio que están a la misma distancia de un punto central.

Example

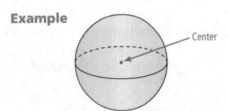

Center

square root A square root of a number is a number that, when multiplied by itself, equals the original number.

raíz cuadrada La raíz cuadrada de un número es un número que, cuando se multiplica por sí mismo, es igual al número original.

Example $\sqrt{9} = 3$, because $3^2 = 9$.

supplementary angles Two angles are supplementary angles if the sum of their measures is 180°. Supplementary angles that are adjacent form a straight angle.

ángulos suplementarios Dos ángulos son suplementarios si la suma de sus medidas es 180°. Los ángulos suplementarios que son adyacentes forman un ángulo llano.

Example

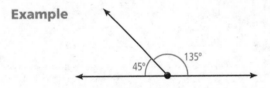

45° 135°

T

terminating decimal A terminating decimal has a decimal expansion that terminates in 0.

decimal finito Un decimal finito tiene una expansión decimal que termina en 0.

Example Both 0.6 and 0.7265 are terminating decimals.

theoretical probability When all outcomes of an action are equally likely, $P(\text{event}) = \frac{\text{number of favorable outcomes}}{\text{number of possible outcomes}}$.

probabilidad teórica Cuando todos los resultados de una acción son igualmente probables, $P(\text{evento}) = \frac{\text{número de resultados favorables}}{\text{número de resultados posibles}}$.

Example The theoretical probability of rolling a 6 on a standard number cube is $\frac{1}{6}$.

ENGLISH

SPANISH

transformation A transformation is a change in position, shape, or size of a figure. Three types of transformations that change position only are translations, reflections, and rotations.

transformación Una transformación es un cambio en la posición, la forma o el tamaño de una figura. Tres tipos de transformaciones que cambian sólo la posición son las traslaciones, las reflexiones y las rotaciones.

Example

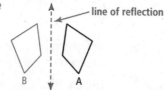

Figure B is a reflection, or flip, of Figure A.

translation A translation, or slide, is a rigid motion that moves every point of a figure the same distance and in the same direction.

traslación Una traslación, o deslizamiento, es un movimiento rígido que mueve cada punto de una figura a la misma distancia y en la misma dirección.

Example A translation 5 units down and 3 units to the right maps square *ABCD* to square *A'B'C'D*.

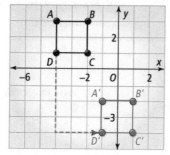

transversal A transversal is a line that intersects two or more lines at different points.

transversal o secante Una transversal o secante es una línea que interseca dos o más líneas en distintos puntos.

Example

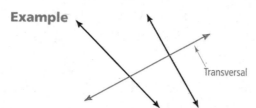

Transversal

trial In a probability experiment, you carry out or observe an action repeatedly. Each observation of the action is a trial.

prueba En un experimento de probabilidad, realizas u observas una acción varias veces. Cada observación de la acción es una prueba.

U

unbiased sample A sample in which every item or individual in the population has an equal chance of being selected.

muestra no sesgada Muestra en la que cada elemento o individuo de la población tiene la misma probabilidad de ser escogido.

ENGLISH

SPANISH

uniform probability model A uniform probability model is a probability model based on using the theoretical probability of equally likely outcomes.

modelo de probabilidad uniforme Un modelo de probabilidad uniforme es un modelo de probabilidad que se basa en el uso de la probabilidad teórica de resultados igualmente probables.

 V

valid inference A valid inference is an inference that is true about the population. Valid inferences can be made when they are based on data from a representative sample.

inferencia válida Una inferencia válida es una inferencia verdadera acerca de una población. Se pueden hacer inferencias válidas si están basadas en los datos de una muestra representativa.

Example If 25% of a representative sample has Characteristic X, then a valid inference is that 25% of the population has Characteristic X.

vertical angles Vertical angles are formed by two intersecting lines and are opposite each other. Vertical angles have equal measures.

ángulos opuestos por el vértice Los ángulos opuestos por el vértice están formados por dos rectas secantes y están uno frente a otro. Los ángulos opuestos por el vértice tienen la misma medida.

Example

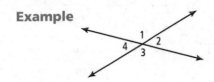

$\angle 1$ and $\angle 3$ are vertical angles.
$\angle 2$ and $\angle 4$ are vertical angles.

 Y

y-intercept The y-intercept of a line is the y-coordinate of the point where the line crosses the y-axis.

intercepto en y El intercepto en y de una recta es la coordenada y del punto por donde la recta cruza el eje de las y.

Example The y-intercept of the line is 4.

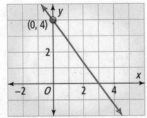

 Z

Zero Exponent Property For any nonzero number a, $a^0 = 1$.

Propiedad del exponente cero Para cualquier número distinto de cero a, $a^0 = 1$.

Example
$$4^0 = 1$$
$$(-3)^0 = 1$$
$$x^0 = 1$$

ACKNOWLEDGEMENTS

Photographs

CVR GLYPHstock/Shutterstock, Akugasahagy/Shutterstock, Primopiano/Shutterstock, Smach2003/Shutterstock, AlexZaitsev/Shutterstock; **3** mycteria/Shutterstock; **4** (penguin) Kotomiti/Fotolia, destina/Fotolia, leona_44/Fotolia, Mr Twister/Fotolia, Siempreverde22/Fotolia; **7** (T) Melana Lettering/Shutterstock, (B) Don Mammoser/Shutterstock; **8** (T) Nadezhda V. Kulagina/Shutterstock, (B) Monkey Business Images/Shutterstock; **9** (BR) Destina/Fotolia, (C) 3dsculptor/Fotolia; **15** (C) Djahan/Fotolia, (CL) Djahan/Fotolia, (T) Rawpixel.com/Fotolia, (TC) Bacalao/Fotolia; **16** (TCR) 103tnn/Fotolia, (TR) Pete Saloutos/Shutterstock; **20** NRT/Shutterstock; **21** Ras slava/Fotolia; **22** (C) Brostock/Fotolia, (T) Violetkaipa/Fotolia; **23** (CR) Nik_Merkulov/Fotolia, (TCR) david_franklin/Fotolia, (TR) Tashka2000/Fotolia; **24** (BCR) Ravenna/Fotolia, (CR) Eric Isselée/Fotolia, (R) Modella/Fotolia; **25** (BCR) dampoint/Fotolia, (BR) Vitaly Krivosheev/Fotolia; **27** castelberry/Fotolia; **41** (C) Natis/Fotolia, (TC) Thomas Barrat/Shutterstock; **43** (TCR) Totophotos/Fotolia, (TR) Igor Mojzes/Fotolia; **47** (C) Nataliia Pyzhova/Fotolia, (TC) Thanakorn Thaneewach/Fotolia; **57** (BCR) Aleksei Lazukov/Shutterstock, (BR) Maximmmmum/Shutterstock; **59** Elvirkin/Fotolia; **67** Georgejmclittle/Fotolia; **65** (TC) Rasulov/Fotolia; **80** Can Yesil/Fotolia; **81** RapidEye/iStock/Getty Images Plus/Getty Images; **83** Hywards/Fotolia; **84** (bulb) Robertovich/Fotolia, (faucet) LYA AKINSHIN/Fotolia, (girl) Maridav/Fotolia, (globe) Somchai Som/Shutterstock, (mineral) marcel/Fotolia, (oil) ptasha/Fotolia, (pump) phive215/Fotolia, (solar panel) lily/Fotolia, (tablet) yossarian6/Fotolia, (tree rings) oscar0/Fotolia, (tree) Givaga/Fotolia, (water) 31moonlight31/Fotolia, (wood) Kletr/Fotolia; **87** (T) Syda Productions/Shutterstock, (B) Ppa/Shutterstock; **88** (T) Denis Belitsky/Shutterstock, (B) Realstock/Shutterstock; **89** (C) Yuri Bizgaimer/Fotolia, (CL) yurakp/Fotolia, (L) Photka/Fotolia, (TC) Jane Kelly/Fotolia; **92** Castleski/Shutterstock; **93** Fotolia; **95** (C) Pongmoji/Fotolia, (CR) Sunnysky69/Fotolia, (TC) Alex Stokes/Fotolia, (TL) Xalanx/Fotolia; **100** Doko/Shutterstock; **101** (TC) Aelita2/123RF, (TL) Richard Laschon/123RF, (TR) Pavel Losevsky/Fotolia; **104** Sakdam/Fotolia; **105** (BCR) Trentemoller/Shutterstock; **107** (C) hrerickson/Fotolia, (CL) Leah Anne Thompson/Fotolia, (TC) andreusK/Fotolia; **111** Perytskyy/Fotolia; **114** (CL) Monkey Business Images/Shutterstock, (TL) Warut Prathaksithorn/123RF; **115** (TCR) Wildarun/Fotolia, (TR) Dirk Ercken/Shutterstock; **121** (C) michaeljung/Fotolia, (CL) Jeka84/Fotolia, (L) Edyta Pawlowska/Fotolia, (TCL) Iarygin Andrii/Fotolia; **122** evelyng23/Shutterstock; **127** (TL) Voyagerix/Fotolia, (TR) mimagephotos/Fotolia; **137** Lev/Fotolia; **140** Tarik GOK/Fotolia; **142** Frender/Fotolia; **143** (C) Jeanne McRight/Fotolia, (TC) Stillfx/Fotolia; **145** Royaltystockphoto/Fotolia; **148** PRinMD68/Fotolia; **149** (C) neirfy/Fotolia, (CL) Brocreative/Fotolia, (CR) Kletr/Fotolia; **152** GRIN/NASA; **161** RapidEye/iStock/Getty Images Plus/Getty Images; **163** (T) Mylisa/Shutterstock, (TC) Foonia/Shutterstcok; **164** (BCR) nito/Fotolia, (BR) yossarian6/Fotolia, (TR) Somchai Som/Shutterstock; **167** (T) Sari ONeal/Shutterstock, (B) Sergey Nivens/Shutterstock; **168** (T) GaudiLab/Shutterstock, (B) Zarya Maxim Alexandrovich/Shutterstock; **171** (C) Scattoselvaggio/Shutterstock, (R) Bernhard Richter/Shutterstock, (TCR) Javier Brosch/Shutterstock, (TR) Javier Brosch/Shutterstock; **173** (BCR) Alphalight Pro Stock/Shutterstock, (BR) Rawpixel/Shutterstock; **175** (Bkgrd) Sorapop Udomsri/Shutterstock, (BC) Takayuki/Shutterstock, (BCR) ChiccoDodiFC/Shutterstock, (BR) kak2s/Shutterstock, (C) kak2s/Shutterstock, (CL) Pete Pahham/Shutterstock, (CR) Leungchopan/Shutterstock, (TC) ChiccoDodiFC/Shutterstock; **176** Technotr/E+/Getty Images; **181** (B) Khunaspix/123RF, (BL) Jiang Hongyan/Shutterstock, (BR) Eric Isselee/Shutterstock, (TL) Somchai Som/Shutterstock, (TR) Quaoar/Shutterstock; **183** Kelly Nelson/123RF; **189** (T) Sergey Nivens/Fotolia, (TC) Blend Images Erik Isakson/Brand X Pictures/Getty Images; **199** luanateutzi/Shutterstock; **200** Maridav/Shutterstock; **205** (BCR) Arina P Habich/Shutterstock, (BR) Arina P Habich/Shutterstock; **207** Purestock/Getty Images; **209** Peter Anderson/Dorling Kindersley Limited; **218** (BCR) Andrey Popov/Fotolia, (BR) yossarian6/Fotolia, (CL) Manaemedia/Fotolia, (CR) Lasse Kristensen/Fotolia, (R) Nikolai Tsvetkov/Fotolia, (TC) Tupungato/Fotolia, (TCL) lucadp/Fotolia, (TCR) Stephen VanHorn/Fotolia, (TR) Andrey Popov/Fotolia; **221** (T) AmazeinDesign/Shutterstock, (B) Jacob Lund/Shutterstock; **222** (T) Rawpixel.com/Shutterstock, (B) Elenabsl/Shutterstock; **223** (Bkgrd) Sergey Yarochkin/Fotolia, (BL) Africa Studio/Fotolia,